CHILTON'S REPAIR & TUNE-UP GUIDE
DODGE D-50
PLYMOUTH ARROW
PICK-UPS
1979-81
All Models

Deleted

Vice President and General Manager JOHN P. KUSHNERICK
Editor-in-Chief KERRY A. FREEMAN, S.A.E.
Managing Editor DEAN F. MORGANTINI, S.A.E.
Senior Editor RICHARD J. RIVELE, S.A.E.
Senior Editor W. CALVIN SETTLE, JR., S.A.E.
Editor MARTIN J. GUNTHER

CHILTON BOOK COMPANY
Radnor, Pennsylvania
19089

SAFETY NOTICE

Proper service and repair procedures are vital to the safe, reliable operation of all motor vehicles, as well as the personal safety of those performing repairs. This book outlines procedures for servicing and repairing vehicles using safe, effective methods. The procedures contain many NOTES, CAUTIONS and WARNINGS which should be followed along with standard safety procedures to eliminate the possibility of personal injury or improper service which could damage the vehicle or compromise its safety.

It is important to note that repair procedures and techniques, tools and parts for servicing motor vehicles, as well as the skill and experience of the individual performing the work vary widely. It is not possible to anticipate all of the conceivable ways or conditions under which vehicles may be serviced, or to provide cautions as to all of the possible hazards that may result. Standard and accepted safety precautions and equipment should be used when handling toxic or flammable fluids, and safety goggles or other protection should be used during cutting, grinding, chiseling, prying, or any other process that can cause material removal or projectiles.

Some procedures require the use of tools specially designed for a specific purpose. Before substituting another tool or procedure, you must be completely satisfied that neither your personal safety, nor the performance of the vehicle will be endangered.

Although information in this guide is based on industry sources and is as complete as possible at the time of publication, the possibility exists that the manufacturer made later changes which could not be included here. While striving for total accuracy, Chilton Book Company cannot assume responsibility for any errors, changes, or omissions that may occur in the compilation of this data.

PART NUMBERS

Part numbers listed in this reference are not recommendations by Chilton for any product by brand name. They are references that can be used with interchange manuals and aftermarket supplier catalogs to locate each brand supplier's discrete part number.

ACKNOWLEDGMENTS

Chilton Book Company wishes to express appreciation to the Chrysler Plymouth Division, Chrysler Motor Corporation, Detroit, Michigan, and the Dodge Division, Chrysler Motors Corporation, Detroit, Michigan for their generous assistance in the preparation of this book.

Manufactured in the United States of America
90   09

Chilton's Repair & Tune-Up Guide: Dodge D-50 and Plymouth Arrow Pick-Ups 1979–81
ISBN 0-8019-7032-6 pbk
Library of Congress Catalog Card No. 80-7043

CONTENTS

Quick Reference Specifications For Your Vehicle

Fill in this chart with the most commonly used specifications for your vehicle. Specifications can be found in Chapters 1 through 3 or on the tune-up decal under the hood of the vehicle.

 Tune-Up

Firing Order_____

Spark Plugs:

    Type_____

    Gap (in.)_____

Point Gap (in.)_____

Dwell Angle (°)_____

Ignition Timing (°)_____

    Vacuum (Connected/Disconnected)_____

Valve Clearance (in.)

    Intake_____   **Exhaust**_____

Capacities

Engine Oil (qts)

    With Filter Change_____

    Without Filter Change_____

Cooling System (qts)_____

Manual Transmission (pts)_____

    Type_____

Automatic Transmission (pts)_____

    Type_____

Front Differential (pts)_____

    Type_____

Rear Differential (pts)_____

    Type_____

Transfer Case (pts)_____

    Type_____

FREQUENTLY REPLACED PARTS

Use these spaces to record the part numbers of frequently replaced parts.

PCV VALVE   **OIL FILTER**   **AIR FILTER**

Manufacturer_____ **Manufacturer**_____ **Manufacturer**_____

Part No._____ **Part No.**_____ **Part No.**_____

General Information and Maintenance

HOW TO USE THIS BOOK

Chilton's Repair & Tune-Up Guide for *Plymouth Arrow/Dodge D-50 Pick-Ups* is intended to help you learn more about the inner workings of your vehicle and save you money on its upkeep and operation.

The first two chapters will be the most used, since they contain maintenance and tune-up information and procedures. Studies have shown that a properly tuned and maintained car can get at least 10% better gas mileage than an out-of-tune car. The other chapters deal with the more complex systems of your car. Operating systems from engine through brakes are covered to the extent that the average do-it-yourselfer becomes mechanically involved. This book will not explain such things as rebuilding the differential for the simple reason that the expertise required and the investment in special tools make this task uneconomical. It will give you detailed instructions to help you change your own brake pads and shoes, replace points and plugs, and do many more jobs that will save you money, give you personal satisfaction, and help you avoid expensive problems.

A secondary purpose of this book is a reference for owners who want to understand their car and/or their mechanics better. In this case, no tools at all are required.

Before removing any bolts, read through the entire procedure. This will give you the overall view of what tools and supplies will be required. There is nothing more frustrating than having to walk to the bus stop on Monday morning because you were short one bolt on Sunday afternoon. So read ahead and plan ahead. Each operation should be approached logically and all procedures thoroughly understood before attempting any work.

All chapters contain adjustments, maintenance, removal and installation procedures, and repair or overhaul procedures. When repair is not considered practical, we tell you how to remove the part and then how to install the new or rebuilt replacement. In this way, you at least save the labor costs. Backyard repair of such components as the alternator is just not practical.

Two basic mechanic's rules should be mentioned here. One, whenever the left side of the car or engine is referred to, it is meant to specify the driver's side of the car. Conversely, the right side of the car means the passenger's side. Secondly, most screws and bolts are removed by turning counterclockwise, and tightened by turning clockwise.

Safety is always the most important rule. Constantly be aware of the dangers involved in working on an automobile and take the proper precautions. (See the section in this chapter "Servicing Your Vehicle Safely" and the SAFETY NOTICE on the acknowledgement page.)

Pay attention to the instructions provided. There are 3 common mistakes in mechanical work:

1. Incorrect order of assembly, disassembly or adjustment. When taking something apart or putting it together, doing things in the wrong order usually justs costs you extra time; however, it CAN break something. Read the entire procedure before beginning disassembly. Do everything in the order in which the instructions say you should do it, even if you can't immediately see a reason for it. When you're taking apart something that is very intricate (for example, a carburetor), you might want to draw a picture of how it looks when assembled at one point in order to make sure you get everything back in its proper position. (We will supply exploded views whenever possible.) When making adjustments, especially tune-up adjustments, do them in order; often, one adjustment affects another, and you cannot expect even satisfactory results unless each adjustment is made only when it cannot be changed by any other.

2. Overtorquing (or undertorquing). While it is more common for overtorquing to cause damage, undertorquing can cause a fastener to vibrate loose causing serious damage. Especially when dealing with aluminum parts, pay attention to torque specifications and utilize a torque wrench in assembly. If a torque figure is not available, remember that if you are using the right tool to do the job, you will probably not have to strain yourself to get a fastener tight enough. The pitch of most threads is so slight that the tension you put on the wrench will be multiplied many, many times in actual force on what you are tightening. A good example of how critical torque is can be seen in the case of spark plug installation, especially where you are putting the plug into an aluminum cylinder head. Too little torque can fail to crush the gasket, causing leakage of combustion gases and consequent overheating of the plug and engine parts. Too much torque can damage the threads, or distort the plug, which changes the spark gap.

There are many commercial products available for ensuring that fasteners won't come loose, even if they are not torqued just right (a very common brand is "Loctite®"). If you're worried about getting something together tight enough to hold, but loose enough to avoid mechanical damage during assembly, one of these products might offer substantial insurance. Read the label on the package and make sure the product is compatible with the materials, fluids, etc. involved before choosing one.

3. Crossthreading. This occurs when a part such as a bolt is screwed into a nut or casting at the wrong angle and forced. Crossthreading is more likely to occur if access is difficult. It helps to clean and lubricate fasteners, and to start threading with the part to be installed going straight in. Then, start the bolt, spark plug, etc. with your fingers. If you encounter resistance, unscrew the part and start over again at a different angle until it can be inserted and turned several turns without much effort. Keep in mind that many parts, especially spark plugs, use tapered threads so that gentle turning will automatically bring the part you're threading to the proper angle if you don't force it or resist a change in angle. Don't put a wrench on the part until it's been turned a couple of turns by hand. If you suddenly encounter resistance, and the part has not seated fully, don't force it. Pull it back out and make sure it's clean and threading properly.

Always take your time and be patient; once you have some experience, working on your car will become an enjoyable hobby.

TOOLS AND EQUIPMENT

Naturally, without the proper tools and equipment it is impossible to properly service your vehicle. It would be impossible to catalog each tool that you would need to perform each or any operation in this book. It would also be unwise for the amateur to rush out and buy an expensive set of tools on the theory that he may need one or more of them at sometime.

The best approach is to proceed slowly, gathering together a good quality set of those tools that are used most frequently. Don't be misled by the low cost of bargain tools. It is far better to spend a little more for better quality. Forged wrenches, 10 or 12 point sockets and fine tooth ratchets are by far preferable to their less expensive counterparts. As any good mechanic can tell you, there are few worse experiences than trying to work on a car or truck with bad tools. Your monetary

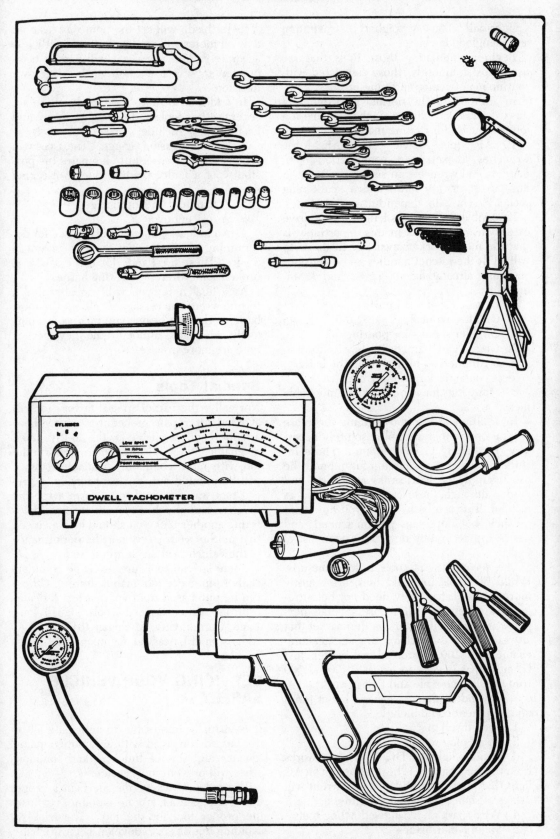

The tools and equipment shown here will handle the majority of the maintenance on your truck

savings will be far outweighed by frustration and mangled knuckles.

Begin accumulating those tools that are used most frequently; those associated with routine maintenance and tune-up.

In addition to the normal assortment of screwdrivers and pliers you should have the following tools for routine maintenance jobs:

1. SAE (or Metric) or SAE/Metric wrenches—sockets and combination open end/box end wrenches in sizes from ⅛ in. (3 mm) to ¾ in. (19 mm); and a spark plug socket $^{13}/_{16}$ or ⅝ in. depending on plug type).

If possible, buy various length socket drive extensions. One break in this department is that the metric sockets available in the U.S. will all fit the ratchet handles and extensions you may already have (¼, ⅜, and ½ in. drive.)

2. Jackstands—for support;
3. Oil filter wrench;
4. Oil filler spout—for pouring oil;
5. Grease gun—for chassis lubrication;
6. Hydrometer—for checking the battery;
7. A container for draining oil;
8. Many rags for wiping up the inevitable mess.

In addition to the above items there are several others that are not absolutely necessary, but handy to have around. These include oil dry, a transmission funnel and the usual supply of lubricants, antifreeze and fluids, although these can be purchased as needed. This is a basic list for routine maintenance, but only your personal needs and desire can accurately determine your list of tools.

The second list of tools is for tune-ups. While the tools involved here are slightly more sophisticated, they need not be outrageously expensive. There are several inexpensive tach/dwell meters on the market that are every bit as good for the average mechanic as a $100.00 professional model. Just be sure that it goes to a least 1,200–1,500 rpm on the tach scale and that it works on 4, 6 or 8 cylinder engines. A basic list of tune-up equipment could include:

1. Tach-dwell meter;
2. Spark plug wrench;
3. Timing light (a DC light that works from the car's battery is best, although an AC light that plugs into 110V house current will suffice at some sacrifice in brightness);
4. Wire spark plug gauge/adjusting tools
5. Set of feeler blades

Here again, be guided by your own needs.

A feeler blade will set the points as easily as a dwell meter will read well, but slightly less accurately. And since you will need a tachometer anyway . . . well, make your own decision.

In addition to these basic tools, there are several other tools and gauges you may find useful. These include:

1. A compression gauge. The screw-in type is slower to use, but eliminates the possibility of a faulty reading due to escaping pressure;
2. A manifold vacuum gauge;
3. A test light;
4. An induction meter. This is used for determining whether or not there is current in a wire. These are handy for use if a wire is broken somewhere in a wiring harness.

As a final note, you will probably find a torque wrench necessary for all but the most basic work. The beam type models are perfectly adequate, although the newer click type are more precise.

Special Tools

Normally, the use of special factory tools is avoided for repair procedures, since these are not readily available for the do-it-yourself mechanic. When it is possible to perform the job with more commonly available tools, it will be pointed out, but occasionally, a special tool was designed to perform a specific function and should be used. Before substituting another tool, you should be convinced that neither your safety nor the performance of the vehicle will be compromised.

Some special tools are available commercially from major tool manufacturers. Others can be purchased from your car/truck dealer or from Miller Special Tools, 32615 Park Lane, Garden City, Michigan 48135, U.S.A. A division of Utica Tool Company Inc.

SERVICING YOUR VEHICLE SAFELY

It is virtually impossible to anticipate all of the hazards involved with automotive maintenance and service but care and common sense will prevent most accidents.

The rules of safety for mechanics range from "don't smoke around gasoline," to "use the proper tool for the job." The trick to avoiding injuries is to develop safe work habits and take every possible precaution.

Do's

• DO keep a fire extinguisher and first aid kit within easy reach.

• DO wear safety glasses or goggles when cutting, drilling, grinding or prying, even if you have 20–20 vision. If you wear glasses for the sake of vision, then they should be made of hardened glass that can serve also as safety glasses, or wear safety goggles over your regular glasses.

• DO shield your eyes whenever you work around the battery. Batteries contain sulphuric acid; in case of contact with the eyes or skin, flush the area with water or a mixture of water and baking soda and get medical attention immediately.

• DO use safety stands for any under-car service. Jacks are for raising vehicles; safety stands are for making sure the vehicle stays raised until you want it to come down. Whenever the vehicle is raised, block the wheels remaining on the ground and set the parking brake.

• DO use adequate ventilation when working with any chemicals. Like carbon monoxide, the asbestos dust resulting from brake lining wear can be poisonous in sufficient quantities.

• DO disconnect the negative battery cable when working on the electrical system. The primary ignition system can contain up to 40,000 volts.

• DO follow manufacturer's directions whenever working with potentially hazardous materials. Both brake fluid and antifreeze are poisonous if taken internally.

• DO properly maintain your tools. Loose hammerheads, mushroomed punches and chisels, frayed or poorly grounded electrical cords, excessively worn screwdrivers, spread wrenches (open end), cracked sockets, slipping ratchets, or faulty droplight sockets can cause accidents.

• DO use the proper size and type of tool for the job being done.

• DO when possible, pull on a wrench handle rather than push on it, and adjust your stance to prevent a fall.

• DO be sure that adjustable wrenches are tightly adjusted on the nut or bolt and pulled so that the face is on the side of the fixed jaw.

• DO select a wrench or socket that fits the nut or bolt. The wrench or socket should sit straight, not cocked.

• DO strike squarely with a hammer—avoid glancing blows.

• DO set the parking brake and block the drive wheels if the work requires that the engine be running.

Dont's

• DON'T run an engine in a garage or anywhere else without proper ventilation—EVER! Carbon monoxide is poisonous; it takes a long time to leave the human body and you can build up a deadly supply of it in your system by simply breathing in a little every day. You may not realize you are slowly poisoning yourself. Always use power vents, windows, fans or open the garage doors.

• DON'T work around moving parts while wearing a necktie or other loose clothing. Short sleeves are much safer than long, loose sleeves and hard-toed shoes with neoprene soles protect your toes and give a better grip on slippery surfaces. Jewelry such as watches, fancy belt buckles, beads or body adornment of any kind is not safe working around a car. Long hair should be hidden under a hat or cap.

• DON'T use pockets for toolboxes. A fall or bump can drive a screwdriver deep into your body. Even a wiping cloth hanging from the back pocket can wrap around a spinning shaft or fan.

• DON'T smoke when working around gasoline, cleaning solvent or other flammable, material.

• DON'T smoke when working around the battery. When the battery is being charged, it gives off explosive hydrogen gas.

• DON'T use gasoline to wash your hands; there are excellent soaps available. Gasoline may contain lead, and lead can enter the body through a cut, accumulating in the body until you are very ill. Gasoline also removes all the natural oils from the skin so that bone dry hands will suck up oil and grease.

• DON'T service the air conditioning system unless you are equipped with the necessary tools and training. The refrigerant, R-12, is extremely cold and when exposed to the air, will instantly freeze any surface it comes in contact with, including your eyes. Although the refrigerant is normally nontoxic, R-12 becomes a deadly poisonous gas in the presence of an open flame. One good whiff of the vapors from burning refrigerant can be fatal.

IDENTIFICATION NUMBERS

Vehicle Identification Number

The vehicle identification number is located on a plate attached to the left top side of the instrument panel and visible through the windshield. All vehicle identification numbers on 1979–80 Models contain 13 digits. The vehicle number is a code which tells the truck line (1st digit), wheelbase and GVW (Gross Vehicle Weight) (2nd digit), price class (3rd digit), body code (4th digit), engine code (5th digit), model year (6th digit), transmission code (7th digit), trim code (8th digit) and vehicle sequential serial number (last five digits). On 1981 models the vehicle identification number contains 17 digits identifying additional information as shown in the illustration.

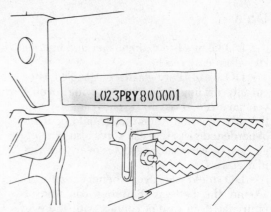

Chassis number location

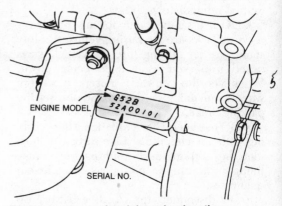

Engine number and serial number location

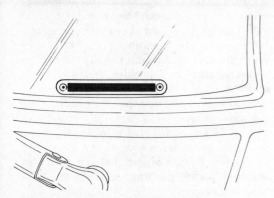

Vehicle identification number location

Chassis Number

The chassis number is stamped on the sidewall of the frame near the rear spring hanger.

Engine Model Number and Serial Number

The engine model number is stamped near the engine serial number on the right front side at the top edge of the cylinder block.

Transmission Serial Number

The manual transmission serial number is stamped on the clutch housing of the transmission case. The automatic transmission serial number is stamped on the lower edge of the transmission case just above the oil pan.

ROUTINE MAINTENANCE

Refer to the maintenance Interval Chart as a guide to schedule periodic maintenance for the following operations.

J	B	7	F	P	2	4	5	1	B	Y	1	0	0	1	0	1

1st Digit	2rd Digit	3rd Digit	4th Digit	5th Digit	6th Digit	7th Digit	8th Digit	9th Digit	10th Digit	11th Digit	12th Digit	13th to 17th Digit
Manufac- turing Country	Sales Channel	Vehicle Type	Other	Vehicle Line	Trim Code	Body Type	Engine Displace- ment	*Check Digits	Model Year	Assem- bly Plant	Trans- mission Code	Sequence Number

1981 vehicle identification number plate

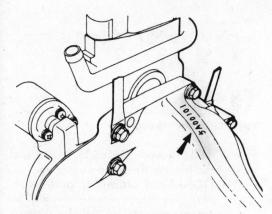

Manual transmission serial number location

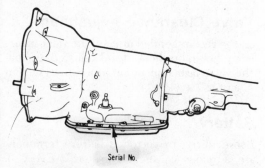

Automatic transmission serial number location

Air Cleaner

A clogged air filter can result in poor engine performance and as much as a 10% increase in fuel consumption by richening the air/fuel mixture. The air filter should be checked and cleaned periodically and replaced as necessary.

REMOVAL, CLEANING AND REPLACEMENT

1. Remove the wing nut and unsnap the finger clips.

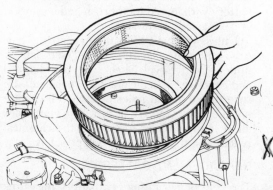

Removing the air filter element

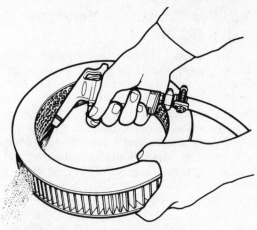

Clean the air filter from the inside out

2. To clean the element, use compressed air and clean from the inside out.
3. Install the air filter, and then install the cover and housing.

NOTE: *Make sure the arrows are aligned.*

4. Tighten the wing nut by hand.

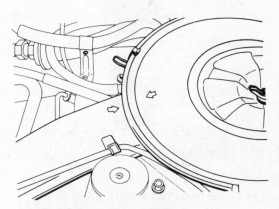

Align the arrows when installing

Engine Identification Chart

Year	Engine Model	Engine Displacement	Location
1979–81	G52B (U-engine)	2.0 liters (121.7 CID)	U.S.A.
1979–81	4G52 (U-engine)	2.0 liters (121.7 CID)	Canada
1979–81	G54B (W-engine)	2.6 liters (155.9 CID)	U.S.A.
1979–80	4G54 (W-engine)	2.6 liters (155.9 CID)	Canada

Positive Crankcase Ventilation Valve (PCV)

On all models a closed type crankcase ventilation system is used to prevent blow-by gas from escaping into the atmosphere. On 1979 and 80 models this system has a small orifice fixed at the intake manifold or at the rocker cover. On 1981 models a P.C.V. valve is utilized at the rocker arm cover. On all models the breather hoses should be inspected and cleaned at regular intervals. On 1981 models the P.C.V. valve can be tested by performing the following test:

With the engine idling, remove the PCV valve from the rocker cover. If the valve is not clogged, a kissing noise will be heard as the air is passed through the valve, and a strong vacuum should be felt when a finger is placed over the valve inlet. A clogged valve should be cleaned with an appropriate solvent or replaced.

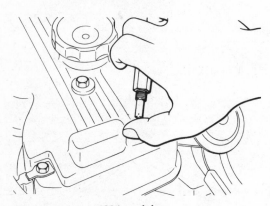

PCV valve test—1981 models

Evaporator Canister

An activated charcoal canister is installed between the fuel tank and the air cleaner. The canister stores carburetor and fuel tank vapors while the engine is off, holding them to be drawn into the engine and burned when the engine is started. If or when the canister filter becomes clogged the canister should be replaced.

Cylinder Head Bolts

At the recommended interval the cylinder head bolts should be retorqued while the en-

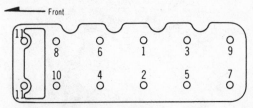

Head bolt tightening sequence

gine is cold. Remove the rocker cover and tighten the bolts in the sequence shown.

CAUTION: *Never attempt to run the engine while the rocker cover is removed or the engine compartment will be sprayed with oil.*

Valve Clearance Adjustment

At the recommended interval the valve clearance should be checked and adjusted. Follow the valve lash adjustment procedure given in Chapter Two.

Battery

Loose, dirty, or corroded battery terminals are a major cause of "no-start". Every 3 months or so, remove the battery terminals and clean them, giving them a light coating of petroleum jelly when you are finished. This will help to retard corrosion.

Check the battery cables for signs of wear or chafing and replace any cable or terminal that looks marginal. Battery terminals can be easily cleaned and inexpensive terminal cleaning tools are an excellent investment that will pay for themselves many times over. They can usually be purchased from any well-equipped auto store or parts department. Side terminal batteries require a different tool to clean the threads in the battery case. The accumulated white powder and corrosion can be cleaned from the top of the battery with an old toothbrush and a solution of baking soda and water.

Unless you have a "maintenance-free" battery, check the electrolyte level (see Battery under Fluid Level Checks in this chapter) and check the specific gravity of each cell. Be sure that the vent holes in each cell cap are not blocked by grease or dirt. The vent holes allow hydrogen gas, formed by the chemical reaction in the battery, to escape safely.

REPLACEMENT BATTERIES

The cold power rating of a battery measures starting performance and provides an approx-

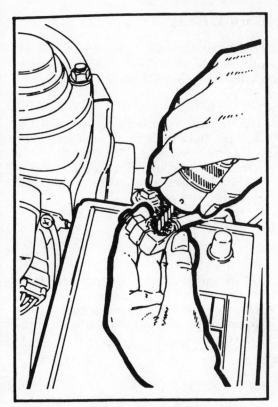

Battery cable cleaning tool—top terminal type

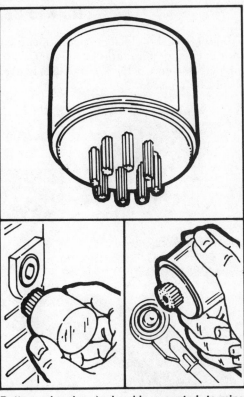

Battery cleaning tool—side mounted terminal battery

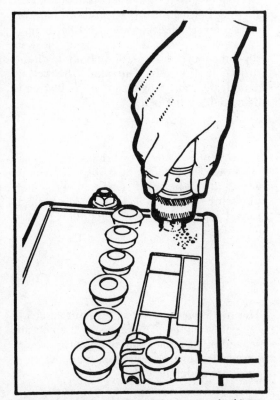

Battery terminal cleaning tool—top terminal type

imate relationship between battery size and engine size. The cold power rating of a replacement battery should match or exceed your engine size in cubic inches.

Belts

TENSION CHECKING AND ADJUSTMENT

Check the drive belts at regular intervals for evidence of wear such as cracking, fraying, and incorrect tension. Determine belt tension at a point halfway between the pulleys by pressing on the belt with moderate thumb

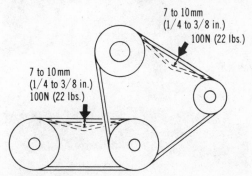

Checking belt tension

How to Spot Worn V-Belts

V-Belts are vital to efficient engine operation—they drive the fan, water pump and other accessories. They require little maintenance (occasional tightening) but they will not last forever. Slipping or failure of the V-belt will lead to overheating. If your V-belt looks like any of these, it should be replaced.

Cracking or weathering

This belt has deep cracks, which cause it to flex. Too much flexing leads to heat build-up and premature failure. These cracks can be caused by using the belt on a pulley that is too small. Notched belts are available for small diameter pulleys.

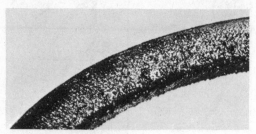

Softening (grease and oil)

Oil and grease on a belt can cause the belt's rubber compounds to soften and separate from the reinforcing cords that hold the belt together. The belt will first slip, then finally fail altogether.

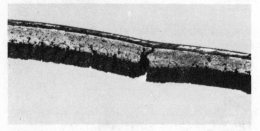

Glazing

Glazing is caused by a belt that is slipping. A slipping belt can cause a run-down battery, erratic power steering, overheating or poor accessory performance. The more the belt slips, the more glazing will be built up on the surface of the belt. The more the belt is glazed, the more it will slip. If the glazing is light, tighten the belt.

Worn cover

The cover of this belt is worn off and is peeling away. The reinforcing cords will begin to wear and the belt will shortly break. When the belt cover wears in spots or has a rough jagged appearance, check the pulley grooves for roughness.

Separation

This belt is on the verge of breaking and leaving you stranded. The layers of the belt are separating and the reinforcing cords are exposed. It's just a matter of time before it breaks completely.

pressure. The deflection should be between ¼ and ⅜ inches. If the deflection is found to be too much or too little, loosen the mounting bolts and make the adjustment.

Hoses
HOSE REPLACEMENT

1. Remove the radiator cap.
2. Drain the coolant from the radiator by opening the radiator petcock, if so equipped, or by disconnecting the lower radiator hose. If your car is equipped with a petcock it might be a good idea to squirt a little penetrating oil on it first.
3. To replace the bottom hose drain all the coolant from the radiator but if only the top hose is to be replaced drain just enough fluid to bring the level down below the level of the top hose. If the fluid is over a year old discard it.
4. Most hoses are attached with screw type hose clamps. If the old clamps are badly rusted or damaged in any way it is always best to replace with new ones.
5. When installing the new hose slide the clamps over each end of the hose then slide the hose over the hose connections. Position each clamp about ¼" from the end of the hose and tighten.
   CAUTION: *Do not over tighten at the radiator connections as it is very easy to crush the metal.*
6. Close the petcock and refill with the old coolant if it is less than a year old or with a new mixture of 50/50, coolant/water.
7. Start the engine and idle it for 15 minutes with the radiator cap off and check for leaks. Add coolant if necessary and install the radiator cap.

Cooling System

At least once every 2 years, the engine cooling system should be inspected, flushed, and refilled with fresh coolant. If the coolant is left in the system too long, it loses its ability to prevent rust and corrosion. If the coolant has too much water, it won't protect against freezing.

The pressure cap should be looked at for signs of age or deterioration. Fan belt and other drive belts should be inspected and adjusted to the proper tension. (See checking belt tension).

Hose clamps should be tightened, and soft or cracked hoses replaced. Damp spots, or accumulations of rust or dye near hoses, water pump or other areas, indicate possible leakage, which must be corrected before filling the system with fresh coolant.

CHECK THE RADIATOR CAP

While you are checking the coolant level, check the radiator cap for a worn or cracked gasket. If the cap doesn't seal properly, fluid will be lost and the engine will overheat.

Worn caps should be replaced with a new one.

CLEAN RADIATOR OF DEBRIS

Periodically clean any debris—leaves, paper, insects, etc.—from the radiator fins. Pick the large pieces off by hand. The smaller pieces can be washed away with water pressure from a hose.

Carefully straighten any bent radiator fins with a pair of needle nose pliers. Be careful— the fins are very soft. Don't wiggle the fins back and forth too much. Straighten them once and try not to move them again.

DRAIN AND REFILL THE COOLING SYSTEM

Completely draining and refilling the cooling system every two years at least will remove accumulated rust, scale and other deposits. Coolant in late model cars is a 50-50 mixture of ethylene glycol and water for year round use. Use a good quality antifreeze with water pump lubricants, rust inhibitors and other corrosion inhibitors along with acid neutralizers.

1. Drain the existing antifreeze and coolant. Open the radiator and engine drain petcocks, or disconnect the bottom radiator hose, at the radiator outlet.
   NOTE: *Before opening the radiator petcock, spray it with some penetrating lubricant.*
2. Close the petcock or re-connect the lower hose and fill the system with water.
3. Add a can of quality radiator flush.
4. Idle the engine until the upper radiator hose gets hot.
5. Drain the system again.
6. Repeat this process until the drained water is clear and free of scale.
7. Close all petcocks and connect all the hoses.
8. If equipped with a coolant recovery system, flush the reservoir with water and leave empty.
9. Determine the capacity of your cool-

How to Spot Bad Hoses

Both the upper and lower radiator hoses are called upon to perform difficult jobs in an inhospitable environment. They are subject to nearly 18 psi at under hood temperatures often over 280°F., and must circulate nearly 7500 gallons of coolant an hour—3 good reasons to have good hoses.

A good test for any hose is to feel it for soft or spongy spots. Frequently these will appear as swollen areas of the hose. The most likely cause is oil soaking. This hose could burst at any time, when hot or under pressure.

Swollen hose

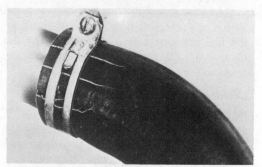

Cracked hoses can usually be seen but feel the hoses to be sure they have not hardened; a prime cause of cracking. This hose has cracked down to the reinforcing cords and could split at any of the cracks.

Cracked hose

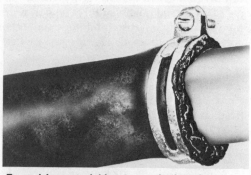

Weakened clamps frequently are the cause of hose and cooling system failure. The connection between the pipe and hose has deteriorated enough to allow coolant to escape when the engine is hot.

Frayed hose end (due to weak clamp)

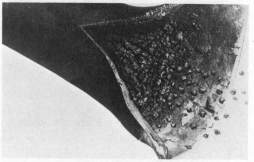

Debris, rust and scale in the cooling system can cause the inside of a hose to weaken. This can usually be felt on the outside of the hose as soft or thinner areas.

Debris in cooling system

ing system (see capacities specifications). Add a 50/50 mix of quality antifreeze (ethylene glycol) and water to provide the desired protection.

10. Run the engine to operating temperature.

11. Stop the engine and check the coolant level.

12. Check the level of protection with an anti-freeze tester, replace the cap and check for leaks.

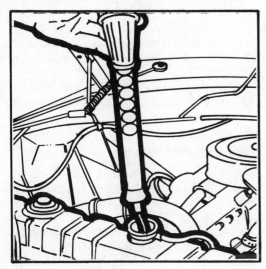

Anti freeze tester

AIR-CONDITIONING SAFETY PRECAUTIONS

There are two particular hazards associated with air conditioning systems and they both relate to the refrigerant gas.

First, the refrigerant gas is an extremely cold substance. When exposed to air, it will instantly freeze any surface it comes in contact with, including your eyes. The other hazard relates to fire. Although normally non-toxic, refrigerant gas becomes highly poisonous in the presence of an open flame. One good whiff of the vapor formed by burning refrigerant can be fatal. Keep all forms of fire (including cigarettes) well clear of the air-conditioning system.

Any repair work to an air conditioning system should be left to a professional. Do not, under any circumstances, attempt to loosen or tighten any fittings or perform any work other than that outlined here.

CHECKING FOR OIL LEAKS

Refrigerant leaks show up as oily areas on the various components because the compressor oil is transported around the entire system along with the refrigerant. Look for oily spots on all the hoses and lines, and especially on the hose and tubing connections. If there are oily deposits, the system may have a leak, and you should have it checked by a qualified repairman.

NOTE: *A small area of oil on the front of the compressor is normal and no cause for alarm.*

CHECK THE COMPRESSOR BELT

Refer to the section in this chapter on "Drive Belts".

KEEP THE CONDENSER CLEAR

Periodically inspect the front of the condenser for bent fins or foreign material (dirt, bugs, leaves, etc.) If any cooling fins are bent, straighten them carefully with needle-nosed pliers. You can remove any debris with a stiff bristle brush or hose.

OPERATE THE A/C SYSTEM PERIODICALLY

A lot of A/C problems can be avoided by simply running the air conditioner at least once a week, regardless of the season. Simply let the system run for at least 5 minutes a week (even in the winter), and you'll keep the internal parts lubricated as well as preventing the hoses from hardening.

REFRIGERANT LEVEL CHECK

There are two ways to check refrigerant level, depending on how your model is equipped.

With Sight Glass

The first order of business when checking the sight glass is to find the sight glass. It will either be in the head of the receiver/drier, or in one of the metal lines leading from the top of the receiver/drier. Once you've found it, wipe it clean and proceed as follows:

1. With the engine and the air conditioning system running, look for the flow of refrigerant through the sight glass. If the air conditioner is working properly, you'll be able to see a continuous flow of clear refrigerant through the sight glass, with perhaps an occasional bubble at very high temperatures.

2. Cycle the air conditioner on and off to make sure what you are seeing is clear refrigerant. Since the refrigerant is clear, it is possible to mistake a completely discharged system for one that is fully charged. Turn the

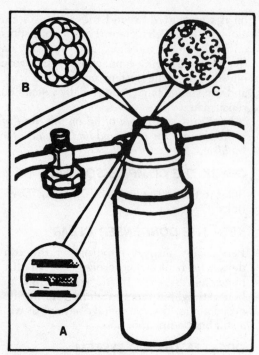

Oil streaks (A), constant bubbles (B) or foam (C) indicate there is not enough refrigerant in the system. Occasional bubbles during initial operation is normal. A clear sight glass indicates a proper charge or no refrigerant at all

system off and watch the sight glass. If there is refrigerant in the system, you'll see bubbles during the off cycle. If you observe no bubbles when the system is running, and the air flow from the unit in the car is delivering cold air, everything is OK.

3. If you observe bubbles in the sight glass while the system is operating, the system is low on refrigerant. Have it checked by a professional.

4. Oil streaks in the sight glass are an indication of trouble. Most of the time, if you see oil in the sight glass, it will appear as a series of streaks, although occasionally it may be a solid stream of oil. In either case, it means that part of the charge has been lost.

Without Sight Glass

On vehicles that are not equipped with sight glasses, it is necessary to feel the temperature difference in the inlet and outlet lines at the receiver/drier to gauge the refrigerant level. Use the following procedure:

1. Locate the receiver/drier. It will generally be up front near the condenser. It is shaped like a small fire extinguisher and will always have two lines connected to it. One

line goes to the expansion valve and the other goes to the condenser.

2. With the engine and the air conditioner running, hold a line in each hand and gauge their relative temperatures. If they are both the same approximate temperature, the system is correctly charged.

3. If the line from the expansion valve to the receiver/drier is a lot colder than the line from the receiver/drier to the condenser, then the system is overcharged. It should be noted that this is an extremely rare condition.

4. If the line that leads from the receiver/drier to the condenser is a lot colder than the other line, the system is undercharged.

5. If the system is undercharged or overcharged, have it checked by a professional air conditioning mechanic.

Windshield Wipers

Intense heat from the sun, snow and ice, road oils and the chemicals used in windshield washer solvents combine to deteriorate the rubber wiper refills. The refills should be replaced about twice a year or whenever the blades begin to streak or chatter.

WIPER REFILL REPLACEMENT

Normally, if the wipers are not cleaning the windshield properly, only the refill has to be replaced. The blade and arm usually require replacement only in the event of damage. It is not necessary (except on new Tridon refills) to remove the arm or the blade to replace the refill (rubber part), though you may have to position the arm higher on the glass. You can do this by turning the ignition switch on and operating the wipers. When they are positioned where they are accessible, turn the ignition switch off.

There are several types of refills and your vehicle could have any kind, since aftermarket blades and arms may not use exactly the same type refill as the original equipment.

Most Trico styles use a release button that is pushed down to allow the refill to slide out of the yoke jaws. The new refill slides in the locks in place. Some Trico refills are removed by locating where the metal backing strip or the refill is wider. Insert a small screwdriver blade between the frame and metal backing strip. Press down to release the refill from the retaining tab.

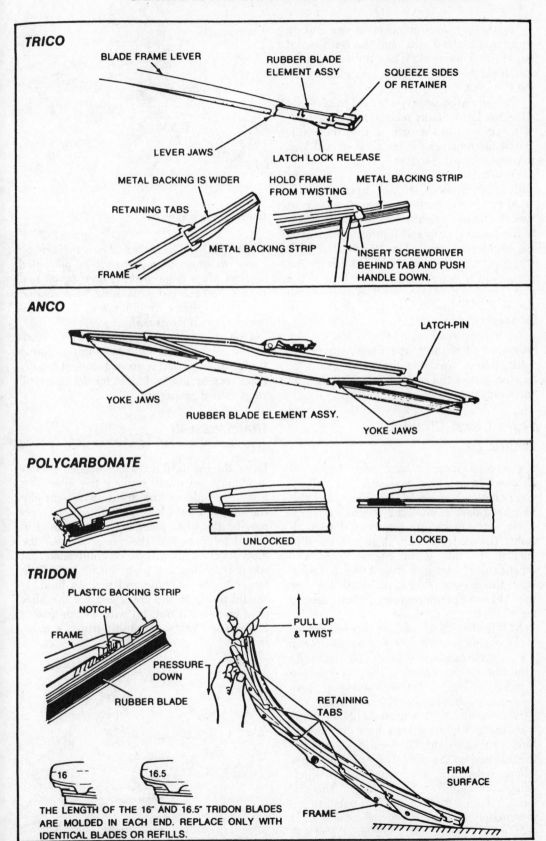

TRICO

BLADE FRAME LEVER

RUBBER BLADE ELEMENT ASSY

SQUEEZE SIDES OF RETAINER

LEVER JAWS

LATCH LOCK RELEASE

METAL BACKING IS WIDER

RETAINING TABS

FRAME

METAL BACKING STRIP

HOLD FRAME FROM TWISTING

METAL BACKING STRIP

INSERT SCREWDRIVER BEHIND TAB AND PUSH HANDLE DOWN.

ANCO

LATCH-PIN

YOKE JAWS

RUBBER BLADE ELEMENT ASSY.

YOKE JAWS

POLYCARBONATE

UNLOCKED

LOCKED

TRIDON

PLASTIC BACKING STRIP

NOTCH

FRAME

PULL UP & TWIST

PRESSURE DOWN

RUBBER BLADE

RETAINING TABS

16

16.5

FIRM SURFACE

FRAME

THE LENGTH OF THE 16" AND 16.5" TRIDON BLADES ARE MOLDED IN EACH END. REPLACE ONLY WITH IDENTICAL BLADES OR REFILLS.

Wiper insert replacement

The Anco style is unlocked at one end by squeezing 2 metal tabs, and the refill is slid out of the frame jaws. When the new refill is installed, the tabs will click into place, locking the refill.

The polycarbonate type is held in place by a locking lever that is pushed downward out of the groove in the arm to free the refill. When the new refill is installed, it will lock in place automatically.

The Tridon refill has a plastic backing strip with a notch about an inch from the end. Hold the blade (frame) on a hard surface so that the frame is tightly bowed. Grip the tip of the backing strip and pull up while twisting counterclockwise. The backing strip will snap out of the retaining tab. Do this for the remaining tabs until the refill is free of the arm. The length of these refills is molded into the end and they should be replaced with identical types.

No matter which type of refill you use, be sure that all of the frame claws engage the refill. Before operating the wipers, be sure that no part of the metal frame is contacting the windshield.

Fluid Level Checks
ENGINE OIL

It's a good idea to have the engine oil checked every time you buy gas. When you're having it checked, it's also a good idea to take a look around the engine compartment just to make sure that everything is alright. The oil level is checked with the dipstick at the side of the engine block. The dipstick protrudes into the oil pan and measures the amount of oil in the crankcase. See the "Oil and Fuel Recommendations" section for which type of oil to use.

NOTE: *The oil should be checked before the engine is started or five minutes after the engine has been shut off. This gives the oil time to drain back to the pan from the valves and upper engine components preventing an inaccurate oil level reading.*

Remove the dipstick from its holder, wipe it clean, and insert it back into the engine. Remove it again and observe the point where the oil stops on the stick. It should fall somewhere between "full" and "add" without going above "full" or below "add." The distance between the two marks is equal to approximately 1 qt, so, if your oil level is right on the "add" mark, the addition of 1 qt will bring the level up to "full."

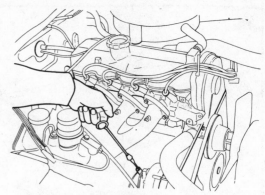

Checking the engine oil

CAUTION: *Overfilling the crankcase by one qt or more may result in oil-fouled spark plugs or oil leaks caused by oil seal failure. To avoid weakening oil seals and gaskets, remove the plug from the oil pan and drain the extra oil.*

Don't be alarmed if a new car uses a moderate amount of oil. Oil consumption during the break-in period is normal since it usually takes several hundred miles for the piston oil rings to seat properly.

TRANSMISSION
Manual

Drive the car until it reaches normal operating temperature and remove the filler plug from the side of the transmission. If the transmission fluid leaks out while you're removing the filler plug, there is no need to completely remove the plug because the fluid level is alright. If no fluid leaks out when removing the plug, insert your little finger in the opening and feel for fluid. It should be up to the lower edge of the filler plug opening; if not, fill with a high-quality SAE 80 or SAE 80–90 multipurpose gear lubricant.

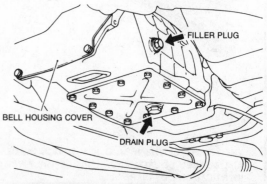

Manual transmission filler plug location

Automatic

1. Drive the truck until it reaches normal operating temperature.

2. Drive to a flat surface and pull on the parking brake lever.

3. Move the selector lever through all positions (P-L) before placing it in the "N" position.

4. The fluid level should be between the notches above "ADD-1-PINT" and below "FULL" inscribed on the dipstick.

CAUTION: *Do not overfill as this can have adverse effects on the operation of the transmission.*

5. When adding fluid use only "DEXRON II" type automatic transmission fluid.

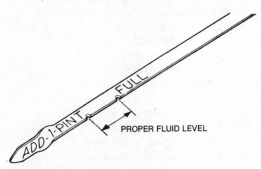

PROPER FLUID LEVEL

Automatic transmission dipstick

BRAKE MASTER CYLINDER

At the recommended interval check the brake fluid level in the master cylinder. The fluid level should be between the upper and lower markings on the fluid reservoir. With disc brakes the fluid level can be expected to fall as the brake pads wear, however, a rapid loss of fluid indicates a leak in the brake system which should be inspected and repaired immediately. Use only a top grade SAE approved brake fluid with the words "DOT-3"

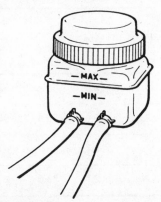

Brake fluid reservoir

on the can and tighten the cap on the reservoir securely.

CAUTION: *Be careful when using brake fluid around painted surfaces; it will quickly dissolve paint if not immediately diluted with water. Never operate the brake pedal with the reservoir cover removed. Fluid pressure created by pushing the pedal will force fluid from the reservoir.*

COOLANT

Since the cooling system is pressurized, the radiator cap should not be removed unless the engine has cooled. To do otherwise involves the risk of being scalded by steam. To check the coolant level; simply note the coolant level in relation to the level marks on the overflow canister.

If the coolant needs to be replenished, refer to the "Anti-Freeze" charts in the Appendix and to the "capacities" chart in this chapter to determine the proper amounts of anti-freeze and water to add to maintain the proper coolant mix.

NOTE: *Even in summer, the coolant mixtures must provide 0° F protection. This is required to prevent rust and to ensure proper operation of the temperature warning light.*

If the coolant level is frequently low, refer to the cooling system section of Chapter 11.

REAR AXLE

It is recommended that the rear axle lubricant level be checked at each engine oil change interval. The proper lubricant is SAE 80 or 90 GL-5 gear lubricant. The filler plug is removed with a ⅜ in. drive ratchet and short extension. When the unit is cold, the level should be ½ in. below the filler plug hole; when it is hot, it should be even with the hole. Lubricant may be added by a suction gun.

STEERING GEAR

The steering gear oil level can be checked by removing the breather plug and inserting a screwdriver into the plug hole at least 1.4 inches. If the tip of the screwdriver is not covered with oil add SAE grade 90 API classification GL-4 lubricant.

POWER STEERING RESERVOIR

1. Place the truck in a level position.
2. Start the engine and turn the steering

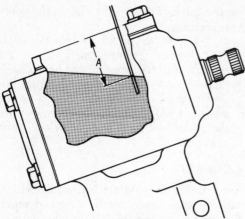

Inspecting steering gear oil level (A = 1.4 in.)

wheel fully to the right and left a few times while idling.

3. Check the reservoir level and add DEXTRON II type AFT fluid if the level is low.

CAUTION: *It is very important that when checking or adding fluid that dirt or grease does not enter the system.*

BATTERY

The electrolyte level in the battery should be checked once every month and more often during hot weather or long trips. If the level is below the bottom of the split ring, distilled water should be added until the level reaches the ring.

Tires

INFLATION PRESSURE

Tire inflation is the most ignored item of auto maintenance. Gasoline mileage can drop as much as .8% for every 1 pound per square inch (psi) of under inflation.

Two items should be a permanent fixture in every glove compartment; a tire pressure gauge and a tread depth gauge. Check the tire air pressure (including the spare) regularly with a pocket type gauge. Kicking the tires won't tell you a thing, and the gauge on the service station air hose is notoriously inaccurate.

The tire pressures recommended for your pick-up are usually found (See Tire Inflation Chart) in the owners manual. Ideally, inflation pressure should be checked when the tires are cool. When the air becomes heated it expands and the pressure increases. Every 10° rise (or drop) in temperature means a difference of 1 psi, which also explains why the tire appears to lose air on a very cold night. When it is impossible to check the tires "cold", allow for pressure build-up due to heat. If the "hot" pressure exceeds the "cold" pressure by more than 15 psi, reduce your speed, load or both. Otherwise internal heat is created in the tire. When the heat approaches the temperature at which the tire was cured, during manufacture, the tread can separate from the body.

CAUTION: *Never counteract excessive pressure build-up by bleeding off air pressure (letting some air out), This will only further raise the tire operating temperature.*

Before starting a long trip with lots of luggage, you can add about 2–4 psi to the tires to make them run cooler, but never exceed the maximum inflation pressure on the side of the tire.

Capacities

Year	Model	Engine Displacement (cc)	Crankcase (qts) With Filter	Crankcase (qts) Without Filter	Transmission (qts) Manual 4-spd	Transmission (qts) Manual 5-spd	Transmission (qts) Automatic	Drive Axle (pts)	Gasoline Tank (gals)	Cooling System (qts) With AC	Cooling System (qts) Without AC
1979–80	All	2000	4.5	4.0	2.2	—	6.8 ①	2.8	15.8	9.5	9.5
		2555	4.5	4.0	—	2.4	6.8 ①	2.8	15.8	9.7	9.7
1981	All	2000	4.5	4.0	2.2	—	7.1	2.7	15.1	9.5	9.5
		2555	4.5	4.0	—	2.4	7.1	2.7	18.0	9.5	9.5

① 1980: 7.2 U.S. quarts

TREAD DEPTH

All tires made since 1968, have 8 built-in tread wear indicator bars that show up as ½" wide smooth bands across the tire when $1/16"$ of tread remains. The appearance of tread wear indicators means that the tires should be replaced. In fact, many states have laws prohibiting the use of tires with less than $1/16"$ tread.

You can check your own tread depth with an inexpensive gauge or by using a Lincoln head penny. Slip the Lincoln penny into several tread grooves. If you can see the top of Lincoln's head in 2 adjacent grooves, the tires have less than $1/16"$ tread left and should be replaced. You can measure snow tires in the same manner by using the "tails" side of the Lincoln penny. If you can see the top of

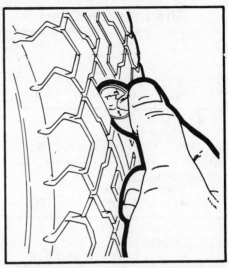

Checking tread depth with a Lincoln head penny

the Lincoln memorial, it's time to replace the snow tires.

TIRE ROTATION

Tire wear can be equalized by switching the position of the tires about every 6000 miles. Including a conventional spare in the rotation pattern can give up to 20% more tire life.

CAUTION: *Do not include the new "Space-Saver®" or temporary spare tires in the rotation pattern.*

There are certain exceptions to tire rotation, however. Studded snow tires should not be rotated, and radials should be kept on the same side of the car (maintain the same direction of rotation). The belts on radial tires get set in a pattern. If the direction of rotation is reversed, it can cause rough ride and vibration.

NOTE: *When radials or studded snows are taken off the car, mark them, so you can maintain the same direction of rotation.*

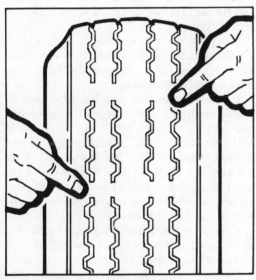

Built-in tread wear indicator bars

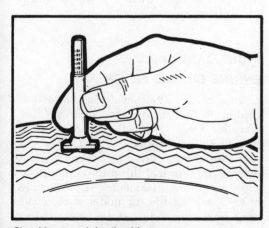

Checking tread depth with a gauge

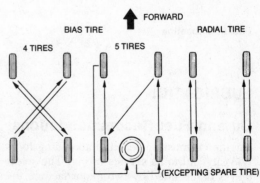

Tire rotation

Tire Inflation Chart

Description	Inflation Pressure (psi)	
Tire size	U-engine 6.00-14-6PR	W-engine 185SR14
No cargo		
Front	26	22
Rear	26	22
Full cargo		
Front	26	22
Rear	46	32

TIRE STORAGE

Store the tires at proper inflation pressures if they are mounted on wheels. All tires should be kept in a cool, dry place. If they are stored in the garage or basement, do not let them stand on a concrete floor; set them on strips of wood.

Fuel Filter

The fuel filter is the cartridge type and should be replaced at the interval specified in the Maintenance Interval Chart. The filter is retained by two hose clamps and can easily be removed with a pair of pliers.

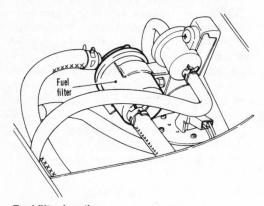

Fuel filter

Fuel filter location

LUBRICATION

Oil and Fuel Recommendations

Engine oil must be selected according to its viscosity and to its service rating. The selection is determined by two major factors: the climate in which the car will be operated and the work the engine will be doing. Engine oils are sold in a variety of viscosities. Each oil can top is stamped with a viscosity number (SAE 20, 30, 10W-30, etc.,) and a service rating (SA, SB, SC, SD, SF, or SE). Oil viscosity refers to the body and thickness of the oil. The Society of Automotive Engineers (SAE) devised an oil viscosity rating system in which the thicker oils receive a higher viscosity number than the thinner oils. SAE 30 oil is a straight-weight, single-viscosity oil having a fairly high viscosity.

As mentioned earlier, engine oil must be selected by viscosity and service rating. An engine oil is refined and then rated according to its ability to lubricate, control deposits, retard oil oxidation, and protect the engine from rust and corrosion.

For your truck, Chrysler Corp. recommends that only engine oils designed for service SE or SF be used. Both the SAE grade and the API service designation can be found on the container.

The gasolines you should use should have a minimum anti-knock index (Octane Value). This designation is comparable to 91 Research Octane Number.

Unleaded gasolines only must be used in trucks equipped with catalyst emission-control systems. All trucks, so equipped, have labels located on the instrument panel and behind the fuel filler lid that state, "UNLEADED GASOLINE ONLY." These trucks also have fuel filler tubes specially designed to accept the smaller diameter unleaded gasoline dispensing nozzles only.

Trucks for Canada not equipped with catalyst emission-control systems were designed to provide optimum efficiency using leaded gasolines having the same minimum anti-knock values shown above. It is recommended that these trucks not be operated exclusively on unleaded gasolines.

Fluid Changes

ENGINE OIL AND FILTER

Engine oil and filter should be changed according to the Maintenance Interval Chart. Chrysler Corp. bases these recommendations on the assumption that your car is being used for average driving. Certain types of driving requires that this interval not exceed three months or 3,000 miles. These include:

1. Operating the car under dusty conditions or during a dust storm. A dust storm may necessitate an immediate oil change.

2. Long periods of idling.

Maintenance Intervals Chart

Maintenance Item	*Maintenance Operation*	*1979*	*1980*	*1981*	*See Chapter Number*
UNDERHOOD					
Cylinder Head Bolts	Retorque—Cold Engine	1st 500 then every 7,500	1st 500 then every 7,500	—	3
Valve Clearance	Check and adjust—Hot Engine	1st 500 then every 15,000	1st 500 then every 15,000	1st 500 then every 15,000	2
Ignition Timing	Check and Adjust	1st 500 then every 24,000	1st 500 then every 24,000	Every 5 yrs or 50,000	2
Fuel Filter	Replace	Every 12 months or 15,000	Every 12 months or 15,000	50,000	1
Air Cleaner Filter	Replace	Every 30,000 ①	Every 30,000 ①	Every 30,000 ①	1
Canister	Replace	Every 30,000	Every 30,000	Every 50,000	1
Exhaust Manifold Bolts	Check & Retorque	Every 15,000	Every 15,000	—	3
Spark Plugs	Replace	Every 15,000	Every 15,000	Every 30,000	2
Drive Belts	Check for tension & wear & adjust or replace as necessary	Every 6 months	Every 6 months	Every 6 months	1
Cooling System	Flush system & change coolant	Every 24 months or 30,000	Every 24 months or 30,000	Every 24 months or 30,000	1
Engine Oil	Change	Every 6 months or 7,500	Every 12 months or 7,500	Every 12 months or 7,500	1
Engine Oil Filter	Replace	Every oil change	Every oil change	Every oil change	1
Brake Fluid	Replace ②	—	Every 24 months or 30,000	Every 4 years	1
Ignition Wires	Check & Replace as required	Every 15,000	Every 15,000	Every 5 yrs. or 50,000	2
Crankcase Emission Control System	Check & clean as required	Every 12 months or 15,000	Every 12 months or 15,000	Every 5 years or 50,000	1

Maintenance Intervals Chart (cont.)

Maintenance Item	Maintenance Operation	1979	1980	1981	See Chapter Number
UNDERHOOD (CONT'D)					
Fuel Water and Vapor Hoses	Check & replace as necessary	Every 6 months	Every 6 months	Every 6 months	—
Carburetor Linkage	Clean	Every 15,000	Every 30,000	Every 30,000	—
UNDER CAR					
Manual Transmission & Rear Axle	Check Fluid Level	Every 6 months	Every 15,000	Every 30,000	1
Automatic Transmission	Change Fluid ③	Every 30,000	Every 30,000	Every 30,000	1
Steering Gear	Fluid Level Check	Every 6 months	—	—	1
Bald Joint and Steering Linkage Seals	Inspect	Every oil change	Every oil change	Every oil change	1
Clutch Pedal	Adjust free play	Every 6 months	—	—	6
OUTSIDE OF VEHICLE					
Tires	Check pressure & wear	Once a month	Once a month	Once a month	1
Front Wheel Bearings	Clean & Lubricate	22,500	30,000	30,000	1
Rear Brake Lining	Inspect for wear	Every oil change	15,000	30,000	9
Disc Brake Pads	Inspect for wear	Every 6 months	Every 7,500	Every 15,000	9
Rear Wheel Cylinders	Check for leaks	Every oil change	15,000	30,000	9
Brake Hoses	Check for leaks	15,000	15,000	15,000	—

① More often under dusty driving conditions
② Check fluid level every six months
③ Severe usage only

3. Trailer hauling.

4. Short trips at freezing temperatures when the engine hasn't had time to warm up sufficiently.

These recommended oil change intervals are based upon the assumption that a high-quality SE or SF oil is used; otherwise the intervals would have to be made shorter for the lower quality oil. Long engine life, low maintenance, and good performance cannot be ensured if these oil changes are not performed at the proper intervals.

Always drain the oil after the engine has been running long enough to bring it to operating temperature. Hot oil will flow easier and more contaminants will be removed along with the oil than if it were drained cold. You will need a large capacity drain pan, which you can purchase at any store which sells automotive parts. Another necessity is containers for the used oil. You will find that plastic bottles, such as those used for bleach or fabric softener, make excellent storage jugs.

After draining your oil you should find some way of disposing of the old oil without damaging the environment. One way to do this would be to ask at your local gas station if you could dump your old oil into his holding tank. Some quantity of the old oil could be kept around for miscellaneous lubrication of things which are exposed to the elements all the time.

Changing Your Oil

1. Run the engine until it reaches normal operating temperature.

2. Jack up the front of the car and support it on safety stands.

3. Slide a drain pan of at least 6 quarts capacity under the oil pan.

4. Loosen the drain plug. Turn the plug out by hand. By keeping an inward pressure on the plug as you unscrew it, oil won't escape past the threads and you can remove it without being burned by hot oil.

5. Allow the oil to drain completely, then wipe clean and install the drain plug. Don't overtighten the plug, or force it in and strip the threads or you'll end up with a headache and a repair bill. If you do happen to damage the plug, there are other types of replacement plugs available from auto supply stores which will do the job.

6. Using a strap wrench, remove the oil filter. Keep in mind that it's holding about one quart of dirty, hot oil.

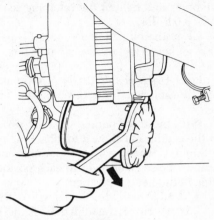

Removing engine oil filter

7. Empty the old filter into the drain pan and dispose of the filter.

8. Using a clean rag, wipe off the filter adapter on the engine block. Be sure that the rag doesn't leave any lint which could clog an oil passage.

9. Coat the rubber gasket on the filter with fresh oil. Spin it onto the engine *by hand;* when the gasket touches the adapter surface give it another ½–¾ turn. No more, or you'll squash the gasket and it will leak.

10. Refill the engine with the correct amount of fresh oil. See the "Capacities" chart.

11. Crank the engine over several times and then start it without touching the accelerator. If the oil pressure "idiot light" doesn't go out or the pressure gauge shows zero, after 10 seconds or so, shut the engine down and find out what's wrong.

12. If the oil pressure is OK and there are no leaks, shut the engine off and lower the car.

13. Wait a few minutes and check the oil level. Add oil, as necessary, to bring the level up to Full.

AUTOMATIC TRANSMISSION

1. Raise the front of the truck either by the use of ramps or a jack and safety stands.

2. Place a suitable drain container under the transmission pan.

3. Loosen the pan bolts and tap the pan at one corner to break it loose allowing the fluid to drain then remove the oil pan.

4. If necessary, adjust the low reverse band by following the procedure given in Chapter 6.

5. Install a new filter on the bottom of the

valve body, and tighten the retaining screws to 2.2–3.6 ft. lbs.

6. Clean the oil pan and reinstall it using a new gasket. Tighten the oil pan bolts to 11–14 ft. lbs.

7. Pour 4 qts. of DEXRON II type automatic transmission fluid through the filler tube.

8. With the truck parked on a flat surface start the engine and allow it to idle for at least two minutes. Then, with the parking brake on, move the selector lever to each position, ending in the neutral position.

9. Add ATF until the fluid level reaches the lower notch of the dipstick. After the transmission has reached normal operating temperature, recheck the fluid level to make sure it is between the notches of the dipstick.

REAR AXLE

1. Drive the truck 5–7 miles to warm the differential oil.

2. Remove both the filler and drain plugs and allow the warm oil to drain into a pan.

3. Install the drain plug and fill the differential up to the bottom of the filler plug hole with SAE 90 hypoid gear oil.

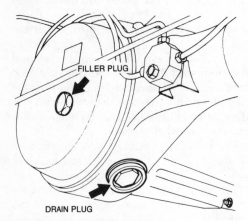

FILLER PLUG

DRAIN PLUG

Rear axle drain and filler plugs

COOLING SYSTEM

See the Cooling System section under Routine Maintenance earlier in this chapter for draining and refilling of the cooling system.

Chassis Greasing

The ball joints and steering linkage are permanently lubricated at the factory and do not require periodic lubrication. Inspect the dust cover and boots for proper sealing or damage and replace if necessary.

Wheel Bearings

For cleaning, packing and adjustment of the front wheel bearings refer to Chapter 9 Front Brake Disc and Wheel Bearing, removal and installation.

PUSHING AND TOWING

Your truck may be pushed for a short distance as long as the transmission is in neutral. If your truck fails to start by jump starting and it is equipped with manual transmission, it may be push started. Trucks equipped with automatic transmission cannot be push started. Keep in mind that the possible mismatching of bumper heights, especially around turns and over rough road surfaces could result in damage to either vehicle. If available, it is wise to tie an old tire either on the back of your truck or on the front of the pushing vehicle.

A truck with automatic transmission may be towed with the selector lever in neutral if the distance to be traveled does not exceed 15 miles and the towing speed does not exceed 30 mph. If the transmission is not operative or the truck is to be towed more than 15 miles, the propeller shaft must be disconnected or the truck towed with the rear wheels off the ground.

CAUTION: *If a towed truck requires steering, the ignition must be in the "ACC" position. If a truck is towed in the "Lock" position, a dolly should be used under the rear wheels and the front wheels should be raised.*

JACKING

The jack supplied with your truck was meant for changing tires. It was not meant to support a vehicle while you crawl under it and work. Whenever it is necessary to get under a vehicle to perform service operations, always be sure that it is adequately supported, preferably by jackstands at the proper points.

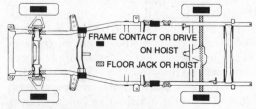

FRAME CONTACT OR DRIVE ON HOIST

FLOOR JACK OR HOIST

Support locations for lifting truck

Jump Starting a Dead Battery

The chemical reaction in a battery produces explosive hydrogen gas. This is the safe way to jump start a dead battery, reducing the chances of an accidental spark that could cause an explosion.

Jump Starting Precautions

1. Be sure both batteries are of the same voltage.
2. Be sure both batteries are of the same polarity (have the same grounded terminal).
3. Be sure the vehicles are not touching.
4. Be sure the vent cap holes are not obstructed.
5. Do not smoke or allow sparks around the battery.
6. In cold weather, check for frozen electrolyte in the battery.
7. Do not allow electrolyte on your skin or clothing.
8. Be sure the electrolyte is not frozen.

Jump Starting Procedure

1. Determine voltages of the two batteries; they must be the same.
2. Bring the starting vehicle close (they must not touch) so that the batteries can be reached easily.
3. Turn off all accessories and both engines. Put both cars in Neutral or Park and set the handbrake.
4. Cover the cell caps with a rag—do not cover terminals.
5. If the terminals on the run-down battery are heavily corroded, clean them.
6. Identify the positive and negative posts on both batteries and connect the cables in the order shown.
7. Start the engine of the starting vehicle and run it at fast idle. Try to start the car with the dead battery. Crank it for no more than 10 seconds at a time and let it cool off for 20 seconds in between tries.
8. If it doesn't start in 3 tries, there is something else wrong.
9. Disconnect the cables in the reverse order.
10. Replace the cell covers and dispose of the rags.

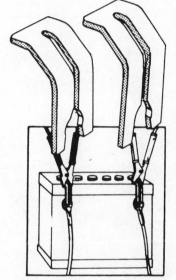

Side terminal batteries occasionally pose a problem when connecting jumper cables. There frequently isn't enough room to clamp the cables without touching sheet metal. Side terminal adaptors are available to alleviate this problem and should be removed after use.

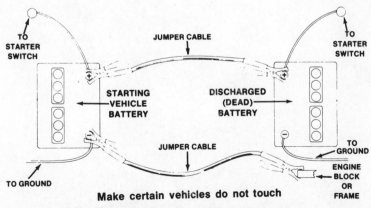

TO STARTER SWITCH

JUMPER CABLE

TO STARTER SWITCH

STARTING VEHICLE BATTERY

DISCHARGED (DEAD) BATTERY

JUMPER CABLE

TO GROUND

TO GROUND

ENGINE BLOCK OR FRAME

Make certain vehicles do not touch

This hook-up for negative ground cars only

Always block the wheels when changing tires.

Some of the service operations in this book require that one or both ends of the vehicle be raised and supported safely. The best arrangement for this, of course, is a grease pit or a vehicle lift, but these items are seldom found in the home garage. However, small hydraulic, screw, or scissors jacks are satisfactory for raising the vehicle.

Heavy wooden blocks or adjustable jackstands should be used to support the vehicle while it is being worked on. Drive-on trestles, or ramps, are also a handy and a safe way to raise the vehicle, assuming their capacity is adequate. These can be bought or constructed from suitable heavy timbers or steel.

In any case, it is always best to spend a little extra time to make sure that your truck is lifted and supported safely.

CAUTION: *Concrete blocks are not recommended. They may crumble if the load is not evenly distributed. Boxes and milk crates of any description must not be used.*

Tune-Up

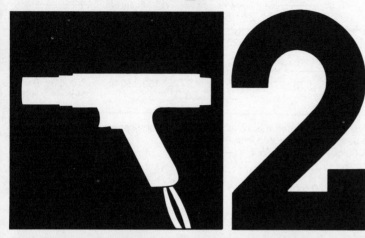

TUNE-UP PROCEDURES

Spark Plugs

A typical spark plug consists of a metal shell surrounding a ceramic insulator. A metal electrode extends downward through the center of the insulator and protrudes a small distance. Located at the end of the plug and attached to the side of the outer metal shell is the side electrode. The side electrode bends in at a 90° angle so that its tip is even with, and parallel to, the tip of the center electrode. The distance between these two electrodes (measured in thousandths of an inch) is called the spark plug gap. The spark plug in no way produces a spark but merely provides a gap across which the current can arc. The coil produces anywhere from 20,000 to 40,000 volts which travels to the distributor where it is distributed through the spark plug wires to the spark plugs. The current passes along the center electrode and jumps the gap to the side electrode, and, in so doing, ignites the air/fuel mixture in the combustion chamber.

SPARK PLUG HEAT RANGE

Spark plug heat range is the ability of the plug to dissipate heat. The longer the insulator (or the farther it extends into the engine), the hotter the plug will operate; the shorter the insulator the cooler it will operate. A plug that absorbs little heat and remains too cool will quickly accumulate deposits of oil and

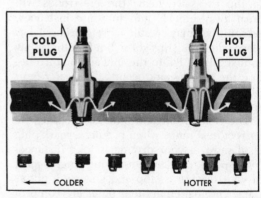

Spark plug heat range system. The higher the number the hotter the plug

	1 2 3 4 5
	R 45 T S X
1 —	R--INDICATES RESISTOR-TYPE PLUG.
2 —	"4" INDICATES 14 mm THREADS.
3 —	HEAT RANGE
4 —	TS--TAPERED SEAT
	S--EXTENDED TIP
5 —	SPECIAL GAP

6221

Spark plug coding using a AC-R45TSX as an example

Tune-Up Specifications

(When analyzing compression test results, look for uniformity among cylinders, rather than specific pressures)

Year	Engine Displacement cu in. (cc)	Spark Plugs		Ignition Timing (deg)		Intake Valve Opens (deg) BTDC	Fuel Pump Pressure (psi)	Idle Speed (rpm)	Valve Clearance (in.)	
		Type ①	Gap (in.)	MT	AT				In	Ex
1979–81	121.7 (2000)	BPR6ES-11	0.039–0.043 ②	5B	5B	25	4.6–6.0	650 ± 50 ④ ⑤	0.006 ③ Hot	0.010 Hot
	155.92 (2555)	BPR5ES-11	0.039–0.043 ②	7B	7B	25	4.6–6.0	750 ± 50 ⑤	0.006 ③ Hot	0.010 Hot

NOTE: *The underhood specifications sticker sometimes reflects tune-up specification changes made in production. Sticker figures must be used if they disagree with this chart.*
① NGK Spark Plugs. For Canada, 2000 cc—BRP6ES: 2555 cc—BPR5ES.
② Canada: 0.028–0.031 in.
③ Jet Valve clearance: 0.006 (Hot)
④ Automatic Transmission: 1979–80 700 ± 50 rpm.
⑤ 1981: 2000 cc—750 ± 100
         2555 cc—800 ± 100
MT: Manual Transmission
AT: Automatic Transmission

carbon since it is not hot enough to burn them off. This leads to plug fouling and consequently to misfiring. A plug that absorbs too much heat will have no deposits, but, due to the excessive heat, the electrodes will burn away quickly and in some instances, preignition may result. Preignition takes place when plug tips get so hot that they glow sufficiently to ignite the fuel/air mixture before the actual spark occurs. This early ignition will usually cause a pinging during low speeds and heavy loads.

The general rule of thumb for choosing the correct heat range when picking a spark plug is: if most of your driving is long distance, high speed travel, use a colder plug; if most of your driving is stop and go, use a hotter plug. Original equipment plugs are compromise plugs, but most people never have occasion to change their plugs from the factory-recommended heat range.

REPLACING SPARK PLUGS

A set of spark plugs usually requires replacement after about 10,000 miles on cars with conventional ignition systems and after about 20,000 to 30,000 miles on cars with electronic ignition, depending on your style of driving. In normal operation, plug gap increases about 0.001 in. for every 1,000–2,500 miles. As the gap increases, the plug's voltage re-

quirement also increases. It requires a greater voltage to jump the wider gap and about two to three times as much voltage to fire a plug at high speeds than at idle.

When you're removing spark plugs, you should work on one at a time. Don't start by removing the plug wires all at once, because unless you number them, they may become mixed up. Take a minute before you begin and number the wires with tape. The best location for numbering is near where the wires come out of the cap.

1. Twist the spark plug boot and remove the boot and wire from the plug. Do not pull on the wire itself as this will ruin the wire.

2. If possible, use a brush or rag to clean the area around the spark plug. Make sure that all the dirt is removed so that none will enter the cylinder after the plug is removed.

3. Remove the spark plug using the proper size socket. Turn the socket counterclockwise to remove the plug. Be sure to hold the socket straight on the plug to avoid breaking the plug, or rounding off the hex on the plug.

4. Once the plug is out, check it against the plugs shown in Chapter 11 (also see the "Color" insert in Chapter Four) to determine engine condition. This is crucial since plug readings are vital signs of engine condition.

5. Use a round wire feeler gauge to check

Engine Tune-Up Specifications
U.S.A. engines

Year	Engine	Transmission	Curb Idle Speed	Curb Idle CO	Enriched Idle Speed	Enriched Idle CO	Ignition Timing
1979–80	49-state U-engine	Manual	650 ± 50 rpm	Below 0.1%	730 ± 10	1.0 ± 0.1%	5° BTDC ± 1°
		Automatic	700 ± 50 rpm	Below 0.1%	780 ± 10	1.0 ± 0.1%	5° BTDC ± 1°
	W-engine	Manual	750 ± 50 rpm	1.0 ± 0.5%*	—	—	7° BTDC ± 1°
		Automatic	750 ± 50 rpm	1.0 ± 0.5%*	—	—	7° BTDC ± 1°
	California U-engine	Manual	650 ± 50 rpm	1.0 ± 0.5%*	—	—	5° BTDC ± 1°
		Automatic	700 ± 50 rpm	1.0 ± 0.5%*	—	—	5° BTDC ± 1°
	W-engine	Manual	750 ± 50 rpm	1.0 ± 0.5%*	—	—	7° BTDC ± 1°
		Automatic	750 ± 50 rpm	1.0 ± 0.5%*	—	—	7° BTDC 1°
1981	U-engine	All	750 ± 100 rpm	0.5 ± 0%*	—	—	5° BTDC ± 10
	W-engine	All	800 ± 100 rpm	0.5 ± 0%*	—	—	7° BTDC ± 1°

*With air injection system disconnected

the plug gap. The correct size gauge should pass through the electrode gap with a slight drag. If you're in doubt, try one size smaller and one larger. The smaller gauge should go through easily while the larger one shouldn't go through at all. If the gap is incorrect, use the electrode bending tool on the end of the gauge to adjust the gap. When adjusting the gap, always bend the side electrode. The center electrode is non-adjustable.

Set the plug gap to .039–.043 in. (U.S.A.), .028–.031 in. (Canada).

6. Squirt a drop of penetrating oil on the threads of the new plug and install it. Don't

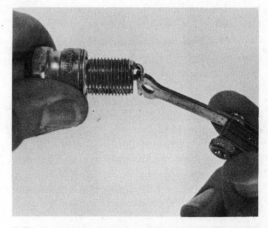

Adjusting the gap with an electrode bending tool

oil the threads too heavily. Turn the plug in clockwise by hand until it is snug.

7. When the plug is finger tight, tighten it with a wrench. If you don't have a torque wrench, tighten the plug as shown.

8. Install the plug boot firmly over the plug. Proceed to the next plug.

CHECKING AND REPLACING SPARK PLUG CABLES

Visually inspect the spark plug cables for burns, cuts, or breaks in the insulation. Check the spark plug boots and the nipples on the distributor cap and coil. Replace any

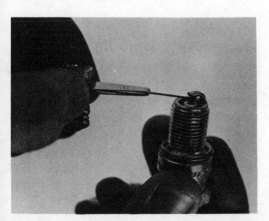

Checking plug gap with a round wire feeler gauge

damaged wiring. If no physical damage is obvious, the wires can be checked with an ohmmeter for excessive resistance. (See the tune-up and troubleshooting section).

When installing a new set of spark plug cables, replace the cables one at a time so there will be no mixup. Start by replacing the longest cable first. Install the boot firmly over the spark plug. Route the wire exactly the same as the original. Insert the nipple firmly into the tower on the distributor cap. Repeat the process for each cable.

SPARK PLUG ANALYSIS

Refer to chapter 11 and the "Color" insert in chapter 4.

Electronic Ignition

All D—50, Ram-50 and Arrow pick-ups are equipped with electronic ignition systems which replace the contact points and condenser with a transistorized integrated circuit. There are no adjustments that can be done on this type of ignition system.

Ignition Timing

1. Warm up the engine. Connect a tachometer and check the engine idle speed. Adjust it as outlined below if it is not within specifications.

If the timing mark on the front pulley is difficult to see, use chalk or a dab of paint to make it more visible.

2. Connect a timing light to the engine, as outlined in the instructions supplied by the manufacturer of the light.

3. Allow the engine to run at the specified idle speed with the gear shift in Neutral and

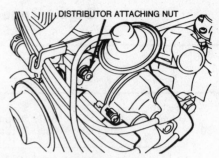

Ignition timing adjusting nut

the air conditioning compressor and lights off.

CAUTION: *Be sure the parking brake is firmly set and that the wheels are chocked.*

4. Point the timing light at the timing marks indicated on the front timing chain cover. With engine at idle, timing should be at the specifications given in the tune-up chart at the beginning of this section. If it is not, loosen the attaching nut at the base of the distributor and rotate the distributor until the correct timing is achieved.

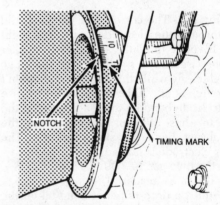

Crankshaft pulley timing mark

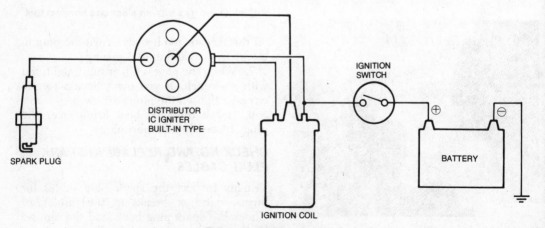

Electronic ignition system

5. Stop the engine and retighten the attaching nut. Start the engine and recheck the timing.

6. Stop the engine and disconnect the timing light and tachometer.

Valve Lash Adjustment

Both the U engine (1995 c.c.) and the W engine (2555 c.c.) which are sold in the United States have a jet valve located beside the intake valve of each cylinder. The jet valve works off the intake valve rocker arm and injects a swirl of air into the combustion chamber to promote more complete burning of fuel.

NOTE: *When adjusting valve clearances, the jet valve must be adjusted before the intake valve.*

1. Start the engine and allow it to reach normal operating temperature (170–190°F).

2. Stop the engine and remove the air cleaner and its hoses. Remove any other cables, hoses, wires, etc., which are attached to the valve cover, and remove the valve cover.

3. Disconnect the high tension coil-to-distributor wire at the coil.

4. Watch the rocker arms for No. 1 cylinder and rotate the crankshaft until the exhaust valve is closing and the intake valve has just started to open. At this point, no. 4 cylinder will be at Top Dead Center (TDC) commencing its firing stroke.

5. Loosen the lock nut on cylinder no. 4 intake valve and back off the intake valve adjusting screw 2 or more turns.

6. Loosen the lock nut on the jet valve adjusting screw.

7. Turn the jet valve adjusting screw counter-clockwise and insert a 0.006 in. feeler gauge between the jet valve stem and the adjusting screw.

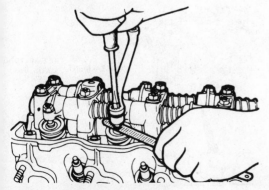

Adjusting the valve clearance

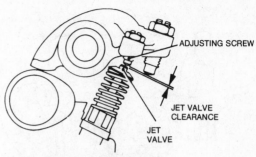

Jet valve clearance adjustment

8. Tighten the adjusting screw until it touches the feeler gauge.

Take care not to press in the valve while adjusting because the jet valve spring is very weak.

NOTE: *If the adjusting screw is tight, special care must be taken to avoid pressing down on the jet valve when adjusting the clearance or a false reading will result.*

9. Tighten the lock nut securely while holding the rocker arm adjusting screw with a screwdriver to prevent it from turning.

10. Make sure that a 0.006 in. feeler gauge can be easily inserted between the jet valve and the rocker arm.

11. Adjust no. 4 cylinder's intake valve to 0.006 in. and its exhaust valve to 0.010 in. Tighten the adjusting screw locknuts and recheck each clearance.

12. Perform step 4 to set up the remaining three cylinders for valve adjustments.

13. Replace the valve cover and all other components. Run the engine and check for oil leaks at the valve cover.

Idle Speed and Mixture Adjustments

NOTE: *The following procedures require the use of a CO meter to adjust their mixture ratios.*

U engine—U.S.A. except 1980 California 1979 W engine

1. place the transmission in "N" (Neutral) position and set the parking brake.

2. Make sure the air conditioner, lights and all accessories are off.

3. Run the engine at idle until the coolant temperature reaches 170–190°F.

4. Adjust the engine speed and idle CO concentration to the enriched idle speed and enriched idle CO as specified in the tune-up chart. Adjust the CO-concentration using the

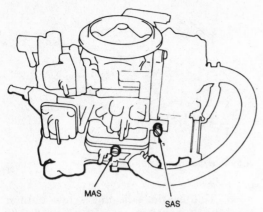

Idle mixture adjusting screw (MAS) and idle speed adjusting screw (SAS)—1979-80 models U.S.A. and Canada, 1981 Canadian models

idle speed adjusting screw (SAS) and the idle mixture adjusting screw (MAS).

5. Reset the engine speed to curb idle speed by adjusting the idle mixture adjusting screw (MAS—See illustration).

6. The engine should now run smoothly.

7. If the adjustment procedure does not bring the CO concentration and speed to specifications, reset the idle mixture adjusting screw or repeat steps 3 through 5.

U engine—1980 California, 1980 W engine

1. Complete steps 1 through 3 under U engine, above.

2. Remove the air hose running from the reed valve to the air cleaner and plug the air inlet of the reed valve with your thumb.

3. Set the engine speed and the idle CO concentration to their respective values given in the chart by adjusting the idle speed adjusting screw (SAS) and the idle mixture adjusting screw (MAS). See illustration.

4. Unplug the air inlet of the reed valve and reconnect the air hose to the reed valve.

5. Reset the engine speed to the chart specifications by adjusting the idle speed adjusting screw if the engine is not running within idling limits.

Canada through 1981

1. Place the transmission in "N" (Neutral) position and set the parking brake.

2. Make sure the air conditioner, lights and accessories are off.

3. Run the engine at idle until the coolant temperature reaches 170–190°F.

4. Set the engine speed to the value specified in the chart by adjusting the idle speed

adjusting screw (SAS), then adjust the idle CO by the idle mixture adjusting screw (MAS). Ideally, the idle CO should be as lean as possible without causing misfiring within the specified values.

Mixture Adjustment

1981 (U.S.A.)

NOTE: *The following procedure requires the use of a CO meter and the removal of the carburetor.*

1. Remove the carburetor from the engine.

2. Place the carburetor on a bench and remove the roll pin and concealment plug.

3. Reinstall the carburetor on the engine without the concealment plug and roll pin.

4. Run the engine until the coolant water temperature is raised to 185–205°F.

5. Disconnect the air hose between the reed valve and the aircleaner. Plug the air hose to stop any secondary air flow into the reed valve.

6. Run the truck for 5 minutes at 30 MPH or run the engine for more than 5 seconds at an engine speed of 2,000–3,000 rpm.

7. Set the idle CO and the engine speed to the value listed below by adjusting the speed adjusting screw and the mixture adjusting screw.

8. The idle CO should be 0.5% at the curb idle speed of 650–850 rpm for the U engine and 800–900 rpm for the W engine. (See the Tune-up Specifications Chart)

9. Unplug the air hose and reconnect to the air cleaner.

10. Reset the engine speed if necessary.

11. Reinstall the roll pin and the concealment plug.

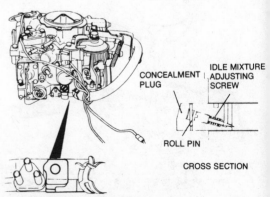

Adjusting idle mixture U.S.A.

Idle Speed Adjustment

1981 models (U.S.A.)

1. Make sure all the lights and accessories are off and the transmission is in neutral.

2. Run the engine until it reaches normal operating temperature.

3. Run the engine at idle for at least 2 minutes.

4. Attach a tachometer to the engine using the manufacturers instructions.

5. Check the idle speed and readjust if necessary using the idle adjusting screw.

6. Idle speed should be 650–850 rpm for the U engine and 800–900 rpm for the W engine. (See the Tune-up Specifications Chart)

7. After completion of the above procedure, lift the throttle opener lever by hand and adjust the throttle opener adjusting screw to —U engine, 1000–1050 rpm, W engine, 1050–1100 rpm.

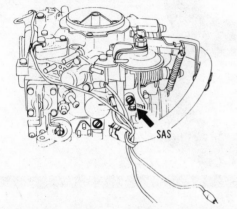

Idle speed adjusting screw (SAS)—1981 models

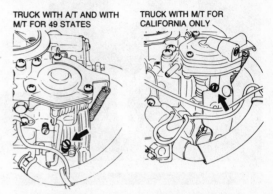

TRUCK WITH A/T AND WITH M/T FOR 49 STATES

TRUCK WITH M/T FOR CALIFORNIA ONLY

Throttle opener adjusting screw—1981 models

Engine and Engine Rebuilding

ENGINE ELECTRICAL

Electronic Ignition Systems

All D-50, Ram 50 and Arrow pick-ups are equipped with electronic ignition systems which replace the contact points and condenser with a transistoized integrated circuit. There are no adjustments that can be done to this type of ignition system.

IGNITION SYSTEM TEST

If you suspect that the ignition system may be defective perform the following test:

1. Remove the distributor cap by inserting a screwdriver in the ends of the two retaining screws, pushing in and turning the screws clockwise.

2. Remove the mounting screws holding the rotor assembly and lift out the rotor assembly.

3. Set the ignition switch to ON.

4. Disconnect the high tension cable from the center terminal of the distributor cap and hold its end about a quarter of an inch away from ground (cylinder block, etc.). Insert a flatblade screwdriver between the reluctor and the stator of the distributor (see illustration). A spark should jump from the high tension wire to ground. If a spark is not produced, a defective control unit, pick-up coil,

ignition coil or faulty wiring may be the problem. Further service should be left to a qualified service technician.

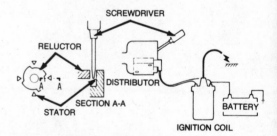

Electronic ignition system test

Distributor
REMOVAL

1. Disconnect the battery ground cable.

2. Disconnect the wiring harness from the distributor control unit.

3. Mark the spark plug cables and pull them off the spark plugs.

NOTE: *Always pull spark plug and coil cables at their caps to avoid breaking the wires inside the cables.*

4. Remove the distributor cap by inserting a screwdriver into the two retaining screws, pushing in and turning clockwise.

5. Match-mark the distributor housing

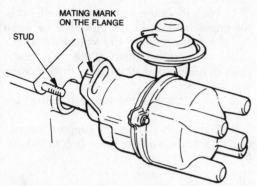

Distributor installation—: align the mark on the flange with the center of the stud

and the engine block; mark the rotor position in the distributor as well. This will aid in correct positioning of the distributor during installation.

6. Disconnect the vacuum hose from the vacuum control unit.

7. Remove the distributor mounting nut and lift off the distributor assembly.

INSTALLATION—ENGINE DISTURBED

1. Turn the engine crankshaft until the No. 1 cylinder is at top dead center on compression stroke. To find No. 1 cylinder, compression stroke, take off the distributor cap and turn over the engine until the rotor assembly is pointing toward the number 1 cylinder lead in the distributor cap. Verify Top Dead Center on the crankshaft pulley.

2. Align the mating mark (line) on the distributor housing with the mating mark (punch mark) on the distributor driven gear.

3. Install the distributor with the mating mark on the distributor attaching flange even with the center of the distributor retaining

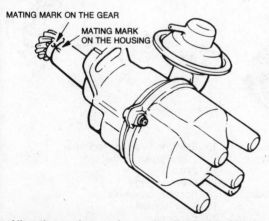

Align the mating marks on the distributor driven gear and housing

stud. Tighten the nut and replace the distributor cap, wires, and plug wires.

4. Set ignition timing as described above.

INSTALLATION—ENGINE NOT DISTURBED

1. Insert the distributor in the engine and align the marks made during removal.

2. Install the mounting nut, distributor cap, wires and plug wires, and vacuum line.

3. Start engine and check ignition timing as outlined above.

Firing Order

To avoid confusion replace spark plug wires one at a time.

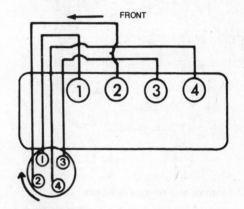

Engine firing order

Alternator

ALTERNATOR PRECAUTIONS

1. Always observe proper polarity of the battery connections; be especially careful when jump-starting the car.

2. Never ground or short out any alternator or alternator regulator terminals.

3. Never operate the alternator with any of its or the battery's leads disconnected.

4. Always remove the battery or disconnect its output lead while charging it.

5. Always disconnect the ground cable when replacing any electrical components.

6. Never subject the alternator to excessive heat or dampness if the engine is being steam-cleaned.

7. Never use arc-welding equipment with the alternator connected.

REMOVAL AND INSTALLATION

1. Disconnect the battery ground cable.

2. Disconnect the cable from terminal "B"

on the back of the alternator. Disconnect the other cables.

3. Remove the alternator brace bolt and the support bolt nut. Remove the drive belt.

4. Pull out the support bolt and remove the alternator assembly.

To install alternator:

1. Align the hole in the alternator leg with the hole in the front case and insert the alternator support bolt from the front bracket side.

2. Install the brace bolt.

3. Install drive belt.

4. Push the alternator toward the front of the engine and check the clearance between the alternator leg and the front case. If the clearance is more than 0.008 in., insert spacers as required. 0.0078 in. thick spacers are available.

5. Adjust the belt tension as described below.

6. Tighten the alternator support bolt nut to 15–18 ft. lb., and the brace bolt to 9–11 ft. lb.

OVERHAUL

1. Remove alternator from vehicle.

2. Remove the three through bolts from the alternator body.

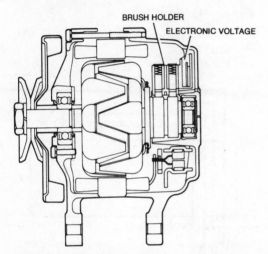

Alternator and voltage regulator

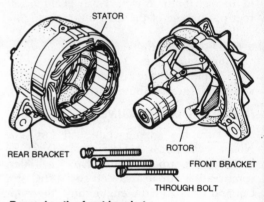

Removing the front bracket

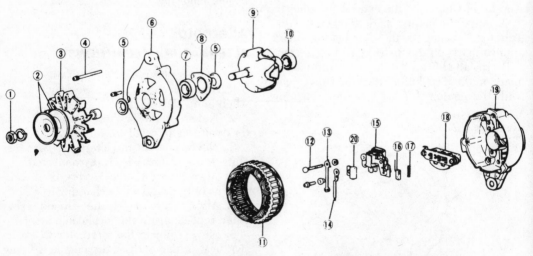

1. Pulley nut	8. Bearing retainer	15. Electronic voltage regulator
2. Pulley	9. Rotor assembly	and brush holder
3. Fan	10. Ball bearing	16. Brush
4. Through bolt	11. Stator assembly	17. Brush spring
5. Seal	12. Terminal "B" bolt	18. Rectifier assembly
6. Front bracket	13. Plate "B"	19. Rear bracket
7. Ball bearing	14. Plate "L"	20. Condenser

Alternator—exploded view

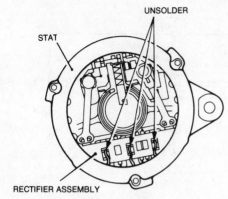

STAT

UNSOLDER

RECTIFIER ASSEMBLY

Removing the stator assembly

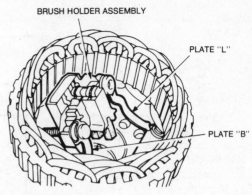

BRUSH HOLDER ASSEMBLY

PLATE "L"

PLATE "B"

Replacing brush

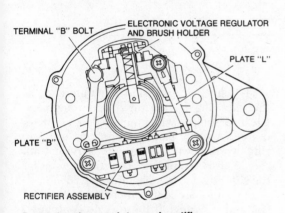

TERMINAL "B" BOLT

ELECTRONIC VOLTAGE REGULATOR AND BRUSH HOLDER

PLATE "L"

PLATE "B"

RECTIFIER ASSEMBLY

Removing the regulator and rectifier

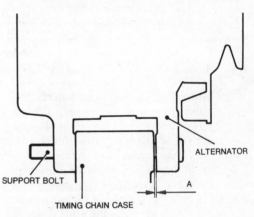

ALTERNATOR

SUPPORT BOLT

TIMING CHAIN CASE

A

Installing the alternator

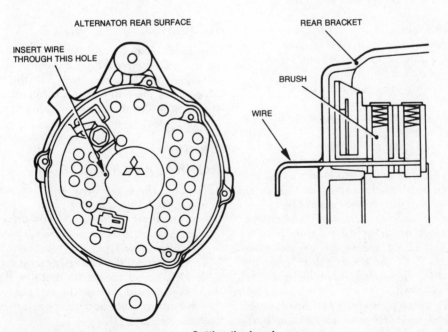

ALTERNATOR REAR SURFACE

INSERT WIRE THROUGH THIS HOLE

REAR BRACKET

BRUSH

WIRE

Setting the brush

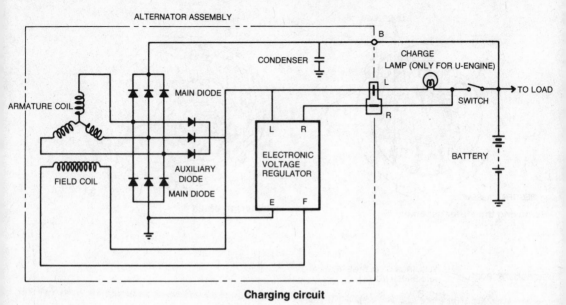

Charging circuit

3. Insert a screwdriver between the front bracket and stator (see illustration). Pry the front bracket away from the stator. Remove the front bracket along with the rotor.

NOTE: *If the screwdriver is inserted too deeply, the stator coil might be damaged.*

4. Hold the rotor in a vise and remove the pulley nut. Then remove the pulley, fan, spacer and seal. Remove the rotor from the front bracket and remove the seal.

5. Unsolder the rectifier from the stator coil lead wires and remove the stator assembly.

NOTE: *Make sure the solder is removed quickly (in less than five seconds). If a diode is heated to more than 150°C, it might be damaged.*

6. Remove the condenser from the terminal "B".

7. Unsolder the plates "B" and "L" from the rectifier assembly.

8. Remove the mounting screw and terminal "B" bolt and remove the electronic voltage regulator and brush holder. The regulator and brush holder cannot be separated.

9. Remove the rectifier assembly.

10. Brush and brush spring replacement; When only a brush or brush spring is to be replaced, it is not necessary to remove the stator, etc. Raise the brush holder assembly and unsolder the wire pigtail of the brush and remove the brush.

NOTE: *Be very careful when bending the plates "B" and "L" so as not to disturb the rectifier moulding.*

11. Check the outside circumference of the slip ring for dirtiness and roughness. Clean or polish with fine sandpaper, if required. A badly damaged slip ring or a slip ring worn down beyond the service limit should also be replaced. The service limit for the slip ring outside diameter is 1.268 in.

12. Check for continuity between the field coil and slip ring. If there is no continuity, the field coil is defective and the rotor must be replaced.

Regulator

The D-50, Ram-50 and Arrow pick-ups use an integrated circuit-type regulator which is contained in the alternator. See the above procedures for removal. Adjustments of the regulator are confined to replacement.

Starter

REMOVAL AND INSTALLATION

NOTE: *There are two types of starters used. Trucks equipped with automatic transmissions use the reduction drive type and those with manual transmissions use the direct drive type.*

1. Disconnect the battery ground cable.

2. Disconnect the starter motor wiring.

3. Loosen and remove the two starter motor mounting bolts and remove the starter motor.

4. Installation is the reverse of removal.

Alternator and Regulator Specifications

Model	Year	Alternator Identification Number	Rated Output @ 5000	Rated Output @ 2500	Brush Length (in.)	Brush Spring Tension (lbs.)	Regulated Voltage
All	1979	AQ2245G	41 amps	34 amps	0.669 ①	2.9–3.7 ②	14.1–14.7
	1980–81	A2T16471	44 amps	37 amps	0.709	0.7–1	14.1–14.7

① Built-in type brush: 0.709 in.   ② Built-in type spring: 0.7–1 lbs.

STARTER DRIVE, SOLENOID AND BRUSH REPLACEMENT

NOTE: *Starter must be removed from the vehicle for this operation*

Direct Drive Type

1. Remove the wire connecting the starter solenoid to the starter.

2. Remove the two screws holding the starter solenoid on the starter-drive housing and remove the solenoid.

3. Remove the two long through bolts at the rear of the starter and separate the armature yoke from the armature.

4. Carefully remove the armature and the starter drive engagement lever from the front bracket, after making a mental note of the way they are positioned along with the attendant spring and spring retainer.

5. Loosen the two screws and remove the rear bracket.

6. Tap the stopper ring at the end of the

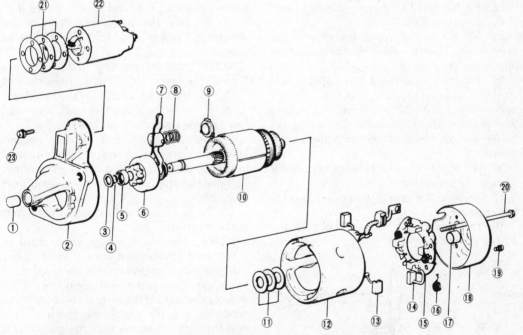

1. Front bearing	9. Spring retainer	18. Rear bracket
2. Front bracket	10. Armature	19. Brush holder tightening
3. Washer	11. Washer set	screw
4. Snap ring	12. Yoke	20. Through bolt
5. Stopper	13. Brush	21. Washer set
6. Overrunning clutch and	14. Brush	22. Magnetic switch
pinion	15. Brush holder	23. Magnetic switch tightening
7. Lever	16. Brush spring	screw
8. Lever spring	17. Rear bearing	

Exploded view of direct drive starter (manual transmission)

drive gear engagement shaft in towards the drive gear to expose the snap ring. Remove the snap ring.

7. Pull the stopper, drive gear and overrunning clutch from the end of the shaft.

Inspect the pinion and spline teeth for wear or damage. If the engagement teeth are damaged, visually check the flywheel ring gear through the starter hole to insure that it is not damaged. It will be necessary to turn the engine over by hand to completely inspect the ring gear.

Check the brushes for wear. Their service limit length is 0.453 in. Replace if necessary.

Assembly is performed in the following manner.

8. Install the spring retainer and spring on the armature shaft.

9. Install the overrunning clutch assembly on the armature shaft.

10. Fit the stopper ring with its open side facing out on the shaft.

11. Install a new snap ring and, using a gear puller, pull the stopper ring into place over the snap ring.

12. Fit the small washer on the front end of the armature shaft.

13. Fit the engagement lever into the overrunning clutch and refit the armature into the front housing.

14. Fit the engagement lever spring and spring retainer into place and slide the armature yoke over the armature. Make sure you position the yoke with the spring retainer cut-out space in line with the spring retainer.

NOTE: *Make sure the brushes are seated on the commutator.*

15. Replace the rear bracket and two retainer screws.

16. Install the two through bolts in the end of the yoke.

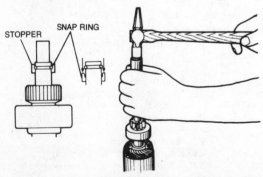

To remove the overrunning clutch tap down the stopper and remove the snap ring

17. Refit the starter solenoid, making sure you fit the plunger over the engagement lever. Install the screws and connect the wire running from the starter yoke to the starter solenoid.

Reduction Drive Type

1. Remove the wire connecting the starter solenoid to the starter.

2. Remove the two screws holding the solenoid and, pulling out, unhook it from the engagement lever.

3. Remove the two through bolts in the end of the starter and remove the two bracket screws. Pull off the rear bracket.

NOTE: *Since the conical spring washer is contained in the rear bracket, be sure to take it out.*

4. Remove the yoke and brush holder assembly while pulling the brush upward.

5. Pull the armature assembly out of the mounting bracket.

6. In the side of the mounting bracket that the armature fits into, there is a small dust cap held by two screws. Remove it and remove the snap ring and washer under it.

7. Remove the remaining bolts in the mounting bracket and split the reduction case.

NOTE: *Several washers will come out when the case is split. These adjust the end play for the pinion shaft. Do not lose them.*

8. Remove the reduction gear, lever and lever spring from the front bracket.

9. Using a brass drift or deep socket, knock the stopper ring on the end of the shaft in toward the pinion. Remove the snap ring. Remove the stopper, pinion and pinion shaft assembly.

10. Remove the ball bearings at both ends of the armature.

NOTE: *The ball bearings are pressed in the front bracket and are not replaceable. Replace them together with the bracket.*

Inspect the pinion and spline teeth for wear or damage. If the engagement teeth are damaged, visually check the flywheel ring gear through the starter hole to insure that it is not damaged also. It will be necessary to turn the engine over by hand to completely inspect the ring gear.

Check the brushes for wear. Their service limit length is 0.0453 in. Replace if necessary.

Assembly is the reverse of disassembly. Be sure to replace all adjusting and thrust washers. When replacing the rear bracket, fit the

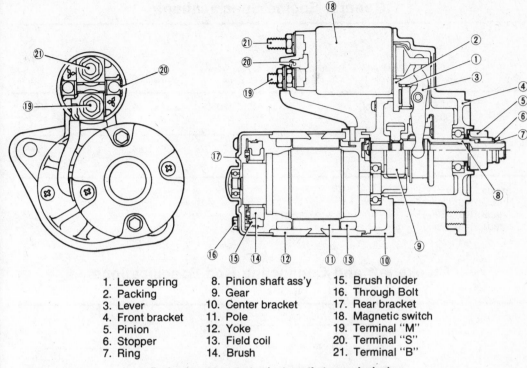

1. Lever spring
2. Packing
3. Lever
4. Front bracket
5. Pinion
6. Stopper
7. Ring
8. Pinion shaft ass'y
9. Gear
10. Center bracket
11. Pole
12. Yoke
13. Field coil
14. Brush
15. Brush holder
16. Through Bolt
17. Rear bracket
18. Magnetic switch
19. Terminal "M"
20. Terminal "S"
21. Terminal "B"

Reduction gear starter (automatic transmission)

conical spring pinion washer with its convex side facing out. Make sure that the brushes seat themselves on the commutator.

Battery

REMOVAL AND INSTALLATION

1. Remove first the negative battery cable, then the positive battery cable.

2. Remove the retaining bracket and remove the battery.

3. Clean the battery terminals and cable terminals before replacing the battery. See Chapter One.

ENGINE MECHANICAL

Design

The 2.0 Liter (121.75 cu. in.) designated the U engine and the 2.6 Liter (155.92 cu. in.) designated the W engine both have silent shaft, and their camshaft and silent shaft are chain driven. The lubrication system consists of a gear type oil pump and a full flow oil filter. The oil pump is mounted on the front surface of the cylinder block. The cooling system includes an aluminum water pump body with a pressed in ball bearing, seal assembly

Battery and Starter Specifications

				Starter				
Year	Engine Model	Battery Amp Hour Capacity	Amps	No Load Test Volts	RPM	Brush Spring Tension (lbs)	Min Brush Length (in.)	Type of Starter
1979–81	U, W w/MT	45, 60 ①	60	11.5	6,600	2.9–3.7	0.453	Direct Drive
	U, W w/AT	45, 60 ①	90 ④	11.5 ③	3,300 ②	2.9–3.7	0.453	Gear Reduction

MT: Manual Transmission
AT: Automatic Transmission
① 60 amp for Canada
② 1979: 4,500 rpm
③ 1979: 11 volts
④ 1979: 62 amps

General Engine Specifications

Year	Engine Displacement cu in. (cc)	Carburetor Type	Horsepower @ rpm	Torque @ rpm (ft. lbs.)	Bore X Stroke (in.)	Compression Ratio	Oil Pressure (psi)
1979–81	121.7 (1995)	1 x 2 bbl	93 @ 5200 ①	108 @ 3000 ②	3.31 x 3.54	8.5 : 1	50–64
	155.92 (2555)	1 x 2 bbl	105 @ 5000 ③	139 @ 2500 ④	3.59 x 3.86	8.2 : 1	50–64

① Canada: 96 @ 5500 HP
② Canada: 109 @ 3500 Torque
③ Canada: 108 @ 5000 HP
④ Canada: 140 @ 2500 Torque

Crankshaft and Connecting Rod Specifications
(All measurements given in inches)

Year	Engine cu in.	Crankshaft				Connecting Rod		
		Main Brg. Journal Diameter	Main Brg Oil Clearance	Shaft End Play	Thrust on No.	Journal Diameter	Oil Clearance	Side Clearance
1979–81	121.7 155.9	2.3622	0.0008–0.0028	0.002–0.007	3	2.0866	0.0008–0.0028	0.004–0.010

Valve Specifications

Year	Engine Displacement cu in. (cc)	Seat Angle (deg)	Face Angle (deg)	Spring Test Pressure (lbs @ in.)	Spring Installed Height (in.)	Stem to Guide Clearance (in.)		Stem Diameter (in.)	
						Intake	Exhaust	Intake	Exhaust
1979–81	121.7 (2000)	45	45	61 @ 1.59	1.590	0.0012–0.0024	0.002–0.0035	0.315	0.315
	155.92 (2555)	45	45	61 @ 1.59	1.590	0.0012–0.0024	0.002–0.0035	0.315	0.315
	Jet Valve	45	45	5.5 @ .846	—	—	—	0.1693	0.1693

Piston and Ring Specifications
(All measurements given in inches)

Year	Engine cu in.	Piston to Bore Clearance	Ring Side Clearance			Ring Gap		
			Top Compression	Bottom Compression	Oil Control	Top Compression	Bottom Compression	Oil Control
1979–81	121.7 155.92	0.0008–0.0016	0.0024–0.0039	0.008–0.0024	—	0.010–0.018	0.010–0.018	0.0078–0.035

Torque Specifications
(All readings in ft. lb.)

Year	Engine Displace- ment cu in. (cc)	Cylinder Head Bolts	Rod Bearing Bolts	Main Bearing Bolts	Crankshaft Pulley Bolt	Flywheel to Crankshaft Bolts	Manifolds	
							Intake	Exhaust
1979–81	All	65–72	33–34	55–61	80–94	94–101	11–14	11–14

and an impeller made of steel stampings. The water pump is mounted on the timing chain case.

REMOVAL AND INSTALLATION

CAUTION: *Be sure the car is supported securely during engine removal.*

NOTE: *The engine and transmission are removed as a unit.*

1. Working inside the engine compartment, remove the slash shield below the engine. Drain the coolant from the radiator and the engine by opening the drain plug at the bottom of the radiator and the drain cock located at the right rear of the cylinder block. Use a suitable container to catch coolant.

NOTE: *It would be wise to drain the radiator in an area other than the one in which the engine is to be removed so that you will not be in contact with coolant when working under the vehicle.*

2. Disconnect and remove the battery.
3. Disconnect the ground strap and the wiring of the ignition coil, fuel cut off solenoid valve, alternator, starter motor, water temperature gauge unit and oil pressure gauge unit.

4. Disconnect the air cleaner breather hose. Remove the air cleaner and disconnect the hot air duct and the vacuum hose.

5. Disconnect the accelerator control cable. For automatic transmissions, disconnect the transmission control rod.

6. Disconnect the radiator hoses by loosening their clips.

7. Disconnect the heater hose.

8. Disconnect the exhaust pipe from the exhaust manifold. The muffler pipe bracket should be detached at the transmission.

9. Disconnect the fuel hoses and vapor hose.

10. Remove the radiator and radiator cowl. Four bolts hold the radiator in place. On vehicles with automatic transmissions, remove and plug the two oil cooling pipes in the bottom of the radiator.

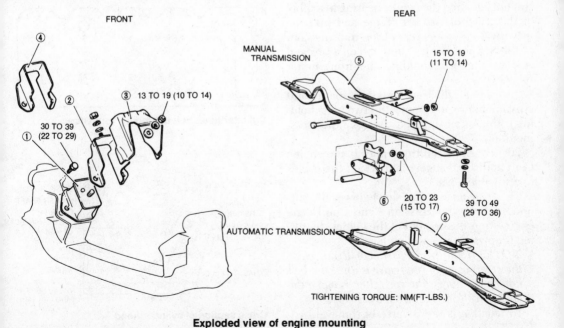

Exploded view of engine mounting

11. For trucks with four and five speed transmissions:

    a. Remove the lock screws and lift up the console box, inside the driver's compartment. In trucks without a console box, remove the carpet.

    b. Remove the attaching screws and lift out the dust cover retainer plate.

    c. Pull up the dust cover and remove the four attaching bolts holding the shift lever to the transmission extension housing. Remove the shift lever control assembly.

NOTE: *On four speed transmissions, remove the gear shift lever with the lever in 2nd speed position. On five speed transmissions, place the lever in 1st speed position.*

12. Mark the position of the hood retaining bolts in relation to the hood and remove the hood.

13. Jack up the vehicle and support it on stands.

14. Disconnect the speedometer cable and backup light switch wiring from the transmission.

15. For trucks with manual transmissions, disconnect the clutch cable from the transmission by removing the cotter key and sliding it off the arm. Disconnect the cable from the cable bracket. For automatic transmissions, remove shift linkage between transmission and shift lever.

16. Drain the transmission.

17. Remove the bolts holding the rear of the driveshaft to the rear axle. Remove the two nuts holding the center bearing assembly of the driveshaft to the frame and pull the driveshaft out of the rear of the transmission.

18. Support the transmission on a jack and remove the bolts holding the front motor mounts.

19. Unbolt the rear transmission mount crossmember and remove the two bolts holding it to the transmission. Remove the crossmember.

20. Attach steel lifting cables to the engine front and rear hangers and attach the cables to a suitable hoist.

21. Have an assistant slowly lower the jack under the transmission and pull the engine/transmission out of the vehicle by tilting it upwards and pulling forward.

NOTE: *If the transmission will not clear the steering relay rod, raise it until the bell housing is above the rod, then remove the engine/transmission from the truck.*

Installation is the reverse of removal. Adjust all transmission and carburetor linkages as detailed in the appropriate sections. Install and adjust the hood. Refill the engine, transmission and radiator to capacity.

NOTE: *Refer to the engine rebuildng section at the end of this book for complete overhaul procedures not covered in this chapter.*

Cylinder Head
REMOVAL AND INSTALLATION

CAUTION: *Do not perform this operation on a warm engine. Remove the head bolts in the sequence shown at the front of this section and in several steps. Loosen the head bolts evenly, not one at a time. Do not attempt to slide the cylinder head off the block, as it is located with dowel pins. Lift the head straight up and off the block.*

1. Disconnect the battery and drain the cooling system. Disconnect the upper radiator hose.

2. Remove the breather hoses and purge hose.

3. Remove the air cleaner and fuel line.

4. Remove the vacuum hose at the distributor and purge control valve.

5. Disconnect the spark plug wires after marking them for reinstallation.

6. Remove the distributor cap, and distributor by removing the retainer nut and pulling the unit out.

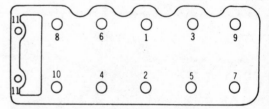

Cylinder head bolt tightening sequence

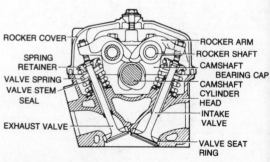

Cross section of cylinder head

7. Disconnect the heater hose at the intake manifold.

8. Disconnect the water temperature gauge unit wire.

9. Place no. 1 piston in the Top Dead Center position to take pressure off the fuel pump rocker arm. Disconnect the fuel hoses and plug the line leading to the gas tank to prevent fuel leakage.

10. Remove the fuel pump mounting nuts or bolts and remove the fuel assembly. Remove the insulator and gaskets.

11. Disconnect the exhaust pipe at the exhaust manifold flange.

12. Remove the rocker cover.

13. Remove its breather and semi-circular seal.

14. After slightly loosening the camshaft sprocket bolt, turn the crankshaft until no. 1 piston is at top dead center on compression stroke (both valves closed).

NOTE: *Never turn the engine over using the camshaft bolt: it puts undue strain on the chain and other components.*

15. Remove the camshaft sprocket bolt and distributor drive gear. Remove the camshaft sprocket and allow it to rest in the chain on the holder below.

16. Remove the cylinder head bolts in the sequence shown in the illustration. Head bolts should be loosened in two or three stages to prevent head warpage.

NOTE: *The cylinder head assembly is located with two dowl pins, front and rear, on the cylinder block. When removing, be careful not to slide it, or twist the camshaft sprocket and chain.*

17. Remove the cylinder head assembly and cylinder head gasket.

Installation is performed in the following manner.

18. Clean all gasket surfaces of cylinder block and cylinder head.

19. Install a new cylinder head gasket. Install the cylinder head assembly.

NOTE: *Do not apply sealant to the head gasket and do not reuse an old heaad gasket.*

NOTE: *The head gasket for the U engine has a number "52" stamped at the front of its upper surface, while the W engine has the number "54" in that position.*

20. Install the ten cylinder head bolts. Starting at top center, tighten all cylinder head bolts to 35 ft. lb. in the sequence shown in the illustration. Repeat the tightening procedure, this time torque the bolts to 65–72 ft. lb. (cold engine), (72–80 ft. lb. hot engine).

21. Tighten the two front bolts (number 11 in illustration) to 11–15 ft. lb.

22. Verify that no. 1 cylinder is at top dead center. Align the dowel pin in the end of the camshaft sprocket with the groove in the top of the front camshaft bearing cap and install the camshaft sprocket and chain while pulling up on the sprocket.

23. Install the distributor drive gear and the sprocket bolt.

24. Turn the crankshaft about 90° back, and tighten the camshaft sprocket bolt to 37–43 ft. lb.

Very slowly turn the engine over two times to make sure the valve timing is correct. If the engine locks at a certain point in these two revolutions, the valve timing is not correct. Repeat steps 22–24.

CAUTION: *At this point, do not turn the engine over using the starter. If the valve timing is off, several of the valves could be bent.*

25. Install the breather and semicircular seal to the cylinder head after applying sealant to surface contact points. Install the rocker cover with a new gasket.

26. Connect the exhaust pipe to the exhaust manifold flange. Tighten the bolts to 11–18 ft. lb.

27. Put no. 1 cylinder at Top Dead Center and install the fuel pump with a new gasket and insulator. Connect all hoses.

28. Connect the water temperature gauge unit wire. Connect the heater hose to the intake manifold.

Install the distributor and spark plug cables. See distributor section, above, for procedure.

29. Connect the vacuum hose to the distributor and purge control valve. Connect the upper radiator hose and fill the cooling system with coolant.

Many mechanics recommend that the engine oil be replaced after the head is removed to avoid water contamination from the coolant.

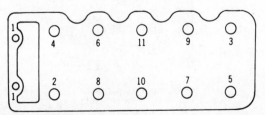

Head bolt removal sequence

Valve Guides and Seats

If it is determined that any valve seat or guide is worn beyond the service limit oversized valve seat inserts and valve guides are available, however installation requires the use of special tools and an alternative would be to have a head serviced at a local automotive machine shop.

Valve and Spring

The intake valves and exhaust valves are made of heat resistant steel and arranged in V with the camshaft on center. The valve stem seal, installed on the upper part of the valve guide, serves to prevent the oil from working down through the clearance between the valve stem and the valve guide.

Removal and Installation

1. Using a valve lifter, remove the retainer lock. Then remove the spring retainer, valve spring, spring seat and valve.
   NOTE: *Keep these parts in proper order so that they can be installed in their original positions.*
2. Pull off the valve stem seals with pliers.
   NOTE: *Never reuse old valve seals.*
3. Using a valve stem seal installer, install the seal on the valve guide by lightly tapping the tool until the seal is in place.
4. Apply engine oil to each valve and insert the valves into the valve guides.
5. Install the springs and the spring retainers. Install the valve springs with the enamel coated side toward the valve spring retainer.
6. Using a valve lifter, compress the spring and install the retainer lock.

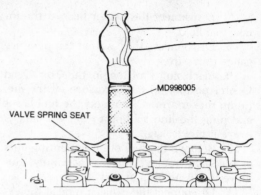

VALVE SPRING SEAT —— MD998005

Installing the valve stem seal

NOTE: *When compressing the spring make sure the valve stem seal is not pressed with the bottom of the retainer. Then start installing the retainer lock.*
7. Install the cylinder head.

Rocker Arms and Shafts
REMOVAL AND INSTALLATION

1. Remove the rocker arm shaft assembly as described under "Camshaft" removal and installation.
2. Remove the bolts from the camshaft bearing caps and remove the bearing caps, rocker arms and springs from the shafts (right and left).
3. To assemble insert the right and left rocker shafts into the front bearing cap, making sure that the mating marks will face the front of the engine and will be aligned with the mating marks on the bearing cap then temporarily insert the bolts to keep the shafts in position.
4. Install the rocker arms, springs and bearing caps in the proper order. After the rear bearing cap has been installed, align the

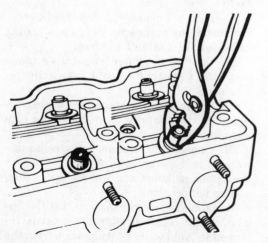

Removing the valve stem seals with pliers

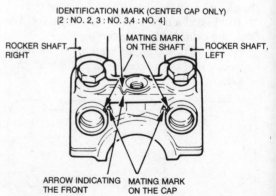

IDENTIFICATION MARK (CENTER CAP ONLY)
[2 : NO. 2, 3 : NO. 3,4 : NO. 4]

ROCKER SHAFT, RIGHT

MATING MARK ON THE SHAFT

ROCKER SHAFT, LEFT

ARROW INDICATING THE FRONT   MATING MARK ON THE CAP

Mating marks on the bearing cap

bolt holes in the bearing cap with the rear-most shaft end bolt holes, and insert the bolts.

5. Install the rocker arm shaft assembly as described under "Camshaft" removal and installation.

Intake Manifold

REMOVAL AND INSTALLATION

1. Drain the cooling system.
2. Remove the air cleaner assembly with its hoses from the engine.
3. Disconnect the fuel line and EGR lines.
4. Disconnect the accelerator linkage and, if so equipped, the automatic transmission shift cables at the carburetor.
5. Remove the water hose at the intake manifold. Remove the water hose at the carburetor.
6. Disconnect the water temperature sending unit.
7. Remove the manifold with the carburetor as a unit.

Installation is the reverse of removal. Tighten manifold nuts to 11–14 ft. lbs.

Exhaust Manifold

REMOVAL AND INSTALLATION

1. Remove air cleaner.
2. Remove the heat shield from the exhaust manifold. Remove the EGR lines and reed valve, if equipped.
3. Unbolt the exhaust flange connection.

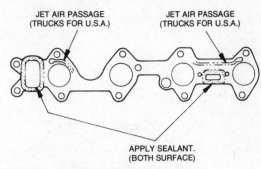

Sealing point of intake manifold gasket

4. Remove nuts holding manifold to cylinder head.
5. Remove manifold.

Installation is the reverse of removal. Tighten flange connection bolts to 11–18 ft. lb. Tighten bolts to 11–14 ft. lb.

Timing Chain, Cover, "Silent Shafts" and Tensioner

REMOVAL AND INSTALLATION

NOTE: *All D-50, Ram-50 and Plymouth Arrow Pickups are equipped with two "Silent shafts" which cancel the vertical vibrating force of the engine and the secondary vibrating forces, which include the sideways rocking of the engine due to the turning direction of the crankshaft and other rolling parts. The secondary vibrating forces can be cancelled if forces equivalent in magnitude but opposite in direction are produced. In these engines, the*

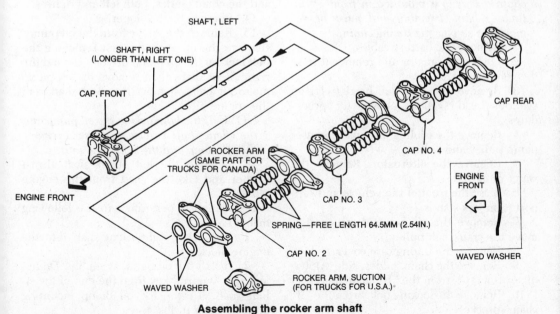

Assembling the rocker arm shaft

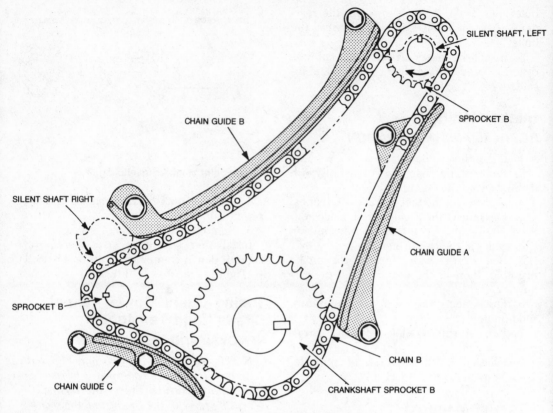

Drive system for "Silent Shaft" system

opposite force is produced by silent shafts located in the upper left and lower right sides in the front of the cylinder block. The shafts are driven by a duplex chain and are turned by the crankshaft. The silent shaft chain assembly is mounted in front of the timing chain assembly and must be removed to service the timing chain.

1. Remove the battery cables.

2. Drain the radiator and remove it from the vehicle.

3. Remove the cylinder head (refer to cylinder head section, above, for procedures).

4. Remove the cooling fan, spacer, water pump pulley and belt.

5. Remove the alternator. Remove the water pump.

6. Raise the front of the vehicle and support it on jack stands.

7. Remove the oil pan and screen. Remove the crankshaft pulley.

8. Remove the timing case cover.

9. Remove the chain guides, side (A), top (b), bottom (C), from the "B" chain (outer).

10. Remove the locking bolts from the "B" chain sprockets.

11. Remove the crankshaft sprocket, silent shaft sprocket and the outer chain.

12. Remove the crankshaft and camshaft sprockets and the timing chain.

13. Remove the camshaft sprocket holder and the chain guides, both left and right.

14. Remove the tensioner.

15. Remove the sleeve from the oil pump. Remove the oil pump by first removing the bolt locking the oil pump driven gear and the right silent shaft, then remove the oil pump mounting bolts. Remove the silent shaft from the engine block.

NOTE: *If the bolt locking the oil pump and the silent shaft is hard to loosen, remove the oil pump and the shaft as a unit.*

16. Remove the left silent shaft thrust washer and take the shaft from the engine block.

Installation is performed in the following manner:

1. Install the right silent shaft into the engine block.

2. Install the oil pump assembly. Do not lose the woodruff key from the end of the silent shaft. Torque the oil pump mounting bolts to 6 to 7 ft. lbs.

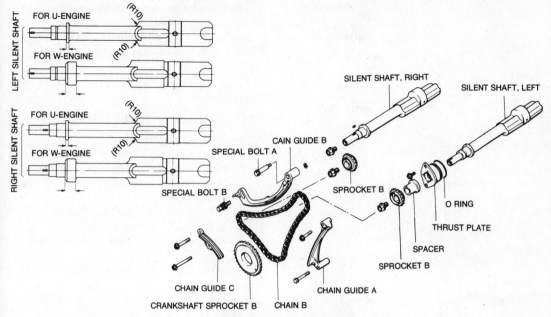

FOR U-ENGINE
FOR W-ENGINE
LEFT SILENT SHAFT
FOR U-ENGINE
FOR W-ENGINE
RIGHT SILENT SHAFT
(R10)

SILENT SHAFT, RIGHT
SILENT SHAFT, LEFT
CAIN GUIDE B
SPECIAL BOLT A
SPROCKET B
O RING
THRUST PLATE
SPACER
SPROCKET B
CHAIN GUIDE A
CHAIN GUIDE C
CRANKSHAFT SPROCKET B
CHAIN B
SPECIAL BOLT B

"Silent Shaft" installation

3. Tighten the silent shaft and the oil pump driven gear mounting bolt.

NOTE: *The silent shaft and the oil pump can be installed as a unit, if necessary.*

4. Install the left silent shaft into the engine block.

5. Install a new "O" ring on the thrust plate and install the unit into the engine block, using a pair of bolts without heads, as alignment guides.

CAUTION: *If the thrust plate is turned to align the bolt holes, the "O" ring may be damaged.*

6. Remove the guide bolts and install the regular bolts into the thrust plate and tighten securely.

7. Rotate the crankshaft to bring no. 1 piston to TDC.

8. Install the cylinder head.

9. Install the sprocket holder and the right and left chain guides.

10. Install the tensioner spring and sleeve on the oil pump body.

11. Install the camshaft and crankshaft sprockets on the timing chain, aligning the sprocket punch marks to the plated chain links.

12. While holding the sprocket and chain as a unit, install the crankshaft sprocket over the crankshaft and align it with the keyway.

13. Keeping the dowel pin hole on the camshaft in a vertical position, install the camshaft sprocket and chain on the camshaft.

NOTE: *The sprocket timing mark and the plated chain link should be at the 2 to 3 O'clock position when correctly installed.*

CAUTION: *The chain must be aligned in the right and left chain guides with the tensioner pushing against the chain. The tension for the inner chain is predetermined by spring tension.*

14. Install the crankshaft sprocket for the outer or "B" chain.

15. Install the two silent shaft sprockets and align the punched mating marks with the plated links of the chain.

16. Holding the two shaft sprockets and chain, install the outer chain in alignment with the mark on the crankshaft sprocket. Install the shaft sprockets on the silent shaft and the oil pump driver gear. Install the lock bolts and recheck the alignment of the punch marks and the plated links.

17. Temporarily install the chain guides, *Side* (A), *Top* (B), and *Bottom* (C).

18. Tighten *side* (A) chain guide securely.

19. Tighten *Bottom* (B) chain guide securely.

20. Adjust the position of the *Top* (B) chain guide, after shaking the right and left sprockets to collect any chain slack, so that when the chain is moved toward the center, the clearance between the chain guide and the chain links will be approximately 9/64 inch. Tighten the *Top* (B) chain guide bolts.

21. Install the timing chain cover using a

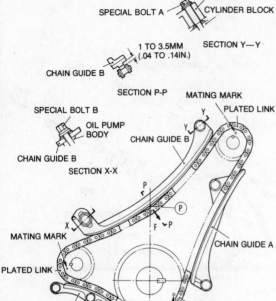

"Silent Shaft" balancing system

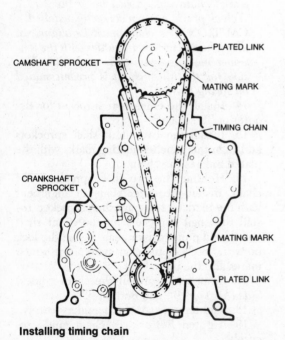

Installing timing chain

new gasket, being careful not to damage the front seal.

22. Install the oil screen and the oil pan, using a new gasket. Torque the bolts to 4.5 to 5.5 ft. lbs.

23. Install the crankshaft pulley, alternator and accessory belts, and the distributor.

24. Install the oil pressure switch, if removed, and install the battery ground cable.

25. Install the fan blades, radiator, fill the system with coolant and start the engine.

Camshaft
REMOVAL AND INSTALLATION

1. Remove the breather hoses and purge hose.

2. Remove the air cleaner and fuel line.

3. Remove the fuel pump. Remove the distributor.

4. Disconnect the spark plug cables.

5. Remove the rocker cover.

6. Remove the breather and semi-circular seal.

7. After slightly loosening the camshaft sprocket bolt, turn the crankshaft until no. 1 piston is at Top Dead Center on compression stroke (both valves closed).

8. Remove the camshaft sprocket bolt and distributor drive gear.

9. Remove the camshaft sprocket with chain and allow it to rest on the camshaft sprocket holder.

10. Remove the camshaft bearing cap tightening bolts. Do not remove the front and rear bearing cap bolts altogether, but keep them inserted in the bearing caps so that the rocker assembly can be removed as a unit.

11. Remove the rocker arms, rocker shafts and bearing caps as an assembly.

12. Remove the camshaft.

Installation is performed in the following manner.

13. Lubricate the camshaft lobes and bearings and fit camshaft into head.

14. Install the assembled rocker arm shaft assembly. The camshaft should be positioned so that the dowel pin on the front end of the cam is in the 12 o'clock position and in line with the notch in the top of the front bearing cap.

15. Install the bearing cap bolts. Starting at the center and working out, tighten the bolts to 7 ft. lb. Repeat the procedure, this time tightening them to 14–15 ft. lb.

16. Install the camshaft sprocket and distributor drive gear onto the camshaft while pulling it upward. Temporarily tighten the locking bolt.

17. Turn the crankshaft about 90° back and tighten the camshaft sprocket bolt to 37–43 ft. lb.

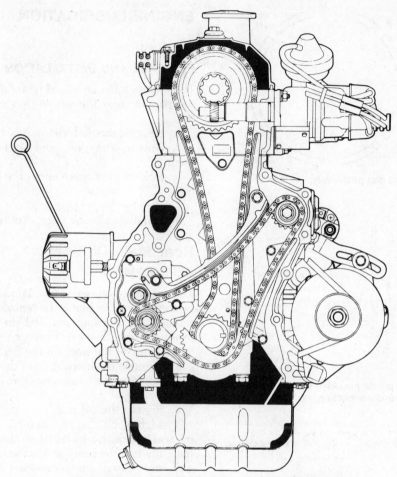

"Silent Shaft" chain mounting in relation to timing chain

18. Temporarily set the valve clearance to cold engine specifications (see Valve Lash section, above).

19. Temporarily install the breather, semicircular seal and rocker cover and start the engine and run it at idle speed.

20. After the engine is at normal operational temperature, adjust the valves to hot engine specifications (see Valve Lash section, above).

21. Install breather and seal and apply sealant to the contact surfaces.

22. Install the rocker cover and tighten to 4–5 ft. lb.

23. Install distributor, fuel pump, air cleaner, fuel line, plug leads and other assemblies.

Pistons and Connecting Rods
REMOVAL AND INSTALLATION

1. Remove the cylinder head assembly as described under "Cylinder Head" removal and installation.

2. Remove the oil pan and oil screen.

3. Remove the crankshaft rear oil seal case.

NOTE: *The rear oil seal case can be split into three parts: the oil seal the separater and the case.*

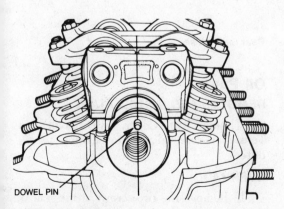

DOWEL PIN

Camshaft installation

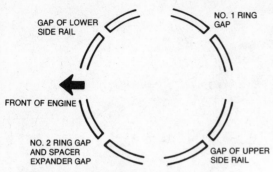

Piston ring end gap positioning

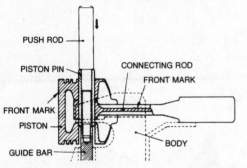

Installing the piston pin. Also shown: front marks on the piston and connecting rod

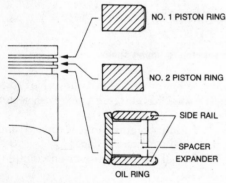

Piston ring installation

4.   Remove the connecting rod caps.

5.   Place a soft piece of wood between the connecting rod and the bearing cap so that the bearing surface is not damaged and push out each piston-rod assembly toward the top of the cylinder. Refer to the Engine Rebuilding section at the end of this chapter.

NOTE: *Rod bearings should be kept in order and not mixed so that they will be reinstalled in their original positions. Make sure the front mark on the top of the piston is facing the front of the engine during installation.*

ENGINE LUBRICATION

Oil Pan
REMOVAL AND INSTALLATION

The engine must be raised off its mounts for the pan to clear the suspension crossmember.

1.   Remove the underbody splash shield.

2.   Unbolt the left and right engine mounts.

3.   Jack up the engine under the bell housing.

4.   Remove the oil pan.

5.   Installation is the reverse of removal.

Rear Main Oil Seal
REPLACEMENT

The rear main oil seal is located in a housing on the rear of the block. To replace the seal, remove the transmission and do the work from underneath the vehicle or remove the engine and do the work on the bench.

1.   Remove the housing from the block.

2.   Remove the separator from the housing.

3.   Pry out the old seal.

4.   Lightly oil the replacement seal. The oil seal should be installed so that the seal plate fits into the inner contact surface of the seal case. Install the separator with the oil holes facing down.

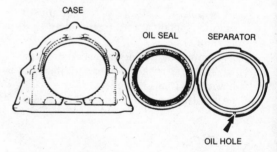

Rear main oil seal

Oil Pump
REMOVAL AND INSTALLATION

See Timing Chain, Cover, "Silent Shaft" and Tensioner removal and installation procedure.

OVERHAUL

1.   Remove the two screws at the rear of the oil pump and remove the cover and gear.

2. Remove the relief valve plug and withdraw the relief spring and plunger.

3. Check the pump for cracks and wear. Check all oil holes for clogging.

4. Clearance between the gears and the pump assembly (tip clearance) should be 0.0043–0.0059 in.

5. Both gears front bearing clearance should be within 0.0008 and 0.0020 in.

6. The rear bearing clearance of the drive gear should be 0.0016–0.0028 in.

NOTE: *When bearing replacement is necessary, replace the oil pump body assembly.*

7. Insert the relief plunger into the pump body and make sure it operates smoothly. Check the relief spring for breakage or sagging.

When reassembling, observe the following:

8. Coat all parts in oil before reassembling.

9. Match the two punch marks on the gears so that they mate where the gears meet.

10. Check for smooth rotation after assembly.

CAUTION: *Make sure the mating marks meet, or the silent shaft will be out of time and cause vibration.*

Before installing the pump, fill the delivery port with clean oil to prime it.

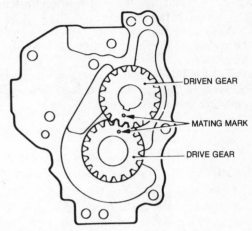

Mating marks of gears

ENGINE COOLING

Radiator

REMOVAL AND INSTALLATION

1. Remove the splash panel from the bottom of the vehicle. Drain the radiator by opening the petcock. Remove the shroud on models so equipped.

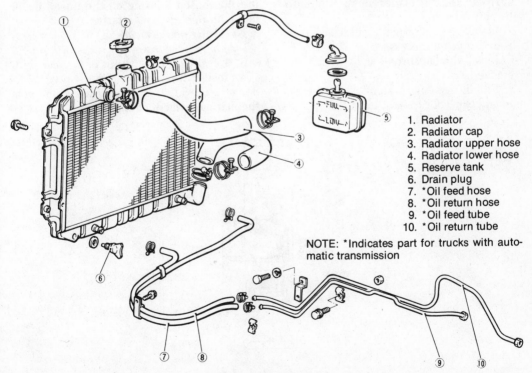

1. Radiator
2. Radiator cap
3. Radiator upper hose
4. Radiator lower hose
5. Reserve tank
6. Drain plug
7. *Oil feed hose
8. *Oil return hose
9. *Oil feed tube
10. *Oil return tube

NOTE: *Indicates part for trucks with automatic transmission

Exploded view of radiator

2. Disconnect the radiator hoses at the engine. On automatic transmission vehicles, disconnect and plug the transmission lines to the bottom of the radiator.

3. Remove the two retaining bolts from either side of the radiator. Lift out the radiator.

4. Install the radiator in the reverse order of removal. Tighten the retaining bolts gradually in a criss-cross pattern.

Water Pump

REMOVAL

1. Drain the cooling system.
2. Remove the fan shroud and radiator if necessary for working room.
3. Remove the alternator and accessory belts.
4. Remove the fan blades and/or automatic hub, if equipped.
5. Remove the water pump assembly from the timing chain case or the cylinder block.

INSTALLATION

1. Install the water pump to the timing chain case or the engine block and tighten the bolts securely.
2. Install the fan blades and/or the automatic clutch fan hub.
3. Install the alternator and accessory belts and adjust as necessary.
4. Install the fan shroud and the radiator, if removed.
5. Fill the cooling system, start the engine, and check for coolant leakage.

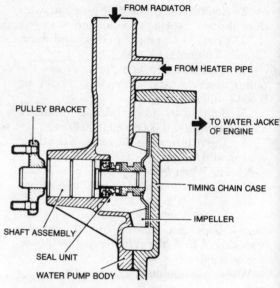

Sectional view of water pump

Thermostat

REMOVAL AND INSTALLATION

The thermostat is located in the intake manifold under the upper radiator hose.

1. Drain the coolant below the level of the thermostat.
2. Remove the two retaining bolts and lift the thermostat housing off the intake manifold with the hose still attached.

NOTE: *If you are careful, it is not necessary to remove the upper radiator hose.*

3. Lift the thermostat out of the manifold.
4. Install the thermostat in the reverse order of removal. Use a new gasket and coat the mating surfaces with sealer.

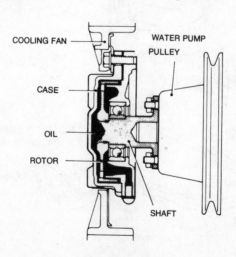

Sectional view of fan clutch

Most procedures involved in rebuilding an engine are fairly standard, regardless of the type of engine involved. This section is a guide to accepted rebuilding procedures. Examples of standard rebuilding practices are illustrated and should be used along with specific details concerning your particular engine, found earlier in this chapter.

The procedures given here are those used by any competent rebuilder. Obviously some of the procedures cannot be performed by the do-it-yourself mechanic, but are provided so that you will be familiar with the services that should be offered by rebuilding or machine shops. As an example, in most instances, it is more profitable for the home mechanic to remove the cylinder heads, buy the necessary parts (new valves, seals, keepers, keys, etc.) and deliver these to a machine shop for the necessary work. In this way you will save the money to remove and install the cylinder head and the mark-up on parts.

On the other hand, most of the work involved in rebuilding the lower end is well within the scope of the do-it-yourself mechanic. Only work such as hot-tanking, actually boring the block or Magnafluxing (invisible crack detection) need be sent to a machine shop.

Tools

The tools required for basic engine rebuilding should, with a few exceptions, be those included in a mechanic's tool kit. An accurate torque wrench, and a dial indicator (reading in thousandths) mounted on a universal base should be available. Special tools, where required, are available from the major tool suppliers. The services of a competent automotive machine shop must also be readily available.

Precautions

Aluminum has become increasingly popular for use in engines, due to its low weight and excellent heat transfer characteristics. The following precautions must be observed when handling aluminum (or any other) engine parts:
—Never hot-tank aluminum parts.
—Remove all aluminum parts (identification tags, etc.) from engine parts before hot-tanking (otherwise they will be removed during the process).

—Always coat threads lightly with engine oil or anti-seize compounds before installation, to prevent seizure.
—Never over-torque bolts or spark plugs in aluminum threads. Should stripping occur, threads can be restored using any of a number of thread repair kits available (see next section).

Inspection Techniques

Magnaflux and Zyglo are inspection techniques used to locate material flaws, such as stress cracks. Magnaflux is a magnetic process, applicable only to ferrous materials. The Zyglo process coats the material with a fluorescent dye penetrant, and any material may be tested using Zyglo. Specific checks of suspected surface cracks may be made at lower cost and more readily using spot check dye. The dye is sprayed onto the suspected area, wiped off, and the area is then sprayed with a developer. Cracks then will show up brightly.

Overhaul

The section is divided into two parts. The first, Cylinder Head Reconditioning, assumes that the cylinder head is removed from the engine, all manifolds are removed, and the cylinder head is on a workbench. The camshaft should be removed from overhead cam cylinder heads. The second section, Cylinder Block Reconditioning, covers the block, pistons, connecting rods and crankshaft. It is assumed that the engine is mounted on a work stand, and the cylinder head and all accessories are removed.

Procedures are identified as follows:
Unmarked—Basic procedures that must be performed in order to successfully complete the rebuilding process.
Starred (*)—Procedures that should be performed to ensure maximum performance and engine life.
Double starred (**)—Procedures that may be performed to increase engine performance and reliability.

When assembling the engine, any parts that will be in frictional contact must be pre-lubricated, to provide protection on initial start-up. Any product specifically formulated for this purpose may be used. NOTE: *Do not use engine oil.* Where semi-permanent (locked but removable) installation of bolts or nuts is desired, threads should be cleaned and located with Loctite® or a similar product (non-hardening).

Repairing Damaged Threads

Several methods of repairing damaged threads are available. Heli-Coil® (shown here), Keenserts® and Microdot® are among the most widely used. All involve basically the same principle—drilling out stripped threads, tapping the hole and installing a pre-wound insert—making welding, plugging and oversize fasteners unnecessary.

Two types of thread repair inserts are usually supplied—a standard type for most Inch Coarse, Inch Fine, Metric Coarse and Metric Fine thread sizes and a spark plug type to fit most spark plug port sizes. Consult the individual manufacturer's catalog to determine exact applications. Typical thread repair kits will contain a selection of pre-wound threaded inserts, a tap (corresponding to the outside diameter threads of the insert) and an installation tool. Spark plug inserts usually differ because they require a tap equipped with pilot threads and a combined reamer/tap section. Most manufacturers also supply blister-packed thread repair inserts separately in addition to a master kit containing a variety of taps and inserts plus installation tools.

Before effecting a repair to a threaded hole, remove any snapped, broken or damaged bolts or studs. Penetrating oil can be used to free frozen threads; the offending item can be removed with locking pliers or with a screw or stud extractor. After the hole is clear, the thread can be repaired, as follows:

Drill out the damaged threads with specified drill. Drill completely through the hole or to the bottom of a blind hole

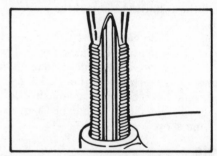

With the tap supplied, tap the hole to receive the thread insert. Keep the tap well oiled and back it out frequently to avoid clogging the threads

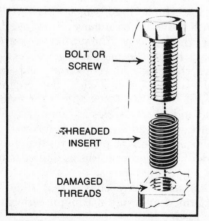

Damaged bolt holes can be repaired with thread repair inserts

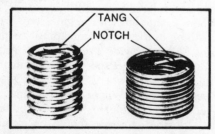

Standard thread repair insert (left) and spark plug thread insert (right)

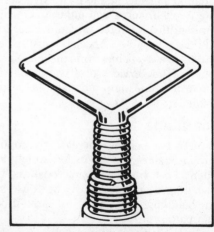

Screw the threaded insert onto the installation tool until the tang engages the slot. Screw the insert into the tapped hole until it is ¼–½ turn below the top surface. After installation break off the tang with a hammer and punch

Standard Torque Specifications and Fastener Markings

The Newton-metre has been designated the world standard for measuring torque and will gradually replace the foot-pound and kilogram-meter. In the absence of specific torques, the following chart can be used as a guide to the maximum safe torque of a particular size/grade of fastener.

- There is no torque difference for fine or coarse threads.
- Torque values are based on clean, dry threads. Reduce the value by 10% if threads are oiled prior to assembly.
- The torque required for aluminum components or fasteners is considerably less.

U. S. BOLTS

SAE Grade Number	1 or 2			5			6 or 7		

Bolt Markings

Manufacturer's marks may vary—number of lines always 2 less than the grade number.

Usage	Frequent			Frequent			Infrequent		
Bolt Size (inches)—(Thread)	Maximum Torque			Maximum Torque			Maximum Torque		
	Ft-Lb	kgm	Nm	Ft-Lb	kgm	Nm	Ft-Lb	kgm	Nm
¼—20	5	0.7	6.8	8	1.1	10.8	10	1.4	13.5
—28	6	0.8	8.1	10	1.4	13.6			
5⁄16—18	11	1.5	14.9	17	2.3	23.0	19	2.6	25.8
—24	13	1.8	17.6	19	2.6	25.7			
⅜—16	18	2.5	24.4	31	4.3	42.0	34	4.7	46.0
—24	20	2.75	27.1	35	4.8	47.5			
7⁄16—14	28	3.8	37.0	49	6.8	66.4	55	7.6	74.5
—20	30	4.2	40.7	55	7.6	74.5			
½—13	39	5.4	52.8	75	10.4	101.7	85	11.75	115.2
—20	41	5.7	55.6	85	11.7	115.2			
9⁄16—12	51	7.0	69.2	110	15.2	149.1	120	16.6	162.7
—18	55	7.6	74.5	120	16.6	162.7			
⅝—11	83	11.5	112.5	150	20.7	203.3	167	23.0	226.5
—18	95	13.1	128.8	170	23.5	230.5			
¾—10	105	14.5	142.3	270	37.3	366.0	280	38.7	379.6
—16	115	15.9	155.9	295	40.8	400.0			
⅞— 9	160	22.1	216.9	395	54.6	535.5	440	60.9	596.5
—14	175	24.2	237.2	435	60.1	589.7			
1— 8	236	32.5	318.6	590	81.6	799.9	660	91.3	894.8
—14	250	34.6	338.9	660	91.3	849.8			

METRIC BOLTS

NOTE: *Metric bolts are marked with a number indicating the relative strength of the bolt. These numbers have nothing to do with size.*

Description	Torque ft-lbs (Nm)			
Thread size x pitch (mm)	Head mark—4		Head mark—7	
6 x 1.0	2.2–2.9	(3.0–3.9)	3.6–5.8	(4.9–7.8)
8 x 1.25	5.8–8.7	(7.9–12)	9.4–14	(13–19)
10 x 1.25	12–17	(16–23)	20–29	(27–39)
12 x 1.25	21–32	(29–43)	35–53	(47–72)
14 x 1.5	35–52	(48–70)	57–85	(77–110)
16 x 1.5	51–77	(67–100)	90–120	(130–160)
18 x 1.5	74–110	(100–150)	130–170	(180–230)
20 x 1.5	110–140	(150–190)	190–240	(160–320)
22 x 1.5	150–190	(200–260)	250–320	(340–430)
24 x 1.5	190–240	(260–320)	310–410	(420–550)

NOTE: *This engine rebuilding section is a guide to accepted rebuilding procedures. Typical examples of standard rebuilding procedures are illustrated. Use these procedures along with the detailed instructions earlier in this chapter, concerning your particular engine.*

Cylinder Head Reconditioning

Procedure	Method
Remove the cylinder head:	See the engine service procedures earlier in this chapter for details concerning specific engines.
Identify the valves:	Invert the cylinder head, and number the valve faces front to rear, using a permanent felt-tip marker.
Remove the camshaft:	See the engine service procedures earlier in this chapter for details concerning specific engines.
Remove the valves and springs:	Using an appropriate valve spring compressor (depending on the configuration of the cylinder head), compress the valve springs. Lift out the keepers with needlenose pliers, release the compressor, and remove the valve, spring, and spring retainer. See the engine service procedures earlier in this chapter for details concerning specific engines.
Check the valve stem-to-guide clearance: 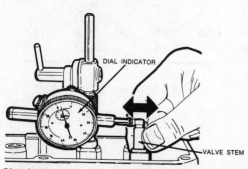 Check the valve stem-to-guide clearance	Clean the valve stem with lacquer thinner or a similar solvent to remove all gum and varnish. Clean the valve guides using solvent and an expanding wire-type valve guide cleaner. Mount a dial indicator so that the stem is at 90° to the valve stem, as close to the valve guide as possible. Move the valve off its seat, and measure the valve guide-to-stem clearance by rocking the stem back and forth to actuate the dial indicator. Measure the valve stems using a micrometer, and compare to specifications, to determine whether stem or guide wear is responsible for excessive clearance. NOTE: *Consult the Specifications tables earlier in this chapter.*

Cylinder Head Reconditioning

Procedure	Method
De-carbon the cylinder head and valves: 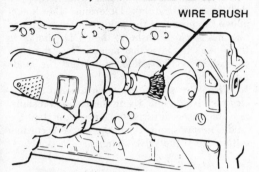WIRE BRUSH **Remove the carbon from the cylinder head with a wire brush and electric drill**	Chip carbon away from the valve heads, combustion chambers, and ports, using a chisel made of hardwood. Remove the remaining deposits with a stiff wire brush. NOTE: *Be sure that the deposits are actually removed, rather than burnished.*
Hot-tank the cylinder head (cast iron heads only): CAUTION: *Do not hot-tank aluminum parts.*	Have the cylinder head hot-tanked to remove grease, corrosion, and scale from the water passages. NOTE: *In the case of overhead cam cylinder heads, consult the operator to determine whether the camshaft bearings will be damaged by the caustic solution.*
Degrease the remaining cylinder head parts:	Clean the remaining cylinder head parts in an engine cleaning solvent. Do not remove the protective coating from the springs.
Check the cylinder head for warpage: 1 & 3 CHECK DIAGONALLY 2 CHECK ACROSS CENTER 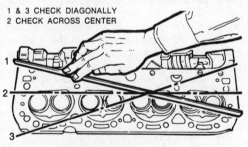 **Check the cylinder head for warpage**	Place a straight-edge across the gasket surface of the cylinder head. Using feeler gauges, determine the clearance at the center of the straight-edge. If warpage exceeds .003″ in a 6″ span, or .006″ over the total length, the cylinder head must be resurfaced. NOTE: *If warpage exceeds the manufacturer's maximum tolerance for material removal, the cylinder head must be replaced.* When milling the cylinder heads of V-type engines, the intake manifold mounting position is altered, and must be corrected by milling the manifold flange a proportionate amount.
*Knurl the valve guides: 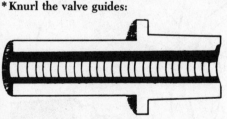 **Cut-away view of a knurled valve guide**	*Valve guides which are not excessively worn or distorted may, in some cases, be knurled rather than replaced. Knurling is a process in which metal is displaced and raised, thereby reducing clearance. Knurling also provides excellent oil control. The possibility of knurling rather than replacing valve guides should be discussed with a machinist.
Replace the valve guides: NOTE: *Valve guides should only be replaced if damaged or if an oversize valve stem is not available.*	See the engine service procedures earlier in this chapter for details concerning specific engines. Depending on the type of cylinder head, valve guides may be pressed, hammered, or shrunk in. In cases where the guides are shrunk into the head, replacement should be left to an equipped machine shop. In other

Cylinder Head Reconditioning

Procedure	Method

Procedure

A—VALVE GUIDE I.D.   B—LARGER THAN THE VALVE GUIDE O.D.

WASHERS

A—VALVE GUIDE I.D.   B—LARGER THAN THE VALVE GUIDE O.D.

Valve guide installation tool using washers for installation

Method

cases, the guides are replaced using a stepped drift (see illustration). Determine the height above the boss that the guide must extend, and obtain a stack of washers, their I.D. similar to the guide's O.D., of that height. Place the stack of washers on the guide, and insert the guide into the boss.

NOTE: *Valve guides are often tapered or beveled for installation.* Using the stepped installation tool (see illustration), press or tap the guides into position. Ream the guides according to the size of the valve stem.

Replace valve seat inserts:

Replacement of valve seat inserts which are worn beyond resurfacing or broken, if feasible, must be done by a machine shop.

Resurface (grind) the valve face:

FOR DIMENSIONS, REFER TO SPECIFICATIONS

CHECK FOR BENT STEM

DIAMETER

VALVE FACE ANGLE

1/32″ MINIMUM

THIS LINE PARALLEL WITH VALVE HEAD

Critical valve dimensions

Using a valve grinder, resurface the valves according to specifications given earlier in this chapter.

CAUTION: *Valve face angle is not always identical to valve seat angle.* A minimum margin of 1/32″ should remain after grinding the valve. The valve stem top should also be squared and resurfaced, by placing the stem in the V-block of the grinder, and turning it while pressing lightly against the grinding wheel.

NOTE: *Do not grind sodium filled exhaust valves on a machine. These should be hand lapped.*

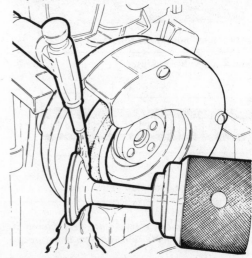

Valve grinding by machine

Cylinder Head Reconditioning

Procedure	Method
Resurface the valve seats using reamers or grinder: 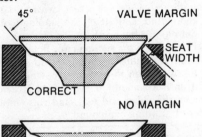 **Valve seat width and centering**  **Reaming the valve seat with a hand reamer**	Select a reamer of the correct seat angle, slightly larger than the diameter of the valve seat, and assemble it with a pilot of the correct size. Install the pilot into the valve guide, and using steady pressure, turn the reamer clockwise. **CAUTION:** *Do not turn the reamer counterclockwise.* Remove only as much material as necessary to clean the seat. Check the concentricity of the seat (following). If the dye method is not used, coat the valve face with Prussian blue dye, install and rotate it on the valve seat. Using the dye marked area as a centering guide, center and narrow the valve seat to specifications with correction cutters. **NOTE:** *When no specifications are available, minimum seat width for exhaust valves should be* $5/64''$, *intake valves* $1/16''$. After making correction cuts, check the position of the valve seat on the valve face using Prussian blue dye. To resurface the seat with a power grinder, select a pilot of the correct size and coarse stone of the proper angle. Lubricate the pilot and move the stone on and off the valve seat at 2 cycles per second, until all flaws are gone. Finish the seat with a fine stone. If necessary the seat can be corrected or narrowed using correction stones.
Check the valve seat concentricity: 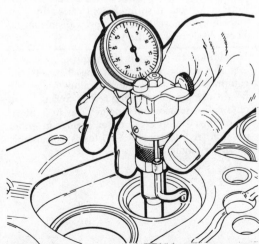 **Check the valve seat concentricity with a dial gauge**	Coat the valve face with Prussian blue dye, install the valve, and rotate it on the valve seat. If the entire seat becomes coated, and the valve is known to be concentric, the seat is concentric. * Install the dial gauge pilot into the guide, and rest of the arm on the valve seat. Zero the gauge, and rotate the arm around the seat. Run-out should not exceed $.002''$.

Cylinder Head Reconditioning

Procedure	Method
*Lap the valves: NOTE: *Valve lapping is done to ensure efficient sealing of resurfaced valves and seats.*	Invert the cyclinder head, lightly lubricate the valve stems, and install the valves in the head as numbered. Coat valve seats with fine grinding compound, and attach the lapping tool suction cup to a valve head. NOTE: *Moisten the suction cup.* Rotate the tool between the palms, changing position and lifting the tool often to prevent grooving. Lap the valve until a smooth, polished seat is evident. Remove the valve and tool, and rinse away all traces of grinding compound.

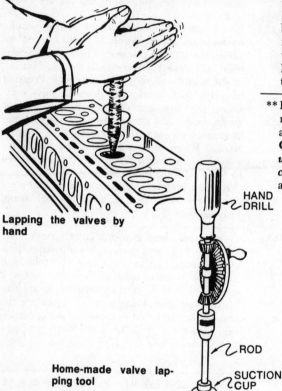

Lapping the valves by hand

HAND DRILL

Home-made valve lapping tool

ROD

SUCTION CUP

**Fasten a suction cup to a piece of drill rod, and mount the rod in a hand drill. Proceed as above, using the hand drill as a lapping tool.
CAUTION: *Due to the higher speeds involved when using the hand drill, care must be exercised to avoid grooving the seat.* Lift the tool and change direction of rotation often.

Procedure	Method
Check the valve springs:	Place the spring on a flat surface next to a square. Measure the height of the spring, and rotate it against the edge of the square to measure distortion. If spring height varies (by comparison) by more than $1/16''$ or if distortion exceeds $1/16''$, replace the spring.

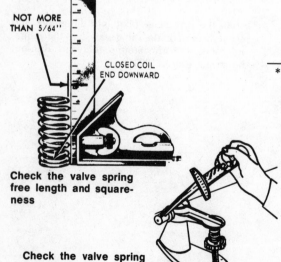

NOT MORE THAN 5/64"

CLOSED COIL END DOWNWARD

Check the valve spring free length and squareness

Check the valve spring test pressure

**In addition to evaluating the spring as above, test the spring pressure at the installed and compressed (installed height minus valve lift) height using a valve spring tester. Springs used on small displacement engines (up to 3 liters) should be ∓ 1 lb of all other springs in either position. A tolerance of ∓ 5 lbs is permissible on larger engines.

Cylinder Head Reconditioning

Procedure	Method

Procedure

***Install valve stem seals:**

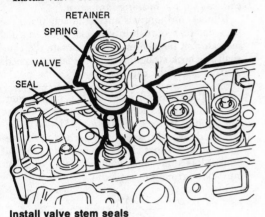

RETAINER
SPRING
VALVE
SEAL

Install valve stem seals

Method

*Due to the pressure differential that exists at the ends of the intake valve guides (atmospheric pressure above, manifold vacuum below), oil is drawn through the valve guides into the intake port. This has been alleviated somewhat since the addition of positive crankcase ventilation, which lowers the pressure above the guides. Several types of valve stem seals are available to reduce blow-by. Certain seals simply slip over the stem and guide boss, while others require that the boss be machined. Recently, Teflon guide seals have become popular. Consult a parts supplier or machinist concerning availability and suggested usages.

NOTE: *When installing seals, ensure that a small amount of oil is able to pass the seal to lubricate the valve guides; otherwise, excessive wear may result.*

Install the valves:

See the engine service procedures earlier in this chapter for details concerning specific engines.

Lubricate the valve stems, and install the valves in the cylinder head as numbered. Lubricate and position the seals (if used) and the valve springs. Install the spring retainers, compress the springs, and insert the keys using needlenose pliers or a tool designed for this purpose.

NOTE: *Retain the keys with wheel bearing grease during installation.*

Check valve spring installed height:

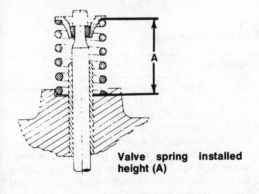

Valve spring installed height (A)

Measure the distance between the spring pad the lower edge of the spring retainer, and compare to specifications. If the installed height is incorrect, add shim washers between the spring pad and the spring.

CAUTION: *Use only washers designed for this purpose.*

GRIND OUT THIS PORTION

Measure the valve spring installed height (A) with a modified steel rule

Clean and inspect the camshaft:

Degrease the camshaft, using solvent, and clean out all oil holes. Visually inspect cam lobes and bearing journals for excessive wear. If a lobe is questionable, check all lobes as indicated below. If a journal or lobe is worn, the camshaft must be reground or replaced.

Cylinder Head Reconditioning

Procedure	Method
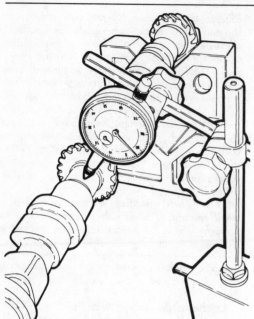

Check the camshaft for straightness | NOTE: *If a journal is worn, there is a good chance that the bushings are worn.*

If lobes and journals appear intact, place the front and rear journals in V-blocks, and rest a dial indicator on the center journal. Rotate the camshaft to check straightness. If deviation exceeds .001″, replace the camshaft.

*Check the camshaft lobes with a micrometer, by measuring the lobes from the nose to base and again at 90° (see illustration). The lift is determined by subtracting the second measurement from the first. If all exhaust lobes and all intake lobes are not identical, the camshaft must be reground or replaced.

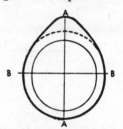

Camshaft lobe measurement |
| Install the camshaft: | See the engine service procedures earlier in this chapter for details concerning specific engines. |
| Install the rocker arms: | See the engine service procedures earlier in this chapter for details concerning specific engines. |

Cylinder Block Reconditioning

Procedure	Method
Checking the main bearing clearance:

PLASTIGAGE®

Plastigage® installed on the lower bearing shell | Invert engine, and remove cap from the bearing to be checked. Using a clean, dry rag, thoroughly clean all oil from crankshaft journal and bearing insert.

NOTE: *Plastigage® is soluble in oil; therefore, oil on the journal or bearing could result in erroneous readings.* Place a piece of Plastigage along the full length of journal, reinstall cap, and torque to specifications.

NOTE: *Specifications are given in the engine specifications earlier in this chapter.*

Remove bearing cap, and determine bearing clearance by comparing width of Plastigage to the scale on Plastigage envelope. Journal taper is determined by comparing width of the Plastigage strip near its ends. Rotate crankshaft 90° and retest, to determine journal eccentricity.

NOTE: *Do not rotate crankshaft with Plastigage installed.* If bearing insert and journal appear in- |

Cylinder Block Reconditioning

Procedure	Method

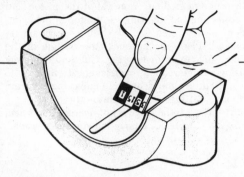

Measure Plastigage® to determine main bearing clearance

tact, and are within tolerances, no further main bearing service is required. If bearing or journal appear defective, cause of failure should be determined before replacement.

*Remove crankshaft from block (see below). Measure the main bearing journals at each end twice (90° apart) using a micrometer, to determine diameter, journal taper and eccentricity. If journals are within tolerances, reinstall bearing caps at their specified torque. Using a telescope gauge and micrometer, measure bearing I.D. parallel to piston axis and at 30° on each side of piston axis. Subtract journal O.D. from bearing I.D. to determine oil clearance. If crankshaft journals appear defective, or do not meet tolerances, there is no need to measure bearings; for the crankshaft will require grinding and/or undersize bearings will be required. If bearing appears defective, cause for failure should be determined prior to replacement.

Check the connecting rod bearing clearance:

Connecting rod bearing clearance is checked in the same manner as main bearing clearance, using Plastigage. Before removing the crankshaft, connecting rod side clearance also should be measured and recorded.

*Checking connecting rod bearing clearance, using a micrometer, is identical to checking main bearing clearance. If no other service is required, the piston and rod assemblies need not be removed.

Remove the crankshaft:

Using a punch, mark the corresponding main bearing caps and saddles according to position (i.e., one punch on the front main cap and saddle, two on the second, three on the third, etc.). Using number stamps, identify the corresponding connecting rods and caps, according to cylinder (if no numbers are present). Remove the main and connecting rod caps, and replace sleeves of plastic tubing or vacuum hose over the connecting rod bolts, to protect the journals as the crankshaft is removed. Lift the crankshaft out of the block.

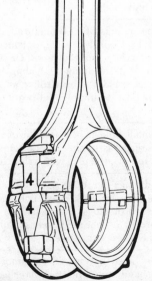

Match the connecting rod to the cylinder with a number stamp

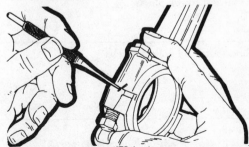

Match the connecting rod and cap with scribe marks

Cylinder Block Reconditioning

Procedure	Method
Remove the ridge from the top of the cylinder: 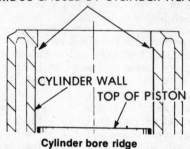 RIDGE CAUSED BY CYLINDER WEAR 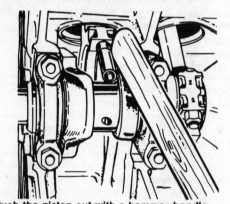 CYLINDER WALL TOP OF PISTON **Cylinder bore ridge**	In order to facilitate removal of the piston and connecting rod, the ridge at the top of the cylinder (unworn area; see illustration) must be removed. Place the piston at the bottom of the bore, and cover it with a rag. Cut the ridge away using a ridge reamer, exercising extreme care to avoid cutting too deeply. Remove the rag, and remove cuttings that remain on the piston. **CAUTION:** *If the ridge is not removed, and new rings are installed, damage to rings will result.*
Remove the piston and connecting rod: **Push the piston out with a hammer handle**	Invert the engine, and push the pistons and connecting rods out of the cylinders. If necessary, tap the connecting rod boss with a wooden hammer handle, to force the piston out. **CAUTION:** *Do not attempt to force the piston past the cylinder ridge* (see above).
Service the crankshaft:	Ensure that all oil holes and passages in the crankshaft are open and free of sludge. If necessary, have the crankshaft ground to the largest possible undersize.
	** Have the crankshaft Magnafluxed, to locate stress cracks. Consult a machinist concerning additional service procedures, such as surface hardening (e.g., nitriding, Tuftriding) to improve wear characteristics, cross drilling and chamfering the oil holes to improve lubrication, and balancing.
Removing freeze plugs:	Drill a small hole in the middle of the freeze plugs. Thread a large sheet metal screw into the hole and remove the plug with a slide hammer.
Remove the oil gallery plugs:	Threaded plugs should be removed using an appropriate (usually square) wrench. To remove soft, pressed in plugs, drill a hole in the plug, and thread in a sheet metal screw. Pull the plug out by the screw using pliers.
Hot-tank the block: **NOTE:** *Do not hot-tank aluminum parts.*	Have the block hot-tanked to remove grease, corrosion, and scale from the water jackets. **NOTE:** *Consult the operator to determine whether the camshaft bearings will be damaged during the hot-tank process.*

Cylinder Block Reconditioning

Procedure	Method
Check the block for cracks:	Visually inspect the block for cracks or chips. The most common locations are as follows: Adjacent to freeze plugs. Between the cylinders and water jackets. Adjacent to the main bearing saddles. At the extreme bottom of the cylinders. Check only suspected cracks using spot check dye (see introduction). If a crack is located, consult a machinist concerning possible repairs.
	** Magnaflux the block to locate hidden cracks. If cracks are located, consult a machinist about feasibility of repair.
Install the oil gallery plugs and freeze plugs:	Coat freeze plugs with sealer and tap into position using a piece of pipe, slightly smaller than the plug, as a driver. To ensure retention, stake the edges of the plugs. Coat threaded oil gallery plugs with sealer and install. Drive replacement soft plugs into block using a large drift as a driver.
	* Rather than reinstalling lead plugs, drill and tap the holes, and install threaded plugs.
Check the bore diameter and surface: 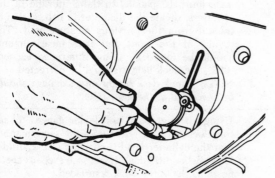 **Measure the cylinder bore with a dial gauge**	Visually inspect the cylinder bores for roughness, scoring, or scuffing. If evident, the cylinder bore must be bored or honed oversize to eliminate imperfections, and the smallest possible oversize piston used. The new pistons should be given to the machinist with the block, so that the cylinders can be bored or honed exactly to the piston size (plus clearance). If no flaws are evident, measure the bore diameter using a telescope gauge and micrometer, or dial gauge, parallel and perpendicular to the engine centerline, at the top (below the ridge) and bottom of the bore. Subtract the bottom measurements from the top to determine taper, and the parallel to the centerline measurements from the perpendicular measurements to determine eccentricity. If the measurements are not within specifications, the cylinder must be bored or honed, and an oversize piston installed. If the measurements are within specifications the cylinder may

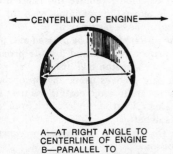

← CENTERLINE OF ENGINE →

A—AT RIGHT ANGLE TO CENTERLINE OF ENGINE
B—PARALLEL TO CENTERLINE OF ENGINE

Cylinder bore measuring points

Measure the cylinder bore with a telescope gauge

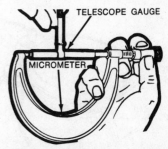

TELESCOPE GAUGE 90° FROM PISTON PIN

TELESCOPE GAUGE

MICROMETER

Measure the telescope gauge with a micrometer to determine the cylinder bore

Cylinder Block Reconditioning

Procedure	Method
	be used as is, with only finish honing (see below). *NOTE: Prior to submitting the block for boring, perform the following operation(s).*
Check the cylinder block bearing alignment: 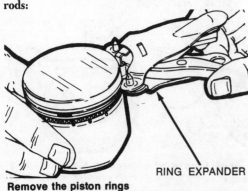 Check the main bearing saddle alignment	Remove the upper bearing inserts. Place a straightedge in the bearing saddles along the centerline of the crankshaft. If clearance exists between the straightedge and the center saddle, the block must be alignbored.
*Check the deck height:	The deck height is the distance from the crankshaft centerline to the block deck. To measure, invert the engine, and install the crankshaft, retaining it with the center maincap. Measure the distance from the crankshaft journal to the block deck, parallel to the cylinder centerline. Measure the diameter of the end (front and rear) main journals, parallel to the centerline of the cylinders, divide the diameter in half, and subtract it from the previous measurement. The results of the front and rear measurements should be identical. If the difference exceeds .005″, the deck height should be corrected. *NOTE: Block deck height and warpage should be corrected at the same time.*
Check the block deck for warpage:	Using a straightedge and feeler gauges, check the block deck for warpage in the same manner that the cylinder head is checked (see Cylinder Head Reconditioning). If warpage exceeds specifications, have the deck resurfaced. *NOTE: In certain cases a specification for total material removal (cylinder head and block deck) is provided. This specification must not be exceeded.*
Clean and inspect the pistons and connecting rods: RING EXPANDER Remove the piston rings	Using a ring expander, remove the rings from the piston. Remove the retaining rings (if so equipped) and remove piston pin. *NOTE: If the piston pin must be pressed out, determine the proper method and use the proper tools; otherwise the piston will distort.* Clean the ring grooves using an appropriate tool, exercising care to avoid cutting too deeply. Thoroughly clean all carbon and varnish from the piston with solvent. *CAUTION: Do not use a wire brush or caustic solvent on pistons.* Inspect the pistons for scuffing, scoring, cracks, pitting, or excessive ringsgroove wear. wear is evident, the piston must be replaced Check the connecting rod length by measuring

Cylinder Block Reconditioning

Procedure	Method

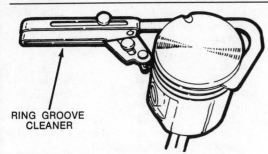

RING GROOVE CLEANER

Clean the piston ring grooves

the rod from the inside of the large end to the inside of the small end using calipers (see illustration). All connecting rods should be equal length. Replace any rod that differs from the others in the engine.

* Have the connecting rod alignment checked in an alignment fixture by a machinist. Replace any twisted or bent rods.

* Magnaflux the connecting rods to locate stress cracks. If cracks are found, replace the connecting rod.

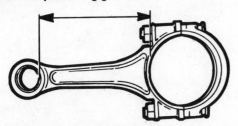

Check the connecting rod length (arrow)

Fit the pistons to the cylinders:

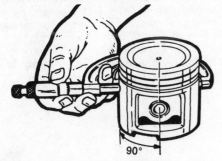

90°

Measure the piston prior to fitting

Using a telescope gauge and micrometer, or a dial gauge, measure the cylinder bore diameter perpendicular to the piston pin, 2½" below the deck. Measure the piston perpendicular to its pin on the skirt. The difference between the two measurements is the piston clearance. If the clearance is within specifications or slightly below (after boring or honing), finish honing is all that is required. If the clearance is excessive, try to obtain a slightly larger piston to bring clearance within specifications. Where this is not possible, obtain the first oversize piston, and hone (of if necessary, bore) the cylinder to size.

Assemble the pistons and connecting rods:

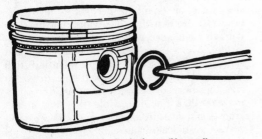

Install the piston pin lock-rings (if used)

Inspect piston pin, connecting rod small end bushing, and piston bore for galling, scoring, or excessive wear. If evident, replace defective part(s). Measure the I.D. of the piston boss and connecting rod small end, and the O.D. of the piston pin. If within specifications, assemble piston pin and rod.
CAUTION: *If piston pin must be pressed in, determine the proper method and use the proper tools; otherwise the piston will distort.*
Install the lock rings; ensure that they seat properly. If the parts are not within specifications, determine the service method for the type of engine. In some cases, piston and pin are serviced as an assembly when either is defective. Others specify reaming the piston and connecting rods for an oversize pin. If the connecting rod bushing is worn, it may in many cases be replaced. Reaming the piston and replacing the rod bushing are machine shop operations.

Cylinder Block Reconditioning

Procedure	Method
Finish hone the cylinders: 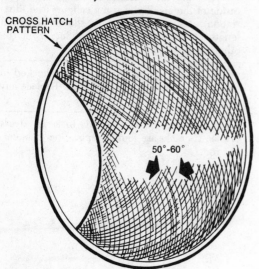	Chuck a flexible drive hone into a power drill, and insert it into the cylinder. Start the hone, and move it up and down in the cylinder at a rate which will produce approximately a 60° cross-hatch pattern. **NOTE:** *Do not extend the hone below the cylinder bore.* After developing the pattern, remove the hone and recheck piston fit. Wash the cylinders with a detergent and water solution to remove abrasive dust, dry, and wipe several times with a rag soaked in engine oil.
Check piston ring end-gap: 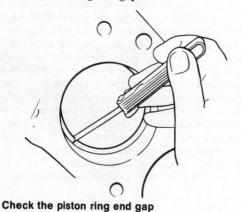 Check the piston ring end gap	Compress the piston rings to be used in a cylinder, one at a time, into that cylinder, and press them approximately 1″ below the deck with an inverted piston. Using feeler gauges, measure the ring end-gap, and compare to specifications. Pull the ring out of the cylinder and file the ends with a fine file to obtain proper clearance. **CAUTION:** *If inadequate ring end-gap is utilized, ring breakage will result.*
Install the piston rings: 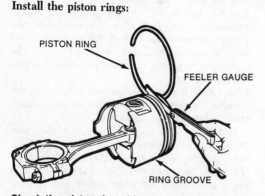 Check the piston ring side clearance	Inspect the ring grooves in the piston for excessive wear or taper. If necessary, recut the groove(s) for use with an overwidth ring or a standard ring and spacer. If the groove is worn uniformly, overwidth rings, or standard rings and spaces may be installed without recutting. Roll the outside of the ring around the groove to check for burrs or deposits. If any are found, remove with a fine file. Hold the ring in the groove, and measure side clearance. If necessary, correct as indicated above. **NOTE:** *Always install any additional spacers above the piston ring.* The ring groove must be deep enough to allow the ring to seat below the lands (see illustration). In many cases, a "go-no-go" depth gauge will be provided with the piston rings. Shallow grooves may be corrected by recutting, while deep

Cylinder Block Reconditioning

Procedure	Method
	grooves require some type of filler or expander behind the piston. Consult the piston ring supplier concerning the suggested method. Install the rings on the piston, lowest ring first, using a ring expander. **NOTE:** *Position the rings as specified by the manufacturer.* Consult the engine service procedures earlier in this chapter for details concerning specific engines.
Install the rear main seal:	See the engine service procedures earlier in this chapter for details concerning specific engines.
Install the crankshaft: 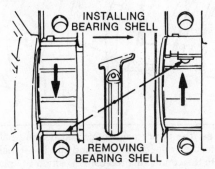 **Remove or install the upper bearing insert using a roll-out pin** 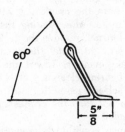 **Home-made bearing roll-out pin**	Thoroughly clean the main bearing saddles and caps. Place the upper halves of the bearing inserts on the saddles and press into position. **NOTE:** *Ensure that the oil holes align.* Press the corresponding bearing inserts into the main bearing caps. Lubricate the upper main bearings, and lay the crankshaft in position. Place a strip of Plastigage on each of the crankshaft journals, install the main caps, and torque to specifications. Remove the main caps, and compare the Plastigage to the scale on the Plastigage envelope. If clearances are within tolerances, remove the Plastigage, turn the crankshaft 90°, wipe off all oil and retest. If all clearances are correct, remove all Plastigage, thoroughly lubricate the main caps and bearing journals, and install the main caps. If clearances are not within tolerance, the upper bearing inserts may be removed, without removing the crankshaft, using a bearing roll out pin (see illustration). Roll in a bearing that will provide proper clearance, and retest. Torque all main caps, excluding the thrust bearing cap, to specifications. Tighten the thrust bearing cap finger tight. To properly align the thrust bearing, pry the crankshaft the extent of its axial travel several times, the last movement held toward the front of the engine, and torque the thrust bearing cap to specifications. Determine the crankshaft end-play (see below), and bring within tolerance with thrust washers.

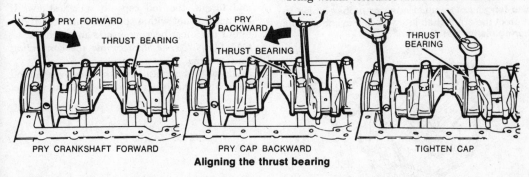
Aligning the thrust bearing

| Measure crankshaft end-play: | Mount a dial indicator stand on the front of the block, with the dial indicator stem resting on the |

Cylinder Block Reconditioning

Procedure	Method

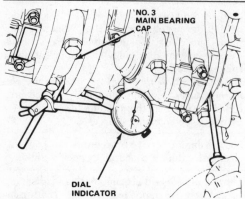

NO. 3 MAIN BEARING CAP

DIAL INDICATOR

Check the crankshaft end-play with a dial indicator

Check the crankshaft end-play with a feeler gauge

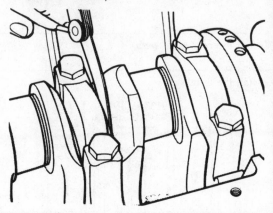

nose of the crankshaft, parallel to the crankshaft axis. Pry the crankshaft the extent of its travel rearward, and zero the indicator. Pry the crankshaft forward and record crankshaft end-play.

NOTE: *Crankshaft end-play also may be measured at the thrust bearing, using feeler gauges (see illustration).*

Install the pistons:

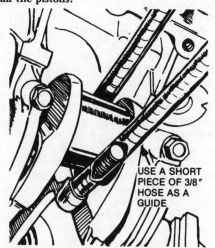

USE A SHORT PIECE OF 3/8" HOSE AS A GUIDE

Use lengths of vacuum hose or rubber tubing to protect the crankshaft journals and cylinder walls during piston installation

Press the upper connecting rod bearing halves into the connecting rods, and the lower halves into the connecting rod caps. Position the piston ring gaps according to specifications (see car section), and lubricate the pistons. Install a ring compresser on a piston, and press two long (8") pieces of plastic tubing over the rod bolts. Using the tubes as a guide, press the pistons into the bores and onto the crankshaft with a wooden hammer handle. After seating the rod on the crankshaft journal, remove the tubes and install the cap finger tight. Install the remaining pistons in the same manner. Invert the engine and check the bearing clearance at two points (90° apart) on each journal with Plastigage.

NOTE: *Do not turn the crankshaft with Plastigage installed.*

If clearance is within tolerances, remove *all* Plastigage, thoroughly lubricate the journals, and torque the rod caps to specifications. If clearance is not within specifications, install different thickness bearing inserts and recheck.

CAUTION: *Never shim or file the connecting rods or caps.*

Always install plastic tube sleeves over the rod bolts when the caps are not installed, to protect the crankshaft journals.

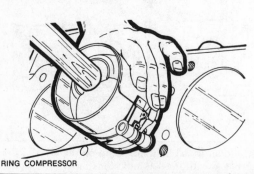

RING COMPRESSOR

Install the piston using a ring compressor

Cylinder Block Reconditioning

Procedure	Method
Check connecting rod side clearance: 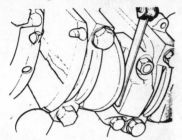 **Check the connecting rod side clearance with a feeler gauge**	Determine the clearance between the sides of the connecting rods and the crankshaft using feeler gauges. If clearance is below the minimum tolerance, the rod may be machined to provide adequate clearance. If clearance is excessive, substitute an unworn rod, and recheck. If clearance is still outside specifications, the crankshaft must be welded and reground, or replaced.
Inspect the timing chain (or belt):	Visually inspect the timing chain for broken or loose links, and replace the chain if any are found. If the chain will flex sideways, it must be replaced. Install the timing chain as specified. Be sure the timing belt is not stretched, frayed or broken. NOTE: *If the original timing chain is to be reused, install it in its original position.* See the engine service procedures earlier in this chapter for details concerning specific engines.

Completing the Rebuilding Process

Following the above procedures, complete the rebuilding process as follows:

Fill the oil pump with oil, to prevent cavitating (sucking air) on initial engine start up. Install the oil pump and the pickup tube on the engine. Coat the oil pan gasket as necessary, and install the gasket and the oil pan. Mount the flywheel and the crankshaft vibration damper or pulley on the crankshaft. NOTE: *Always use new bolts when installing the flywheel.* Inspect the clutch shaft pilot bushing in the crankshaft. If the bushing is excessively worn, remove it with an expanding puller and a slide hammer, and tap a new bushing into place.

Position the engine, cylinder head side up. Install the cylinder head, and torque it as specified. Install the rocker arms and adjust the valves.

Install the intake and exhaust manifolds, the carburetor(s), the distributor and spark plugs. Adjust the point gap and the static ignition timing. Mount all accessories and install the engine in the car. Fill the radiator with coolant, and the crankcase with high quality engine oil.

Break-in Procedure

Start the engine, and allow it to run at low speed for a few minutes, while checking for leaks. Stop the engine, check the oil level, and fill as necessary. Restart the engine, and fill the cooling system to capacity. Check the point dwell angle and adjust the ignition timing and the valves. Run the engine at low to medium speed (800–2500 rpm) for approximately ½ hour, and retorque the cylinder head bolts. Road test the car, and check again for leaks.

Follow the manufacturer's recommended engine break-in procedure and maintenance schedule for new engines.

Emission Controls and Fuel System

EMISSION CONTROLS

Crankcase Emission Control System

On all models a closed-type crankcase ventilation system is used to prevent engine blow-by gases from escaping into the atmosphere.

On 1979–80 models a small fixed orifice, located in the intake manifold, is connected to the rear section of the rocker arm cover by a hose.

A larger hose is connected from the front of the rocker arm cover to the air cleaner as-

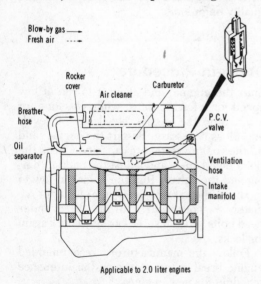

Applicable to 2.0 liter engines

1. Front insulator
2. Roll restrictor
3. Heat deflection plate
   (Trucks for U.S.A. right side only)

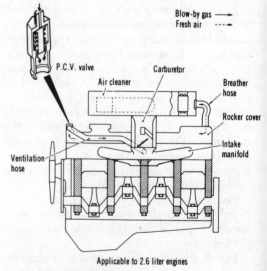

Applicable to 2.6 liter engines

4. Roll restrictor
   (Trucks for Canada right side only)
5. No. 2 crossmember
6. Rear insulator

1981— Crankcase emission control system, 121.7 cu. in. (2000 cc) engine shown

sembly. Under light to medium carburetor throttle opening, the blow-by gases are drawn through the fixed orifice and the large hose route the gases into the engine.

The only maintenance required is to regularly check the breather hose condition, clean the orifice in the intake manifold, and clean the steel wool filter, in the air cleaner.

On 1981 models a replaceable PCV valve is utilized in the valve cover. Refer to Chapter one for testing of the PCV valve.

Fuel Evaporation Control System

This system is designed to prevent hydrocarbons from escaping into the atmosphere from the fuel tank, due to normal evaporation.

The parts of the system are as follow:

Separator Tank   Located near the gasoline tank, used to accommodate expansion, and to allow maximum condensation of the fuel vapors.

Canister   Located in the engine compartment to trap and retain gasoline vapors while the engine is not operating. When the engine is started, fresh air is drawn into the canister, removing the stored vapors, and is directed to the air cleaner.

Two-way Valve   Because of different methods of tank venting and the use of sealed gasoline tank cap, the two-way valve is used in the vapor lines. The valve relieves either pressure or vacuum in the tank.

Purge Control Valve   The purge control valve replaces the check valve used in previous years. During idle, the valve closes off the vapor passage to the air cleaner.

Fuel Check Valve   This valve is used to prevent fuel leakage in case of roll over. It is in-

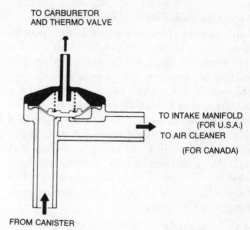

Purge control valve

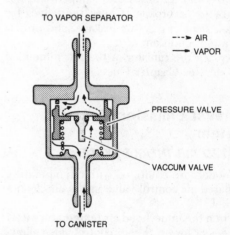

Two—way valve

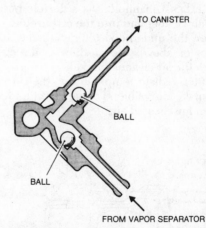

Fuel check valve construction

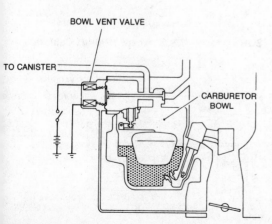

Bowl vent system

stalled in the vapor line between the separator and the two-way valve.

Fuel Bowl Vent Valve   This valve controls the carburetor bowl vapors on later models except in Canada. The valve is opened when the intake manifold vacuum working on the diaphragm of the valve exceeds the present value (after the ignition is turned on), and is kept open by the solenoid valve. When the ignition is turned off the valve is closed.

Thermo Valve This valve used on later models senses the coolant temperature at the intake manifold and closes the purge control valve when the coolant temperature is lower than a preset value, in order to reduce CO and HC emissions under engine warm-up conditions, and opens the purge control valve when the coolant temperature exceeds the pre-set temperature.

MAINTENANCE

Be sure that all hoses are clamped and not dry-rotted or broken. Check the valves for cracks, signs of gasoline leakage, and proper operating condition.

Replace the canister at the recommended interval. See Chapter One.

Exhaust Emission Control System

HEATED AIR INTAKE SYSTEM

All models are equipped with a temperature regulated air control valve in the air cleaner snorkel.

When the underhood air temperature is 41 degrees or lower, the air control valve allows preheated air to flow through the heat cowl of the exhaust manifold, via a flexible hose, to the air cleaner and into the carburetor.

When the underhood temperature is 108 degrees or above, the air flow is directed through the air cleaner snorkel.

At intermediate temperatures, the carburetor intake air is a blend of the direct underhood and preheated air.

Maintenance

Visually check the control valve assembly when the engine is cold, to be sure that the valve is closed.

Warm up the engine and check that the control valve opens to the outside air.

SECONDARY AIR SUPPLY SYSTEM

This system supplies air for the further combustion of unburned gases in the thermal reactor (California only) or exhaust manifold and consists of a reed valve, air hoses, and air passages built into the cylinder head.

The reed valve is operated by exhaust pulsations in the exhaust manifold. It draws fresh air through the air cleaner and supplies it to the exhaust ports.

Maintenance

Check for damages to the air hoses and air pipes. Make sure the air passages are open in the head.

EXHAUST GAS RECIRCULATION SYSTEM

The EGR system recirculates part of the exhaust gases into the combustion chambers. This dilutes the air/fuel mixture, reducing formation of oxides of nitrogen in the exhaust

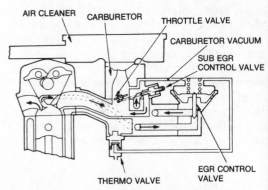

EGR system—U.S.A. except 1980–81 California

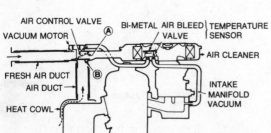

Heated air intake system

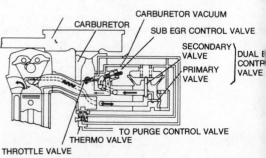

EGR system—1980–81 California

CHILTON'S
FUEL ECONOMY
& TUNE-UP TIPS

Tune-up • Spark Plug Diagnosis • Emission Controls

Fuel System • Cooling System • Tires and Wheels

General Maintenance

CHILTON'S FUEL ECONOMY & TUNE-UP TIPS

Fuel economy is important to everyone, no matter what kind of vehicle you drive. The maintenance-minded motorist can save both money and fuel using these tips and the periodic maintenance and tune-up procedures in this Repair and Tune-Up Guide.

There are more than 130,000,000 cars and trucks registered for private use in the United States. Each travels an average of 10-12,000 miles per year, and, and in total they consume close to 70 billion gallons of fuel each year. This represents nearly ⅔ of the oil imported by the United States each year. The Federal government's goal is to reduce consumption 10% by 1985. A variety of methods are either already in use or under serious consideration, and they all affect you driving and the cars you will drive. In addition to "down-sizing", the auto industry is using or investigating the use of electronic fuel delivery, electronic engine controls and alternative engines for use in smaller and lighter vehicles, among other alternatives to meet the federally mandated Corporate Average Fuel Economy (CAFE) of 27.5 mpg by 1985. The government, for its part, is considering rationing, mandatory driving curtailments and tax increases on motor vehicle fuel in an effort to reduce consumption. The government's goal of a 10% reduction could be realized — and further government regulation avoided — if every private vehicle could use just 1 less gallon of fuel per week.

How Much Can You Save?

Tests have proven that almost anyone can make at least a 10% reduction in fuel consumption through regular maintenance and tune-ups. When a major manufacturer of spark plugs sur-

TUNE-UP

1. Check the cylinder compression to be sure the engine will really benefit from a tune-up and that it is capable of producing good fuel economy. A tune-up will be wasted on an engine in poor mechanical condition.

2. Replace spark plugs regularly. New spark plugs alone can increase fuel economy 3%.

3. Be sure the spark plugs are the correct type (heat range) for your vehicle. See the Tune-Up Specifications.

Heat range refers to the spark plug's ability to conduct heat away from the firing end. It must conduct the heat away in an even pattern to avoid becoming a source of pre-ignition, yet it must also operate hot enough to burn off conductive deposits that could cause misfiring.

The heat range is usually indicated by a number on the spark plug, part of the manufacturer's designation for each individual spark plug. The numbers in bold-face indicate the heat range in each manufacturer's identification system.

Periodically, check the spark plugs to be sure they are firing efficiently. They are excellent indicators of the internal condition of your engine.

Manufacturer	Typical Designation
AC	R **45** TS
Bosch (old)	WA **145** T30
Bosch (new)	HR **8** Y
Champion	RBL **15** Y
Fram/Autolite	4**15**
Mopar	P-**62** PR
Motorcraft	BRF-**42**
NGK	BP **5** ES-15
Nippondenso	W **16** EP
Prestolite	14GR **5** 2A

On AC, Bosch (new), Champion, Fram/Autolite, Mopar, Motorcraft and Prestolite, a higher number indicates a hotter plug. On Bosch (old), NGK and Nippondenso, a higher number indicates a colder plug.

4. Make sure the spark plugs are properly gapped. See the Tune-Up Specifications in this book.

5. Be sure the spark plugs are firing efficiently. The illustrations on the next 2 pages show you how to "read" the firing end of the spark plug.

6. Check the ignition timing and set it to specifications. Tests show that almost all cars have incorrect ignition timing by more than 2°.

veyed over 6,000 cars nationwide, they found that a tune-up, on cars that needed one, increased fuel economy over 11%. Replacing worn plugs alone, accounted for a 3% increase. The same test also revealed that 8 out of every 10 vehicles will have some maintenance deficiency that will directly affect fuel economy, emissions or performance. Most of this mileage-robbing neglect could be prevented with regular maintenance.

Modern engines require that all of the functioning systems operate properly for maximum efficiency. A malfunction anywhere wastes fuel. You can keep your vehicle running as efficiently and economically as possible, by being aware of your vehicle's operating and performance characteristics. If your vehicle suddenly develops performance or fuel economy problems it could be due to one or more of the following:

PROBLEM	POSSIBLE CAUSE
Engine Idles Rough	Ignition timing, idle mixture, vacuum leak or something amiss in the emission control system.
Hesitates on Acceleration	Dirty carburetor or fuel filter, improper accelerator pump setting, ignition timing or fouled spark plugs.
Starts Hard or Fails to Start	Worn spark plugs, improperly set automatic choke, ice (or water) in fuel system.
Stalls Frequently	Automatic choke improperly adjusted and possible dirty air filter or fuel filter.
Performs Sluggishly	Worn spark plugs, dirty fuel or air filter, ignition timing or automatic choke out of adjustment.

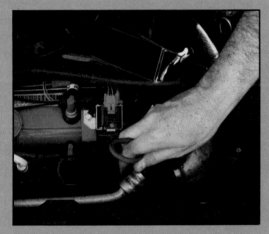

Check spark plug wires on conventional point type ignition for cracks by bending them in a loop around your finger.

Be sure that spark plug wires leading to adjacent cylinders do not run too close together. (Photo courtesy Champion Spark Plug Co.)

7. If your vehicle does not have electronic ignition, check the points, rotor and cap as specified.

8. Check the spark plug wires (used with conventional point-type ignitions) for cracks and burned or broken insulation by bending them in a loop around your finger. Cracked wires decrease fuel efficiency by failing to deliver full voltage to the spark plugs. One misfiring spark plug can cost you as much as 2 mpg.

9. Check the routing of the plug wires. Misfiring can be the result of spark plug leads to adjacent cylinders running parallel to each other and too close together. One wire tends to pick up voltage from the other causing it to fire "out of time".

10. Check all electrical and ignition circuits for voltage drop and resistance.

11. Check the distributor mechanical and/or vacuum advance mechanisms for proper functioning. The vacuum advance can be checked by twisting the distributor plate in the opposite direction of rotation. It should spring back when released.

12. Check and adjust the valve clearance on engines with mechanical lifters. The clearance should be slightly loose rather than too tight.

SPARK PLUG DIAGNOSIS

Normal

APPEARANCE: This plug is typical of one operating normally. The insulator nose varies from a light tan to grayish color with slight electrode wear. The presence of slight deposits is normal on used plugs and will have no adverse effect on engine performance. The spark plug heat range is correct for the engine and the engine is running normally.

CAUSE: Properly running engine.

RECOMMENDATION: Before reinstalling this plug, the electrodes should be cleaned and filed square. Set the gap to specifications. If the plug has been in service for more than 10-12,000 miles, the entire set should probably be replaced with a fresh set of the same heat range.

Oil Deposits

APPEARANCE: The firing end of the plug is covered with a wet, oily coating.

CAUSE: The problem is poor oil control. On high mileage engines, oil is leaking past the rings or valve guides into the combustion chamber. A common cause is also a plugged PCV valve, and a ruptured fuel pump diaphragm can also cause this condition. Oil fouled plugs such as these are often found in new or recently overhauled engines, before normal oil control is achieved, and can be cleaned and reinstalled.

RECOMMENDATION: A hotter spark plug may temporarily relieve the problem, but the engine is probably in need of work.

Incorrect Heat Range

APPEARANCE: The effects of high temperature on a spark plug are indicated by clean white, often blistered insulator. This can also be accompanied by excessive wear of the electrode, and the absence of deposits.

CAUSE: Check for the correct spark plug heat range. A plug which is too hot for the engine can result in overheating. A car operated mostly at high speeds can require a colder plug. Also check ignition timing, cooling system level, fuel mixture and leaking intake manifold.

RECOMMENDATION: If all ignition and engine adjustments are known to be correct, and no other malfunction exists, install spark plugs one heat range colder.

Photos Courtesy Fram Corporation

Carbon Deposits

APPEARANCE: Carbon fouling is easily identified by the presence of dry, soft, black, sooty deposits.

CAUSE: Changing the heat range can often lead to carbon fouling, as can prolonged slow, stop-and-start driving. If the heat range is correct, carbon fouling can be attributed to a rich fuel mixture, sticking choke, clogged air cleaner, worn breaker points, retarded timing or low compression. If only one or two plugs are carbon fouled, check for corroded or cracked wires on the affected plugs. Also look for cracks in the distributor cap between the towers of affected cylinders.

RECOMMENDATION: After the problem is corrected, these plugs can be cleaned and reinstalled if not worn severely.

MMT Fouled

APPEARANCE: Spark plugs fouled by MMT (Methycyclopentadienyl Maganese Tricarbonyl) have reddish, rusty appearance on the insulator and side electrode.

CAUSE: MMT is an anti-knock additive in gasoline used to replace lead. During the combustion process, the MMT leaves a reddish deposit on the insulator and side electrode.

RECOMMENDATION: No engine malfunction is indicated and the deposits will not affect plug performance any more than lead deposits (see Ash Deposits). MMT fouled plugs can be cleaned, regapped and reinstalled.

High Speed Glazing

APPEARANCE: Glazing appears as shiny coating on the plug, either yellow or tan in color.

CAUSE: During hard, fast acceleration, plug temperatures rise suddenly. Deposits from normal combustion have no chance to fluff-off; instead, they melt on the insulator forming an electrically conductive coating which causes misfiring.

RECOMMENDATION: Glazed plugs are not easily cleaned. They should be replaced with a fresh set of plugs of the correct heat range. If the condition recurs, using plugs with a heat range one step colder may cure the problem.

Ash (Lead) Deposits

APPEARANCE: Ash deposits are characterized by light brown or white colored deposits crusted on the side or center electrodes. In some cases it may give the plug a rusty appearance.

CAUSE: Ash deposits are normally derived from oil or fuel additives burned during normal combustion. Normally they are harmless, though excessive amounts can cause misfiring. If deposits are excessive in short mileage, the valve guides may be worn.

RECOMMENDATION: Ash-fouled plugs can be cleaned, gapped and reinstalled.

Detonation

APPEARANCE: Detonation is usually characterized by a broken plug insulator.

CAUSE: A portion of the fuel charge will begin to burn spontaneously, from the increased heat following ignition. The explosion that results applies extreme pressure to engine components, frequently damaging spark plugs and pistons.

Detonation can result by over-advanced ignition timing, inferior gasoline (low octane) lean air/fuel mixture, poor carburetion, engine lugging or an increase in compression ratio due to combustion chamber deposits or engine modification.

RECOMMENDATION: Replace the plugs after correcting the problem.

EMISSION CONTROLS

13. Be aware of the general condition of the emission control system. It contributes to reduced pollution and should be serviced regularly to maintain efficient engine operation.

14. Check all vacuum lines for dried, cracked or brittle conditions. Something as simple as a leaking vacuum hose can cause poor performance and loss of economy.

15. Avoid tampering with the emission control system. Attempting to improve fuel econ-

FUEL SYSTEM

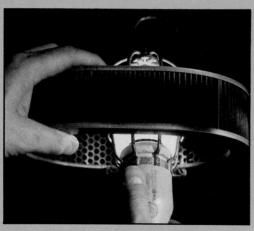

Check the air filter with a light behind it. If you can see light through the filter it can be reused.

Extremely clogged filters should be discarded and replaced with a new one.

18. Replace the air filter regularly. A dirty air filter richens the air/fuel mixture and can increase fuel consumption as much as 10%. Tests show that ⅓ of all vehicles have air filters in need of replacement.

19. Replace the fuel filter at least as often as recommended.

20. Set the idle speed and carburetor mixture to specifications.

21. Check the automatic choke. A sticking or malfunctioning choke wastes gas.

22. During the summer months, adjust the automatic choke for a leaner mixture which will produce faster engine warm-ups.

COOLING SYSTEM

29. Be sure all accessory drive belts are in good condition. Check for cracks or wear.

30. Adjust all accessory drive belts to proper tension.

31. Check all hoses for swollen areas, worn spots, or loose clamps.

32. Check coolant level in the radiator or expansion tank.

33. Be sure the thermostat is operating properly. A stuck thermostat delays engine warm-up and a cold engine uses nearly twice as much fuel as a warm engine.

34. Drain and replace the engine coolant at least as often as recommended. Rust and scale

TIRES & WHEELS

38. Check the tire pressure often with a pencil type gauge. Tests by a major tire manufacturer show that 90% of all vehicles have at least 1 tire improperly inflated. Better mileage can be achieved by over-inflating tires, but never exceed the maximum inflation pressure on the side of the tire.

39. If possible, install radial tires. Radial tires deliver as much as ½ mpg more than bias belted tires.

40. Avoid installing super-wide tires. They only create extra rolling resistance and decrease fuel mileage. Stick to the manufacturer's recommendations.

41. Have the wheels properly balanced.

omy by tampering with emission controls is more likely to worsen fuel economy than improve it. Emission control changes on modern engines are not readily reversible.

16. Clean (or replace) the EGR valve and lines as recommended.

17. Be sure that all vacuum lines and hoses are reconnected properly after working under the hood. An unconnected or misrouted vacuum line can wreak havoc with engine performance.

23. Check for fuel leaks at the carburetor, fuel pump, fuel lines and fuel tank. Be sure all lines and connections are tight.

24. Periodically check the tightness of the carburetor and intake manifold attaching nuts and bolts. These are a common place for vacuum leaks to occur.

25. Clean the carburetor periodically and lubricate the linkage.

26. The condition of the tailpipe can be an excellent indicator of proper engine combustion. After a long drive at highway speeds, the inside of the tailpipe should be a light grey in color. Black or soot on the insides indicates an overly rich mixture.

27. Check the fuel pump pressure. The fuel pump may be supplying more fuel than the engine needs.

28. Use the proper grade of gasoline for your engine. Don't try to compensate for knocking or "pinging" by advancing the ignition timing. This practice will only increase plug temperature and the chances of detonation or pre-ignition with relatively little performance gain.

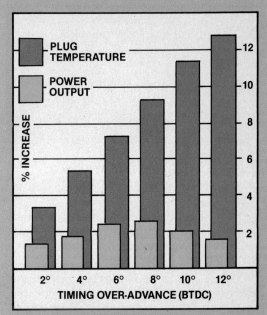

Increasing ignition timing past the specified setting results in a drastic increase in spark plug temperature with increased chance of detonation or preignition. Performance increase is considerably less. (Photo courtesy Champion Spark Plug Co.)

that form in the engine should be flushed out to allow the engine to operate at peak efficiency.

35. Clean the radiator of debris that can decrease cooling efficiency.

36. Install a flex-type or electric cooling fan, if you don't have a clutch type fan. Flex fans use curved plastic blades to push more air at low speeds when more cooling is needed; at high speeds the blades flatten out for less resistance. Electric fans only run when the engine temperature reaches a predetermined level.

37. Check the radiator cap for a worn or cracked gasket. If the cap does not seal properly, the cooling system will not function properly.

42. Be sure the front end is correctly aligned. A misaligned front end actually has wheels going in differed directions. The increased drag can reduce fuel economy by .3 mpg.

43. Correctly adjust the wheel bearings. Wheel bearings that are adjusted too tight increase rolling resistance.

Check tire pressures regularly with a reliable pocket type gauge. Be sure to check the pressure on a cold tire.

GENERAL MAINTENANCE

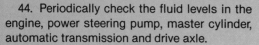

Check the fluid levels (particularly engine oil) on a regular basis. Be sure to check the oil for grit, water or other contamination.

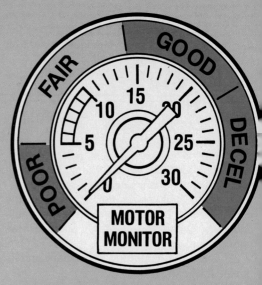

A vacuum gauge is another excellent indicator of internal engine condition and can also be installed in the dash as a mileage indicator.

44. Periodically check the fluid levels in the engine, power steering pump, master cylinder, automatic transmission and drive axle.

45. Change the oil at the recommended interval and change the filter at every oil change. Dirty oil is thick and causes extra friction between moving parts, cutting efficiency and increasing wear. A worn engine requires more frequent tune-ups and gets progressively worse fuel economy. In general, use the lightest viscosity oil for the driving conditions you will encounter.

46. Use the recommended viscosity fluids in the transmission and axle.

47. Be sure the battery is fully charged for fast starts. A slow starting engine wastes fuel.

48. Be sure battery terminals are clean and tight.

49. Check the battery electrolyte level and add distilled water if necessary.

50. Check the exhaust system for crushed pipes, blockages and leaks.

51. Adjust the brakes. Dragging brakes or brakes that are not releasing create increased drag on the engine.

52. Install a vacuum gauge or miles-per-gallon gauge. These gauges visually indicate engine vacuum in the intake manifold. High vacuum = good mileage and low vacuum = poorer mileage. The gauge can also be an excellent indicator of internal engine conditions.

53. Be sure the clutch is properly adjusted. A slipping clutch wastes fuel.

54. Check and periodically lubricate the heat control valve in the exhaust manifold. A sticking or inoperative valve prevents engine warm-up and wastes gas.

55. Keep accurate records to check fuel economy over a period of time. A sudden drop in fuel economy may signal a need for tune-up or other maintenance.

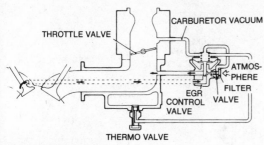

EGR system—Canada

gases by lowering the peak combustion temperatures.

The parts of the EGR system are:

EGR Valve Operated by vacuum drawn from a point above the carburetor throttle plate. The vacuum controls the raising and lowering of the valve pintle to allow exhaust gases to pass from the exhaust system to the intake manifold.

Thermo Valve Used to stop EGR valve operation below approximately 131 degrees, in order to improve cold driveability and starting.

DUAL EGR CONTROL VALVE

The EGR vacuum flow is suspended during idle and wide open throttle operation.

The primary valve controls EGR flow when the throttle valve opening is relatively narrow, while the secondary control valve operates at wider openings.

Sub EGR Control Valve Linked to the throttle valve to closely modulate the EGR gas flow.

EGR MAINTENANCE WARNING LIGHT

A light in the speedometer assembly to alert the driver to the need for EGR system maintenance.

This device has a mileage sensor to light the visual signal at 15,000 mile intervals.

Upon completion of the required EGR system maintenance, the warning light can be turned off by resetting the switch. It is in the speedometer cable, under the instrument panel.

Maintenance

1. Check all vacuum hoses for cracks, breakage and correct installation.
2. Check EGR valve operation by applying vacuum to the EGR valve vacuum nipple with the engine idling. The idle should become rough.
3. Check the passages in the cylinder head and intake manifold for clogging. Clean as necessary.
4. Cold start the engine. The EGR port nipple should be open. When the coolant is warmed to over 131 degrees, the port should be closed.

CATALYTIC CONVERTER

This unit replaces the thermal reactor. It is filled with catalyst to oxidize hydrocarbons and carbon monoxide in the exhaust gases.

Maintenance

1. Check the core for cracks and damages.
2. If the idle carbon monoxide and hydrocarbon content exceeds specifications and the ignition timing and idle mixture are correct, the converter must be replaced.

Jet Air System

A jet air passage is provided in the carburetor, intake manifold, and cylinder head to direct air to a jet valve, operated simultaneously with the intake valve.

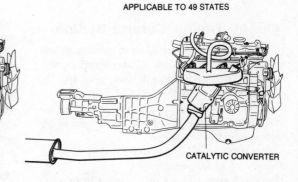

Catalytic converter system-typical

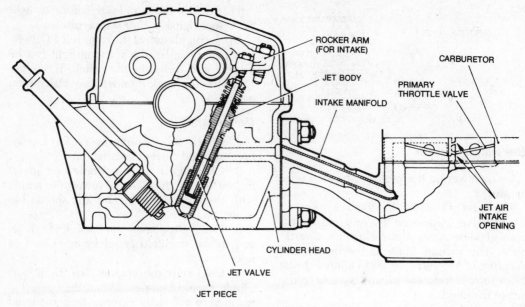

Jet air system

On the intake stroke, jet air is forced into the combustion chamber because of the pressure difference between the ends of the air jet passage.

This jet of air produces a strong swirl in the combustion chamber scavenging the residual gases around the spark plug.

The jet air volume lessens with increased throttle opening. It is at a maximum at idle.

Maintenance

NOTE: *Refer to Valve Lash Adjustment for adjusting jet valve clearance.*

No maintenance is required other than clearance adjustment during valve adjustment. The valve can be removed from the cylinder head for service or replacement.

Ignition Timing Control System

When the engine is idling or operating at low speeds under light load or deceleration, the exhaust gas temperature is low, resulting in incomplete combustion of the air/fuel mixture. To prevent this, ignition timing is retarded under these conditions to maintain high exhaust gas temperature.

The units in the Ignition Timing Control system are as follow:

Thermo Valve This valve is used to protect the engine from overheating. When coolant temperature reaches 203 degrees, the ad-

vance unit is allowed to operate, causing an increase in engine speed and a decrease in coolant temperature.

Single Diaphragm Distributor This distributor has a single diaphragm vacuum advance unit, which advances the ignition timing as engine vacuum dictates. The single diaphragm distributor must not be interchanged with the dual diaphragm distributor. The distributor operating curves are different and would cause increased emissions. A thermo valve is *not* used with this type of distributor.

DECELERATION DEVICE

Closing of the throttle valve on deceleration is delayed in order to burn the air/fuel mixture more thoroughly. A vacuum controlled dashpot, attached to the carburetor linkage is used.

A servo valve detects intake manifold vacuum and closes if vacuum exceeds a preset value. Since the air in the dash pot diaphragm chamber can not escape, the throttle linkage opening is temporarily retained. If the vacuum is below the preset value, the servo valve opens and the dashpot works normally.

Maintenance

Inspect the hoses for breaks and damage, and the valve body for cracks.

Adjustment

1. Have the engine running, brakes locked, and a tachometer attached.

2. Push the dashpot rod, connected to the carburetor arm, upward and into the dashpot until it stops.

3. Note the rpm at the dashpot stop and adjust to specifications. Note the time required between suddenly releasing the dashpot rod and the return to normal curb idle.

MIXTURE CONTROL VALVE

This control valve is used to supply additional air into the intake manifold to decrease manifold vacuum during deceleration, and is activated by the intake manifold vacuum level.

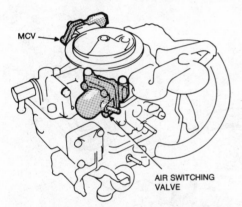

Mixture control valve and Air switching valve used on earlier models

MANUAL ALTITUDE COMPENSATION SYSTEM

An off-on valve is used to increase the air supply to the carburetor to lean the mixture and decrease the EGR flow for high altitude operation.

Maintenance

The required maintenance is to inspect any vacuum hoses and routing for kinks, breakage and cracks. The off-on valve should be on for high altitude and off for driving under 4000 ft.

COASTING AIR VALVE AND AIR SWITCHING VALVE

These deceleration devices are built into the carburetor on later models and are used to decrease HC emissions during truck deceleration.

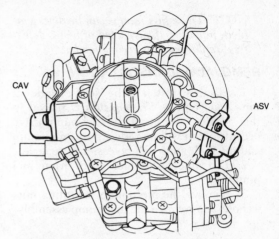

Coasting air valve and air switching valve used on later models

FUEL SYSTEM

Fuel Pump

The fuel pump on all models is a mechanical diaphragm type driven by an eccentric cam on the camshaft.

FUEL PUMP TEST (ON TRUCK)

If the fuel pump is suspected of not supplying enough fuel to the carburetor the following test should be made before removing the fuel pump from the truck.

1. Disconnect the fuel hose from the outlet nipple and connect a pressure gauge to the nipple.

2. Start the engine and run at idle. If the pressure is too low a weak diaphragm main spring, or an improper assembly of the diaphragm may be the cause. If pressure is too high, the main spring is too strong or the air vent is plugged.

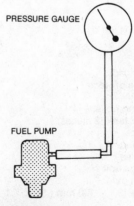

Pressure testing fuel pump

NOTE: *These fuel pumps can be disassembled, however, if suspected of being defective, replacement is recommended.*

REMOVAL AND INSTALLATION

1. Place the piston in the No. 1 cylinder at top dead center. When piston is placed in this position, the lift of the fuel pump drive eccentric cam will be reduced to a minimum and the fuel pump will be easier to remove.

2. Disconnect the fuel hoses from fuel pump.

3. Remove the fuel pump mounting nuts or bolts and remove the fuel pump assembly.

4. Remove the insulator and gaskets.

5. To install, place the piston in the No. 1 cylinder at top dead center on compression stroke and reverse the removal procedure.

Carburetors
REMOVAL AND INSTALLATION

1. Disconnect the negative battery cable.
2. Remove the solenoid valve wiring.
3. Disconnect the air cleaner breather hose, air duct and vacuum tube.
4. Remove the air cleaner.
5. Remove the air cleaner case.

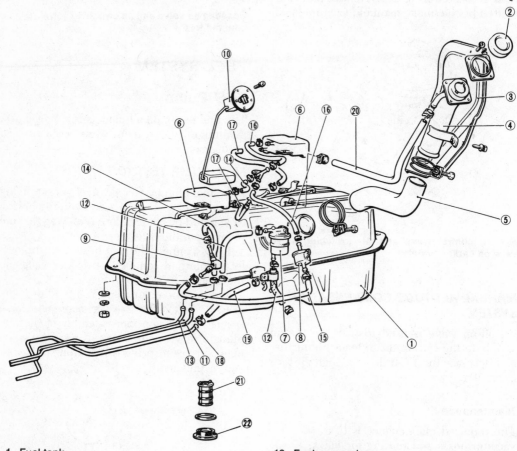

1. Fuel tank
2. Fuel filler cap
3. Filler hose protector
4. Filler neck
5. Connecting hose
6. Separator tank (2 pieces)
7. Fuel filter
8. Overfill limiter
9. Check valve
10. Fuel gauge unit
11. Fuel main pipe
12. Fuel hose [8φ × 180 mm (.31 × 7.1 in.)]
13. Fuel vapor pipe
14. Vapor hose [6φ × 180 mm (.24 × 7.1 in.)]
15. Vapor hose [6φ × 260 mm (.24 × 10.2 in.)]
16. Vapor hose [6φ × 240 mm (.24 × 9.4 in.)]
17. Vapor hose [6φ × 160 mm (.24 × 6.3 in.)]
18. Fuel return pipe
19. Soft vinyl tube [6φ × 170 mm (.24 × 6.7 in.)]
20. Breather hose [10φ × 480 mm (.39 × 18.9 in.) in.)]
21. Fuel filter (in tank)
22. Fuel drain plug

Exploded view of fuel tank

6. Disconnect the accelerator and shift cables (automatic transmission) at the carburetor.

7. Disconnect the purge valve hose; remove the vacuum compensator, and fuel lines.

8. Drain the coolant.

9. Remove the water hose between the carburetor and the cylinder head.

10. Remove the carburetor.

11. Installation is the reverse of removal.

OVERHAUL

Whenever wear or dirt causes a carburetor to perform poorly, there are two possible solutions to the problem. The simplest is to trade in the old unit for a rebuilt one. The other cheaper alternative is to purchase a carburetor overhaul kit and rebuild the original unit. Some of the better overhaul kits contain complete step by step instructions along with exploded views and gauges. Other kits, probably intended for the professional, have only a few general overhaul hints. The second type can be moderately confusing to the novice, especially since a kit may have extra parts so that one kit can cover several variations of the same carburetor. In any event, it is inadvisable to dismantle any carburetor without at least replacing all the gaskets.

FLOAT AND FUEL LEVEL ADJUSTMENT

A sight glass is fitted at the float chamber and the fuel level can be checked without disassembling the carburetor. Normal fuel level is within the level mark on the sight glass.

The fuel level adjustment is corrected by increasing or decreasing the number of needle valve packings. The float level may be

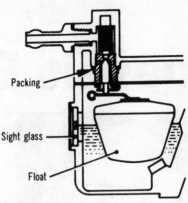

Packing

Sight glass

Float

Float adjustment

off 0.160 inch, above or below the level mark and the operation of the engine would not be affected.

Fuel Tank

REMOVAL AND INSTALLATION

1. Make sure the ignition switch is off.

2. Remove the fuel filler cap to release any pressure in the tank.

3. Remove the drain plug from the fuel tank.

4. Disconnect the fuel hoses from the tank.

5. Support the tank with a jack, remove the retaining nuts and remove the tank.

6. Remove the separator tanks from the tank.

7. To install, connect the hoses and the filler neck to the body.

8. Apply a small amount of sealant to both sides of the packing when replacing the gauge unit.

9. The remainder of the installation is the reverse of removal.

Chassis Electrical

HEATER

Blower Motor Without Air Conditioning

REMOVAL AND INSTALLATION

1. Remove the cluster panel.
2. Disconnect the cable between the motor and the heater unit.
3. Remove the three bolts holding the motor in the heater unit and pull out the fan.

NOTE: *It may be necessary to unfasten the fan from the motor to remove them from under the dashboard.*

Installation is the reverse of removal.

Blower Motor With Air Conditioning

REMOVAL AND INSTALLATION

The air conditioning system used on D-50, RAM 50 and Plymouth Arrow pick-up trucks utilizes the blower motor assembly of the heater unit. See above for removal and installation procedures. However, it may be necessary to remove some of the air conditioning components to gain access to the motor. If this is the case, never attempt to loosen any of the air conditioning hoses during your work. They contain refrigerant un-

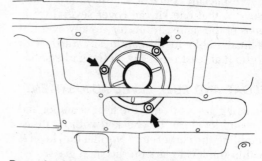

Removing blower motor assembly

der pressure, which could severely damage your eyes or skin on contact.

Heater Unit Without Air Conditioning

REMOVAL AND INSTALLATION

1. Drain the cooling system.
2. Place the hot water flow control lever in the off position.
3. Remove the glove box, the center ventilation grille and duct, and the defroster duct.
4. Disconnect all control cables at the heater side.
5. Disconnect the water hoses.
6. Disconnect the harness from the heater fan motor.

7. Remove the top mounting bolts and the center mounting nuts, and remove the heater assembly.

Heater Unit With Air Conditioning

REMOVAL AND INSTALLATION

Removing the heater unit with air conditioning attached is similar to procedures used on units without air conditioning. It may be necessary to loosen or remove certain components of the air conditioning system to facilitate heater unit removal, however, *never* loosen the refrigerant pipes that lead into the

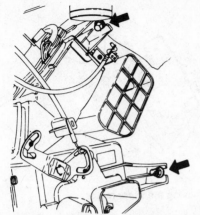

Removing the heater assembly mounting bolts

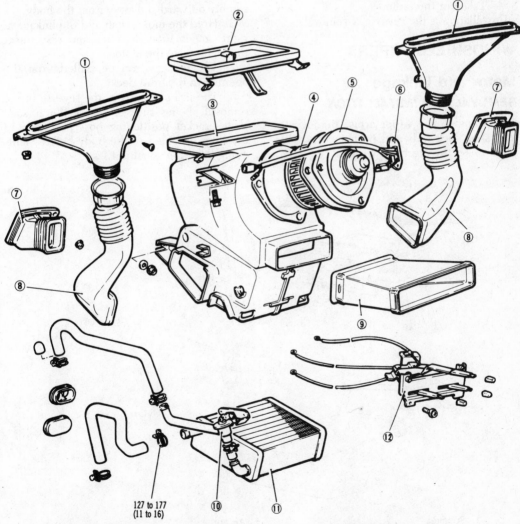

1. Defroster nozzle
2. Ventilator assembly
3. Heater assembly
4. Turbo fan
5. Motor
6. Heater resistor
7. Side ventilator duct
8. Defroster duct
9. Center ventilator duct
10. Water valve
11. Heater core
12. Heater control panel assembly

Exploded view of the heater and ventilator

air conditioning evaporator assembly. They are filled with a noxious fluid which, under certain conditions, could cause severe damage to your face or skin. Always leave all air conditioning work to skilled professionals.

RADIO

REMOVAL AND INSTALLATION

1. Remove the instrument cluster bezel.
2. Remove the radio bracket attaching screws from the instrument panel, and remove the radio bracket.
3. Pull the radio out slightly, disconnect the antenna lead-in, speaker connector and the power supply connector.
4. Take out the radio.
Installation is the reverse of removal.

WINDSHIELD WIPERS

Motor and Linkage

REMOVAL AND INSTALLATION

1. Remove the wiper arms. Remove the arm shaft lock nuts and push in the shafts. Disconnect the electrical wiring.

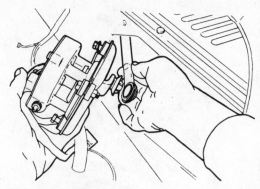

Removing the wiper motor

2. Remove the bolts holding the motor bracket to the body and pull the wiper assembly outward and away from the body.
3. Hold the motor shaft and the linkage at right angles to each other and disconnect them. Remove the motor.
4. The linkages can be pulled from the opening in the front deck.
5. The installation is in the reverse of the removal, being sure to insert the linkage shaft bracket positioning boss positively in the hole provided in the body before tightening the wiper shaft nut.

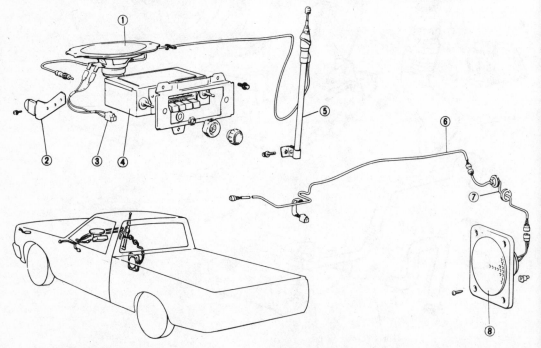

1. Speaker
2. Radio stay
3. Speaker wiring harness
4. AM radio
4. AM/FM MPX radio (for sports model)

5. Antenna
6. Speaker wiring harness (for sports model)
7. Door wiring harness (for sports model)
8. Speaker (for sports model)

Radio System

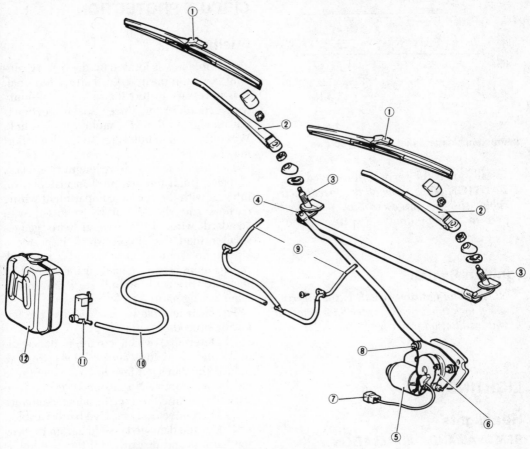

1. Wiper blade
2. Wiper arm
3. Pivot shaft
4. Wiper linkage
5. Wiper motor
6. Motor gear box
7. Motor wire connector
8. Wiper motor assembly grounding point
9. Washer nozzle
10. Washer tube
11. Washer motor assembly
12. Washer liquid tank

Windshield wiper and washer components

6. Locate the wiper blades in the stopped position approximately ½ to ¾ inch above the bottom moulding or sealer of the windshield.

INSTRUMENT CLUSTER

REMOVAL AND INSTALLATION

1. Disconnect the negative battery cable.
2. Remove the heater fan control knob, heater control knobs and the radio knobs.
3. Remove the ash tray and remove the two screws behind it holding the instrument panel bezel. Remove the two screws at the top of the bezel and remove the bezel.
4. Remove the four screws in the corners of the meter case.

5. Disconnect the speedometer cable and connectors from the back of the meter, and remove the meter assembly.

Installation is the reverse of removal.

SPEEDOMETER CABLE REPLACEMENT

1. Unfasten the speedometer cable from the rear of the speedometer. The instrument panel may have to be removed.

NOTE: *The cable is fastened to the speedometer via a snap clip, which must be pressed down while the cable is being unfastened.*

2. Unfasten the speedometer cable from the transmission.
3. Remove the bands holding the cable with the wiring harness and withdraw the cable through the engine compartment.

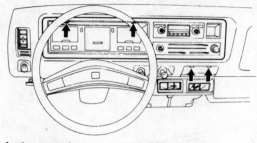

Instrument cluster panel retaining screws

Installation is the reverse of removal.
CAUTION: *Always install the speedometer cable with the largest radius possible to prevent cable binding and noise.*

Ignition Switch

NOTE: *The ignition switch is the steering wheel lock type. See Chapter 8 for removal and installation procedures.*

LIGHTING

Headlights

REMOVAL AND INSTALLATION

1. Remove the screws from the radiator grille and remove the grille.
2. Remove the screws from the inner retaining ring and remove the ring.
NOTE: *Do not disturb the headlight adjusting screws.*
3. Pull out the sealed beam unit and unplug the connector by pulling straight off.
4. Installation is the reverse of removal.

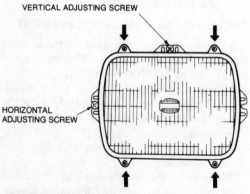

VERTICAL ADJUSTING SCREW

HORIZONTAL
ADJUSTING SCREW

Headlight retaining screws

CIRCUIT PROTECTION

Fusible Link

The fusible link is located on the battery running from the positive (+) battery terminal. It is necessary to test the link for continuity with a circuit tester, since visual inspection is not enough to detect a melted fusible link. When the fusible link is melted, a dead short may be the cause.

The fuse link is a short length of special, Hypalon (high temperature) insulated wire, integral with the engine compartment wiring harness and should not be confused with standard wire. It is several wire gauges smaller than the circuit which it protects. Under no circumstances should a fuse link replacement repair be made using a length of standard wire cut from bulk stock or from another wiring harness.

To repair any blown fuse link use the following procedure:

1. Determine which circuit is damaged, its location and the cause of the open fuse link. If the damaged fuse link is one of three fed by a common No. 10 or 12 gauge feed wire, determine the specific affected circuit.
2. Disconnect the negative battery cable.
3. Cut the damaged fuse link from the wiring harness and discard it. If the fuse link is one of three circuits fed by a single feed wire, cut it out of the harness at each splice end and discard it.
4. Identify and procure the proper fuse link and butt connectors for attaching the fuse link to the harness.
5. To repair any fuse link in a 3-link group with one feed:
   a. After cutting the open link out of the harness, cut each of the remaining undamaged fuse links close to the feed wire weld.
   b. Strip approximately ½ inch of insulation from the detached ends of the two good fuse links. Then insert two wire ends into one end of a butt connector and carefully push one stripped end of the replacement fuse link into the same end of the butt connector and crimp all three firmly together.
NOTE: *Care must be taken when fitting the three fuse links into the butt connector as the internal diameter is a snug fit for three wires. Make sure to use a proper crimping tool. Pliers, side cutters, etc. will not apply the proper crimp to retain the wires and withstand a pull test.*

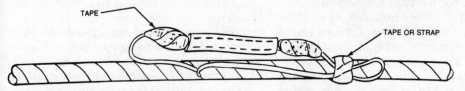

REMOVE EXISTING VINYL TUBE SHIELDING
REINSTALL OVER FUSE LINK BEFORE CRIMPING
FUSE LINK TO WIRE ENDS

TAPE

TAPE OR STRAP

TYPICAL REPAIR USING THE SPECIAL #17 GA. (9.00" LONG-YELLOW) FUSE LINK REQUIRED FOR THE AIR/COND.
CIRCUITS LOCATED IN THE ENGINE COMPARTMENT

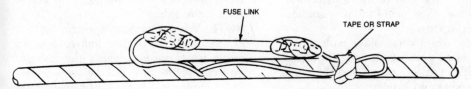

FUSE LINK

TAPE OR STRAP

TYPICAL REPAIR FOR ANY IN-LINE FUSE LINK USING THE SPECIFIED GAUGE FUSE LINK FOR THE SPECIFIC CIRCUIT

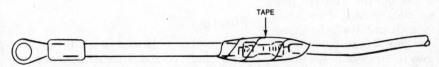

TAPE

TYPICAL REPAIR USING THE EYELET TERMINAL FUSE LINK OF THE SPECIFIED GAUGE FOR ATTACHMENT TO A CIRCUIT WIRE END

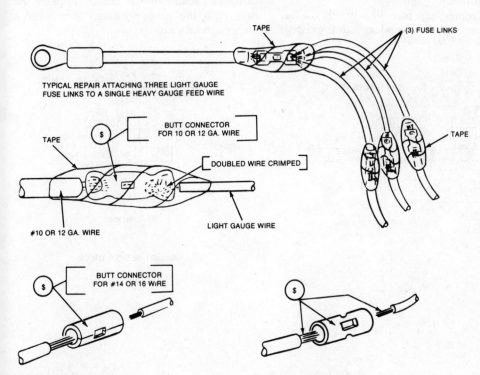

TAPE

(3) FUSE LINKS

TYPICAL REPAIR ATTACHING THREE LIGHT GAUGE
FUSE LINKS TO A SINGLE HEAVY GAUGE FEED WIRE

BUTT CONNECTOR
FOR 10 OR 12 GA. WIRE

TAPE

$

DOUBLED WIRE CRIMPED

TAPE

#10 OR 12 GA. WIRE

LIGHT GAUGE WIRE

BUTT CONNECTOR
FOR #14 OR 16 WIRE

$

$

FUSIBLE LINK REPAIR PROCEDURE

General fuse link repair procedure

c. After crimping the butt connector to the three fuse links, cut the weld portion from the feed wire and strip approximately ½ inch of insulation from the cut end. Insert the stripped end into the open end of the butt connector and crimp very firmly.

d. To attach the remaining end of the replacement fuse link, strip approximately ½ inch of insulation from the wire end of the circuit from which the blown fuse link was removed, and firmly crimp a butt connector or equivalent to the stripped wire. Then, insert the end of the replacement link into the other end of the butt connector and crimp firmly.

e. Using rosin core solder with a consistency of 60 percent tin and 40 percent lead, solder the connectors and the wires at the repairs and insulate with electrical tape.

6. To replace any fuse link on a single circuit in a harness, cut out the damaged portion, strip approximately ½ inch of insulation from the two wire ends and attach the appropriate replacement fuse link to the stripped wire ends with two proper size butt connectors. Solder the connectors and wires and insulate with tape.

7. To repair any fuse link which has an eyelet terminal on one end such as the charg-

ing circuit, cut off the open fuse link behind the weld, strip approximately ½ inch of insulation from the cut end and attach the appropriate new eyelet fuse link to the cut stripped wire with an appropriate size butt connector. Solder the connectors and wires at the repair and insulate with tape.

8. Connect the negative battery cable to the battery and test the system for proper operation.

NOTE: *Do not mistake a resistor wire for a fuse link. The resistor wire is generally longer and has print stating, "Resistor—don't cut or splice."*

NOTE: *When attaching a single No. 16, 17, 18 or 20 gauge fuse link to a heavy gauge wire, always double the stripped wire end of the fuse link before inserting and crimping it into the butt connector for positive wire retention.*

Fuses

The fuse box is located below the hood release handle on the driver's side of the vehicle. When a fuse is burnt out, locate the cause and eliminate the defect. Replace the fuse with the proper rating. Never use a larger capacity fuse.

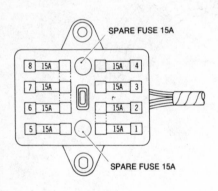

Fuse block

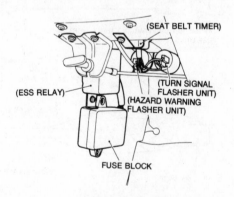

Location of fuse block

Key for 1979 Wiring Diagram

Symbol	Coloring	Connected circuit	System	Color used in wiring diagram
B BW BY BR	Black Black/white Black/yellow Black/red	Grounding Ignition, Meter illumination and Washer motor Starter Ignition	Starting	Black
W WB	White White/black	Charging, ESS relay, Tachometer and Ammeter Ammeter	Charging	White
R RW RB RY RL	Red Red/white Red/black Red/yellow Red/blue	Headlamp, upper beam and Backup switch Headlamp, lower beam Passing switch, Doom light and Seat belt warning Meter illumination, Wiper/washer switch ill. and Radio Backup light	Lighting	Red
G GW GR GY GB GL	Green Green/white Green/red Green/yellow Green/black Green/blue	Stop light, Hazard flasher unit and Horn Tail light, Parking light, Front & rear side marker light and licence plate light Dome light, Door switch and Lighting switch R.H. turn signal lights (front & rear) and indicator light Horn L.H. turn signal lights (front & rear) and indicator light	Signal	Green
Y YR YB YG YW	Yellow Yellow/red Yellow/black Yellow/green Yellow/white	Fuel gauge and Oil pressure gauge or light Water temp. gauge Seat belt warning light Parking brake Charging indicator light and Seat belt switch	Gauge and indicator	Yellow
L LW LR LB LY LO	Blue Blue/white Blue/red Blue/black Blue/yellow Blue/orange	Wiper/washer switch, Alternator (S terminal) and Air-con relay (B) terminal Radio, Cigarette lighter, Wiper motor and Heater switch Heater fan switch and Oil pressure gauge Heater switch and Air-con (B) terminal Heater switch Wiper motor	Others	Blue

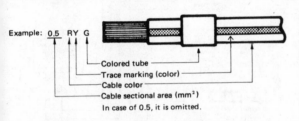

Example: 0.5 RY G

- Colored tube
- Trace marking (color)
- Cable color
- Cable sectional area (mm²)

In case of 0.5, it is omitted.

Nominal size (designated by sectional area in mm² of wire)	SAE gauge No.	Permissible current	
		Within engine compartment	Other areas
0.5	20	7A	13A
0.85	18	9A	17A
1.25	16	12A	22A
2.0	14	16A	30A
3.0	12	21A	40A
5.0	10	31A	54A

Note: The boxed symbols on diagram denote the locations of the parts, ground, etc. as shown in the following table. CB, CE, CG and CI in the symbols indicate body, engine compartment, grounding point and instrument panel, respectively.

Symbol	Part name	Location	Symbol	Part name	Location
CB–1	ESS (Engine Speed Sensor) relay	Lower part of left side front pillar (Above the fuse block)	CE–3 CE–4	Solenoid valve EIC (Electronic Ignition Control) unit	Beside the ignition coil Side of distributor body
CB–2	Parking brake lever switch	Above the guide roller for parking brake cable	CE–5	EVR (Electronic Voltage Regulator)	Inside of the alternator
CB–3	Seat belt switch	Inside of driver's seat belt buckle	CG–1	Body grounding point (Front)	Side of battery support
CB–4	Fuse block	Lower part of left side front pillar	CG–2	Frame grounding point (Front)	Slide of left frame, engine compartment
CB–5	Inhibitor switch	Inside of gearshift lever bracket	CG–3	Engine grounding point (Front)	Left side of cylinder block
CB–6	Backup light switch	Rear upper side of transmission	CG–4	Body grounding point (Cabin)	Fore of driver, under the Instrument panel
CB–7	Stop light switch	Brake pedal support bracket	CI–1	Air-con (B) terminal	One the wiring harness, side of left reinforcement
CB–8	Connector of front and frame	Under floor mat, right side of passenger's seat	CI–2	Air-con relay (B) terminal	Along with the air-con (B) terminal
CB–9	Connector of frame and rear body wiring harness	Rear part of right side rear body frame	CI–3	Seat belt warning timer	Left under side of instrument panel
CB–10	Door switch L.H.	Lower part of left side rear pillar	CI–4	Seat belt warning buzzer	Back side of combination meter case
CB–11	Door switch R.H.	Lower part of right side rear pillar	CI–5	Turn signal flasher unit	Fore of driver, under the instrument panel
CB–12	Fuel gauge unit	Left upper side of fuel tank	CI–6	Hazard warning flasher unit	Along the turn signal flasher unit
CE–1 CE–2	Wiper motor Washer motor	Left side of front deck Lower side of washer liquid tank			

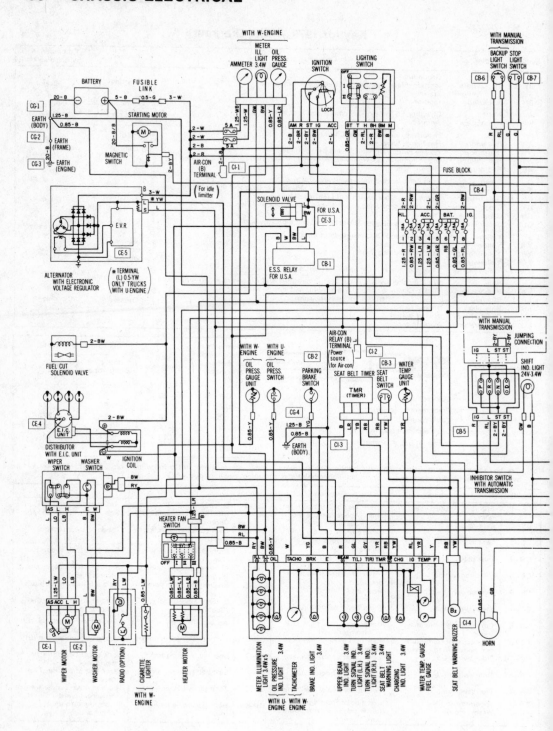

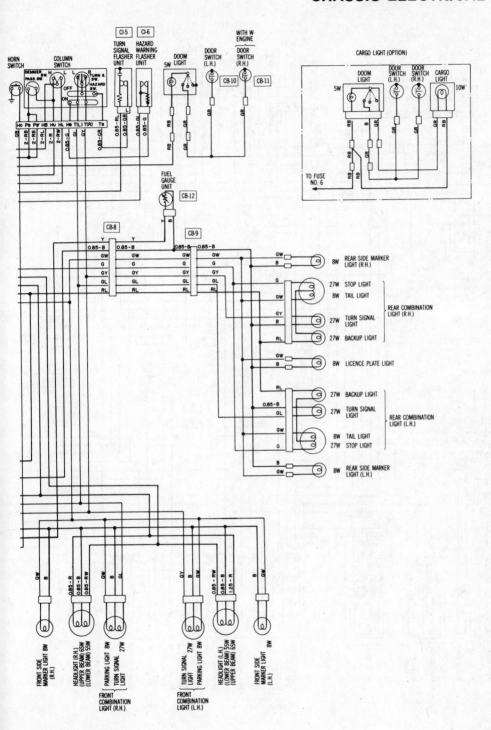

1979 Wiring diagram

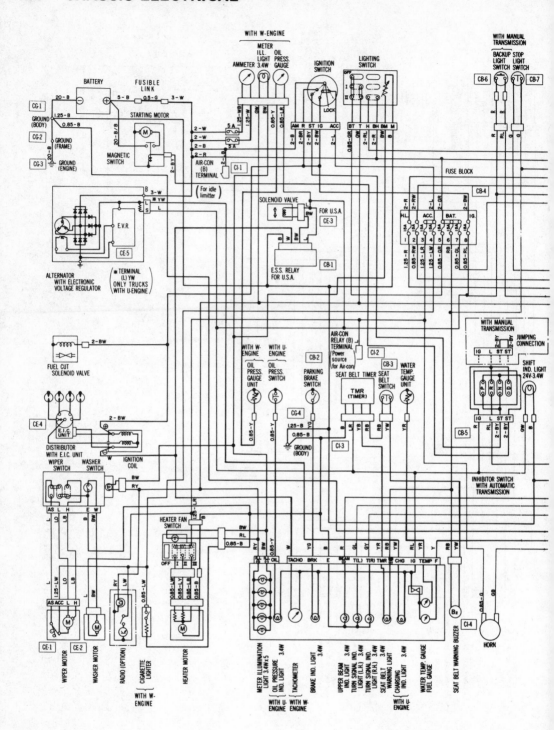

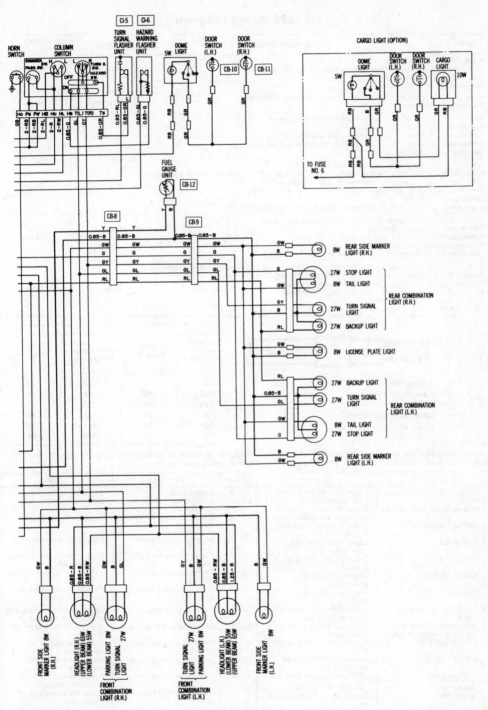

1980 Wiring diagram

Key for 1980 Wiring Diagram

Symbol	Coloring	Connected circuit	System	Color used in wiring diagram
B	Black	Grounding		
BW	Black/white	Ignition, Meter illumination and Washer motor	Starting	Black
BY	Black/yellow	Starter		
BR	Black/red	Ignition		
W	White	Charging, E.S.S. relay, Tachometer and Ammeter	Charging	White
WB	White/black	Ammeter		
R	Red	Headlight, upper beam and Backup switch		
RW	Red/white	Headlight, lower beam		
RB	Red/black	Passing switch, Dome light and Seat belt warning	Lighting	Red
RY	Red/yellow	Meter illumination, Wiper/washer switch ill. and Radio		
RL	Red/blue	Backup light		
G	Green	Stop light, Hazard flasher unit and Horn		
GW	Green/white	Tail light, Parking light, Front & rear side marker light and license plate light		
GR	Green/red	Dome light, Door switch and Lighting switch	Signal	Green
GY	Green/yellow	R.H. turn signal lights (front & rear) and indicator light		
GB	Green/black	Horn		
GL	Green/blue	L.H. turn signal lights (front & rear) and indicator light		
Y	Yellow	Fuel gauge and Oil pressure gauge or light		
YR	Yellow/red	Water temp. gauge	Gauge	
YB	Yellow/black	Seat belt warning light	and	Yellow
YG	Yellow/green	Parking brake	indicator	
YW	Yellow/white	Charging indicator light and Seat belt switch		
L	Blue	Wiper/washer switch, Alternator (S terminal) and Air-con relay (B) terminal		
LW	Blue/white	Radio, Cigarette lighter, Wiper motor and Heater switch		
LR	Blue/red	Heater fan switch and Oil pressure gauge	Others	Blue
LB	Blue/black	Heater switch and Air-con (B) terminal		
LY	Blue/yellow	Heater switch		
LO	Blue/orange	Wiper motor		

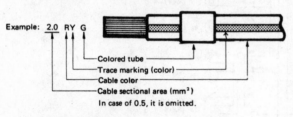

Example: 2.0 RY G

Colored tube
Trace marking (color)
Cable color
Cable sectional area (mm²)

In case of 0.5, it is omitted.

Nominal size (designated by sectional area in mm² of wire)	SAE gauge No.	Permissible current	
		Within engine compartment	Other areas
0.5	20	7A	13A
0.85	18	9A	17A
1.25	16	12A	22A
2.0	14	16A	30A
3.0	12	21A	40A
5.0	10	31A	54A

Note: The boxed symbols on diagram denote the locations of the parts, ground, etc. as shown in the following table. CB, CE, CG and CI in the symbols indicate body, engine compartment, grounding point and instrument panel, respectively.

Symbol	Part name	Location	Symbol	Part name	Location
CB–1	E.S.S. (Engine Speed Sensor) relay	Lower part of left side front pillar (Above the fuse block)	CE–3	Solenoid valve	Beside the ignition coil
CB–2	Parking brake lever switch	Above the guide roller for parking brake cable	CE–4	E.I.C. (Electronic Ignition Control) unit	Side of distributor body
CB–3	Seat belt switch	Inside of driver's seat belt buckle	CE–5	E.V.R. (Electronic Voltage Regulator)	Inside of the alternator
CB–4	Fuse block	Lower part of left side front pillar	CG–1	Body grounding point (Front)	Side of battery support
CB–5	Inhibitor switch	Inside of gearshift lever bracket	CG–2	Frame grounding point (Front)	Slide of left frame, engine compartment
CB–6	Backup light switch	Rear upper side of transmission	CG–3	Engine grounding point (Front)	Left side of cylinder block
CB–7	Stop light switch	Brake pedal support bracket	CG–4	Body grounding point (Cabin)	Fore of driver, under the Instrument panel
CB–8	Connector of front and frame	Under floor mat, right side of passenger's seat	CI–1	Air-con (B) terminal	One the wiring harness, side of left reinforcement
CB–9	Connector of frame and rear body wiring harness	Rear part of right side rear body frame	CI–2	Air-con relay (B) terminal	Along with the air-con (B) terminal
CB–10	Door switch L.H.	Lower part of left side rear pillar	CI–3	Seat belt warning timer	Left under side of instrument panel
CB–11	Door switch R.H.	Lower part of right side rear pillar	CI–4	Seat belt warning buzzer	Back side of combination meter case
CB–12	Fuel gauge unit	Left upper side of fuel tank	CI–5	Turn signal flasher unit	Fore of driver, under the instrument panel
CE–1	Wiper motor	Left side of front deck	CI–6	Hazard warning flasher unit	Along the turn signal flasher unit
CE–2	Washer motor	Lower side of washer liquid tank			

Key for 1981 Wiring Diagram

Symbol	Coloring	Connected circuit	System	Color used in wiring diagram
B	Black	Grounding		
BW	Black/white	Ignition, Meter illumination and Washer motor	Starting	Black
BY	Black/yellow	Starter		
BR	Black/red	Ignition		
W	White	Charging, E.S.S. relay, Tachometer and Ammeter	Charging	White
WB	White/black	Ammeter		
R	Red	Headlight, upper beam and Backup switch		
RW	Red/white	Headlight, lower beam		
RB	Red/black	Passing switch, Dome light and Seat belt warning	Lighting	Red
RY	Red/yellow	Meter illumination, Wiper/washer switch ill. and Radio		
RL	Red/blue	Backup light		
G	Green	Stop light, Hazard flasher unit and Horn		
GW	Green/white	Tail light, Parking light, Front & rear side marker light and License plate light		
GR	Green/red	Dome light, Door switch and Lighting switch	Signal	Green
GY	Green/yellow	R.H. turn signal lights (front & rear) and Indicator light		
GB	Green/black	Horn		
GL	Green/blue	L.H. turn signal lights (front & rear) and Indicator light		
Y	Yellow	Fuel gauge and Oil pressure gauge or light		
YR	Yellow/red	Water temp. gauge	Gauge	
YB	Yellow/black	Seat belt warning light	and	Yellow
YG	Yellow/green	Parking brake	indicator	
YW	Yellow/white	Charging indicator light and Seat belt switch		
L	Blue	Wiper/washer switch, Alternator (S terminal) and Air-con. relay (B) terminal		
LW	Blue/white	Radio, Cigarette lighter, Wiper motor and Heater switch		
LR	Blue/red	Heater fan switch and Oil pressure gauge	Others	Blue
LB	Blue/black	Heater switch and Air-con. (B) terminal		
LY	Blue/yellow	Heater switch		
LO	Blue/orange	Wiper motor		

Example: 2.0 RY

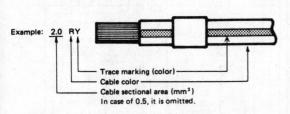

Trace marking (color)
Cable color
Cable sectional area (mm²)
In case of 0.5, it is omitted.

Nominal size (designated by sectional area in mm² of wire)	SAE gauge No.	Permissible current	
		Within engine compartment	Other areas
0.5	20	7A	13A
0.85	18	9A	17A
1.25	16	12A	22A
2.0	14	16A	30A
3.0	12	21A	40A
5.0	10	31A	54A

Note: The boxed symbols on diagram denote the locations of the parts, ground, etc. as shown in the following table. CB, CE, CG and CI in the symbols indicate body, engine compartment, grounding point and instrument panel, respectively.

Symbol	Part name	Location	Symbol	Part name	Location
CB–1	E.S.S. (Engine Speed Sensor) relay	Lower part of left side front pillar (Above the fuse block)	CE–3	Solenoid valve	Beside the ignition coil
CB–2	Parking brake lever switch	Above the guide roller for parking brake cable	CE–4	E.I.C. (Electronic Ignition Control) unit	Side of distributor body
CB–3	Seat belt switch	Inside of driver's seat belt buckle	CE–5	E.V.R. (Electronic Voltage Regulator)	Inside of the alternator
CB–4	Fuse block	Lower part of left side front pillar	CG–1	Body grounding point (Front)	Side of battery support
CB–5	Inhibitor switch	Inside of gearshift lever bracket	CG–2	Frame grounding point (Front)	Side of left frame, engine compartment
CB–6	Backup light switch	Rear outer side of transmission	CG–3	Engine grounding point (Front)	Left side of cylinder block
CB–7	Stop light switch	Brake pedal support bracket	CG–4	Body grounding point (Cabin)	Fore of driver, under the Instrument panel
CB–8	Connector of front and frame	Under floor mat, right side of passenger's seat	CI–1	Air-con. (B) terminal	One the wiring harness, side of left reinforcement
CB–9	Connector of frame and rear body wiring harness	Rear part of right side rear body frame	CI–2	Air-con. relay (B) terminal	Along with the air-con. (B) terminal
CB–10	Door switch L.H.	Lower part of left side rear pillar	CI–3	Seat belt warning timer	Left under side of instrument panel
CB–11	Door switch R.H.	Lower part of right side rear pillar	CI–4	Seat belt warning buzzer	Back side of combination meter case
CB–12	Fuel gauge unit	Left upper side of fuel tank	CI–5	Turn signal flasher unit	Fore of driver, under the instrument panel
CE–1	Wiper motor	Left side of front deck	CI–6	Hazard warning flasher unit	Along the turn signal flasher unit
CE–2	Washer motor	Lower side of washer liquid tank			

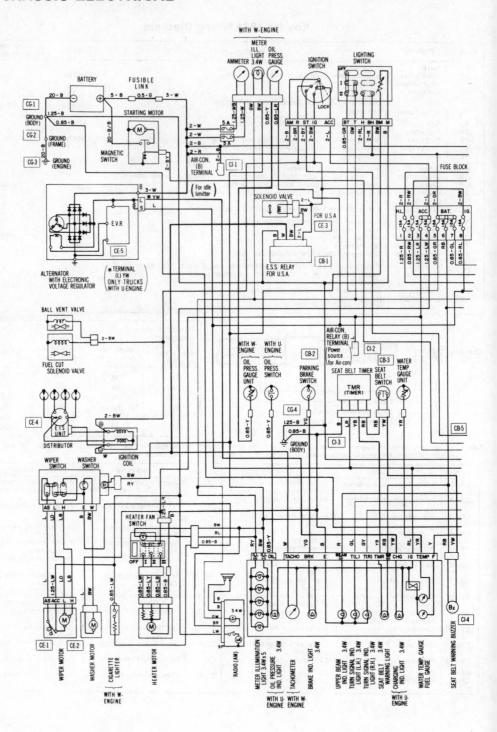

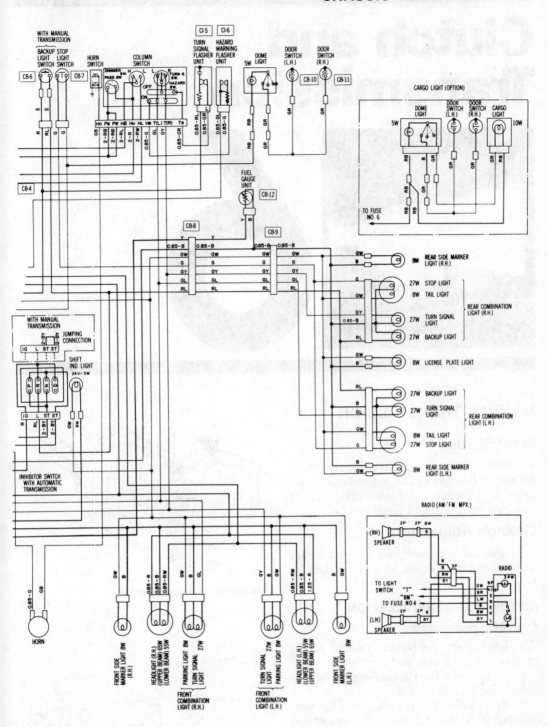

1981 Wiring diagram

Clutch and Transmission

6

MANUAL TRANSMISSION

Identification

A transmission serial number is stamped on the clutch housing of the transmission case. Refer to Chapter 1 for an explanation of transmission model and serial numbers.

Linkage Adjustment

Gear shifting is done by an internal shifter shaft, therefore there is no external linkage to adjust.

REMOVAL AND INSTALLATION
Four and Five Speed

1. Disconnect the battery ground cable, remove the air cleaner and the starter.
2. Remove the top transmission mounting bolts from the bell housing.
3. From inside the vehicle, raise the console assembly, if equipped, or the carpet and remove the dust cover retaining plate at the shift lever.
4. Place the four speed transmission in second gear and the five speed transmission in first gear. Remove the control lever assembly.
5. Raise the vehicle and support it safely. Drain the transmission. Disconnect the speedometer and the back up light switch.

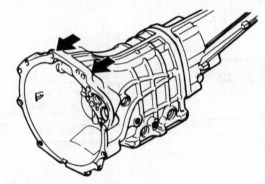

Transmission mounting bolts

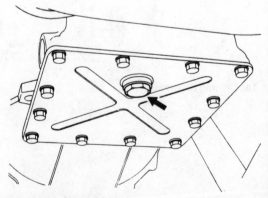

Transmission drain plug

6. Remove the drive shaft, exhaust pipe, and the clutch cable.

7. Support the transmission and remove the engine rear support bracket.

8. Remove the bell housing cover and bolts, move the transmission rearward, and lower it carefully to the floor. Remove the transmission from under the vehicle.

9. To install the transmission, reverse the removal procedure. Make sure the transmission is in the proper gear before installing the gear shift lever.

CLUTCH

PEDAL HEIGHT ADJUSTMENT

1. Adjust the pedal height to the standard value with the adjusting bolt (see illustration), and check the pedal stroke and distance "A."

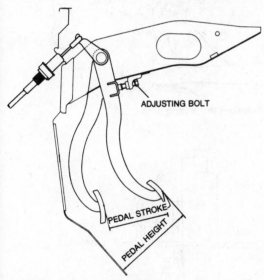

Clutch pedal height adjustment

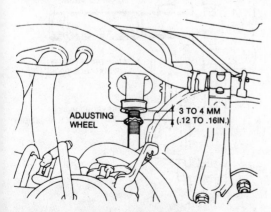

Clutch pedal free play adjustment

CAUTION: *Insufficient pedal stroke results in only partial clutch release, causing hard gear shifting and gear grinding when shifting.*

2. In the engine compartment, at the fire wall, pull out the clutch cable a little and adjust the cable by turning the adjusting wheel until it is 0.12–0.16 in from the insulator.

3. Clutch pedal free play should be within 0.8–1.4 in.

Clutch Cable

REMOVAL AND INSTALLATION

1. Loosen the cable adjusting wheel inside the engine compartment.

2. Loosen the clutch pedal adjusting bolt locknut and loosen the adjusting bolt.

3. Remove the cable end from the clutch throwout lever.

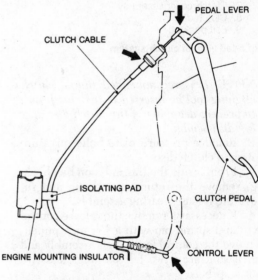

Clutch cable removal and installation

4. Remove the cable end from the clutch pedal.

5. Installation is the reverse of removal.

NOTE: *Apply engine oil to the cable before replacing. Make sure the isolating pad is fitted on the cable after installation to keep the cable from rubbing the motor mount during operation.*

Clutch Assembly

REMOVAL AND INSTALLATION

1. Remove the transmission as outlined in the Manual Transmission Removal and Installation section.

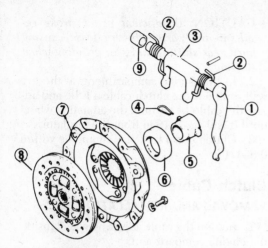

1. Clutch control lever and shaft assembly
2. Return spring
3. Clutch shift arm
4. Return clip
5. Release bearing carrier
6. Release bearing
7. Clutch cover assembly
8. Clutch disc
9. Felt packing

Exploded view of clutch system

NOTE: *It is recommended that a clutch aligning tool be inserted in the clutch hub to prevent dropping of the clutch disc during disassembly.*

2. Remove pressure plate bolts, pressure plate and clutch disc.

3. From inside the transmission bell housing, remove the return spring clip and remove the release bearing assembly.

4. If necessary, remove the release control lever and spring pin with a ³/₁₆ inch punch. Remove the control lever shaft assembly and clutch shift arm, two felt packings and two return springs.

5. Installation is the reverse of removal.

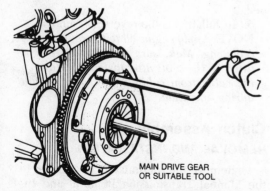

Removing the clutch assembly retaining bolts

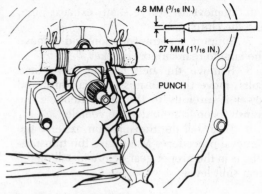

Removing the spring pins

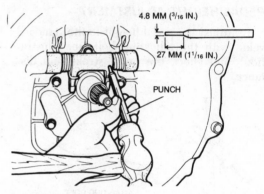

Installing the spring pins

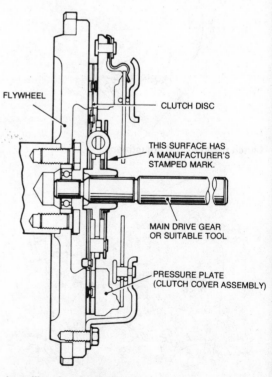

Installing the clutch disc

AUTOMATIC TRANSMISSION

Identification

All models use a Torqueflite three speed automatic transmission. The transmission serial number is stamped on the lower edge of the transmission case just above the oil pan.

Pan and Filter

REMOVAL AND INSTALLATION

1. Raise and support vehicle.
2. Loosen the pan bolts from one end to the other allowing the fluid to drain out.
3. Unbolt the old filter from the pan.
4. Clean the pan and install a new filter. Tighten filter bolts to 35 in. lb.
5. Install the pan and new gasket. Torque pan bolts to 6–9 ft. lb.
6. Add four quarts of Dexron fluid, start the engine and move the lever through all positions, pausing momentarily in each. Add enough fluid to bring the level to the full mark on the dipstick.

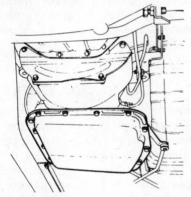

Transmission oil pan

KICKDOWN BAND ADJUSTMENT

The kickdown band adjusting screw is located on the left side of the transmission case.

1. Loosen locknut and back off approximately 5 turns. Test adjusting screw for free turning in the transmission case.
2. Tighten the adjusting screw to 72 in. lbs.
3. Back off adjusting screw 3 turns from Step 2. Tighten the locknut to 35 ft. lbs.

LOW AND REVERSE BAND ADJUSTMENT

1. Raise vehicle, drain transmission fluid and remove the pan.

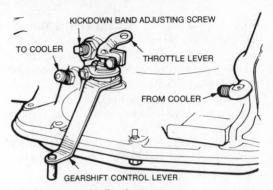

Kickdown band adjusting screw

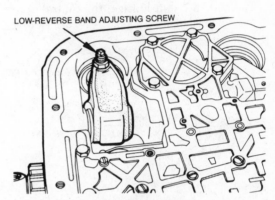

Low and reverse band adjustment

2. This transmission has an allen socket adjustment screw at the servo end of lever. After removing the locknut this screw is tightened to 41 in. lbs. torque then backed off 7½ turns. Tighten locknut to 30 ft. lbs.
3. Reinstall the pan.

NEUTRAL SAFETY SWITCH TEST AND ADJUSTMENT

1. When testing the safety switch, check to see if the switch has been properly installed. Move the selector lever into N position and adjust the switch by moving it so

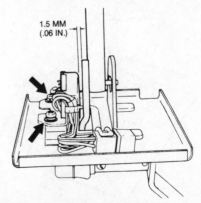

Installed position of the neutral safety switch

that the pin on the forward end of the rod assembly will be in the position near the lobe of detent plate and that this position will be at the front end of the range of N connection of the switch. Temporarily tighten the attaching screws. After adjusting the selection lever clearance to 0.06 in. securely tighten the screws.

2. Test the continuity of the switch circuit by using a test light with switch connector disconnected.

SHIFT LINKAGE ADJUSTMENT

To adjust the shift linkage, the control cover must be removed.

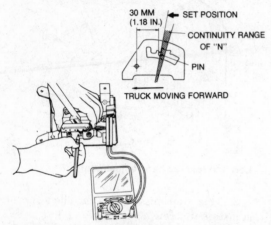

Measuring the continuity between the switch terminals of the neutral safety switch

Removal and Installation

1. Remove the shift handle assembly from the lever.

2. Take the position indicator assembly out upward.

Removing the shift lever handle

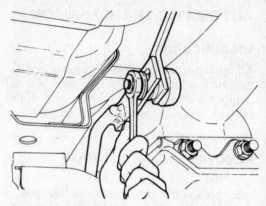

Control rod adjustment

Remove the position indicator lamp.

3. Disconnect the control rod from the arm.

Remove the lever bracket assembly.

4. Installation is the reverse of removal.

If the proper turning effort (13–29 in. lbs) is not obtained, adjust it by using a selective wave-washer of proper size.

CAUTION: *When the turning effort at the pivot is checked, the pin at the forward end of the rod assembly must not slide with the detent plate. If the arm is loose, the bushing should be replaced.*

THROTTLE LINKAGE ADJUSTMENT

The throttle rod adjustment is very important to proper transmission operation. This adjustment positions a valve which controls shift speed, shift quality and part throttle-down shift sensitivity. If the setting is too short, early shifts and slippage between shifts may occur. If the setting is too long, shifts may be delayed and part throttle-down shifts may be very sensitive.

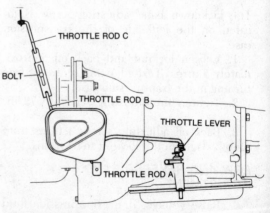

Throttle linkage adjustment

To adjust the throttle rod:

1. Warm up the engine until it reaches the normal operating temperature. With the carburetor automatic choke disengaged from the fast idle cam, adjust the engine idle speed by rotating speed adjusting screw (SAS). See "Tune-up Procedures" in Chapter 2.

2. Loosen the bolts on the linkage so that both rod "B" and "C" can slide properly.

3. Lightly push rod "A" or the transmission throttle lever and rod "C" toward the idle stopper, and set the rods to the idle position. Tighten the bolt securely that connects rods "B" and "C."

4. Make sure that when the carburetor throttle valve is wide-open, the transmission throttle lever smoothly moves from the IDLE to the WIDE OPEN position (from

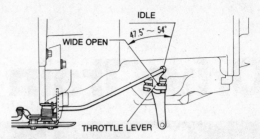

Throttle linkage adjustment

47.5° to 54°), and that there is some range in the lever stroke.

5. Also make sure that when the throttle linkage alone is slowly returned from the fully closed position, the transmission throttle lever completely returns to *idle* by return spring force.

Drive Train

7

DRIVELINE

Driveshaft and U-Joints
REMOVAL AND INSTALLATION

1. Make mating marks on the flange yoke and the differential companion flange.

2. Remove the bolts connecting the flange yoke to the differential companion flange, and remove the nuts attaching the center bearing assembly.

3. Remove the propeller shaft by drawing it out. Installation is reverse of removal.

NOTE: *When the sleeve yoke end of the*

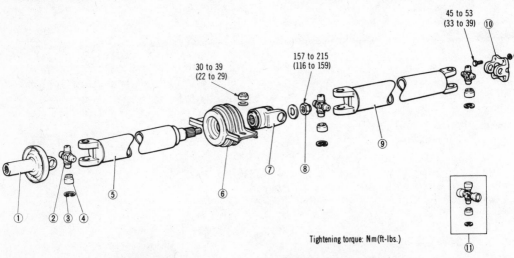

45 to 53 (33 to 39)

30 to 39 (22 to 29)

157 to 215 (116 to 159)

Tightening torque: Nm(ft-lbs.)

1. Sleeve yoke
2. Universal joint journal
3. Snap ring
4. Needle bearing
5. Front propeller shaft
6. Center bearing assembly
7. Center yoke
8. Center yoke attaching nut
9. Rear propeller shaft
10. Propeller shaft flange yoke
11. Universal joint journal kit

Driveshaft assembly

propeller shaft is pulled out from the transmission extension housing, transmission oil will flow out it if the front of the truck is raised higher, than the rear.
CAUTION: *When removing the propeller shaft be careful not to damage the oil seal lip and see that no foreign substance is present in the lip area.*

U-JOINT OVERHAUL

1. Remove the bearing retainer snap rings from the flange yoke.
2. With a vise and suitable sockets, force one needle bearing cup outward from the yoke, using the cross as a ram.
3. Grasp the protruding bearing with pliers or vise grips and remove it from the yoke.
NOTE: *If the needle bearing is hard to remove, strike the yoke with a plastic hammer.*

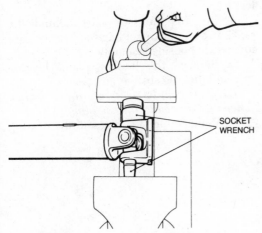

SOCKET WRENCH

Forcing out the needle bearing using a vise

It may be necessary to remove the needle bearings using a plastic hammer

4. Reverse the sockets and again using the cross as a ram, force the opposite bearing outward from the yoke and remove it with pliers or vise grips.
5. Follow the same procedure to remove the remaining bearing in the yoke.
6. To install, place the cross in the yoke and start a bearing cup into the yoke collar, engaging the cross arm.
7. With the aid of a vise, force the bearing cup into the yoke collar until it bottoms. Install the opposite bearing cup in the same manner.
NOTE: *Sockets may be used to force the bearing cup inward so that the retaining snap rings can be installed.*
8. Different thickness snap rings are used to control the clearance between the bearing and the snap ring.
9. Install a snap ring and measure the clearance with a feeler gauge. Replace the snap ring with one of the proper thickness to have a total clearance tolerance of .000 to .001 inch.
Snap ring selection range:
 • No color—0.0504 inch
 • Yellow—0.0561 inch
 • Blue—0.0528 inch
 • Purple—0.0539 inch
NOTE: *When snap rings are installed, press each bearing towards the opposite side to measure the maximum clearance.*

Center Bearing
REMOVAL AND INSTALLATION

1. Remove driveshaft.
2. Disconnect the center universal joint.
3. Remove the nut holding the center yoke and remove the yoke. Remove the center bearing bracket from the bearing by prying on it.
4. Remove the center bearing using a gear puller.
NOTE: *The center bracket and the mount-*

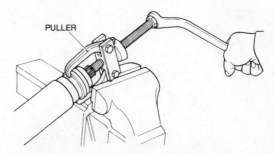

PULLER

Removing the center bearing using a puller

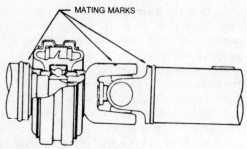

Mating marks of the yoke and shaft

ing rubber are welded together and must be replaced as a unit.

To assemble:

5. Fill the bearing grease cavity with multipurpose grease.

6. Partially insert the center bearing into the shaft and install the bracket to the bearing.

7. Verify that the bracket mounting rubber is properly fitted in the bearing groove.

8. Refit the center yoke, making sure you align the notch on the yoke with the notch on the front propeller shaft. Replace the attaching nut and tighten to 116–159 ft. lb.

9. Replace the center universal joint, making sure you align the notch on the rear propeller shaft with the notch on the yoke.

10. Install the driveshaft.

NOTE: *The manufacturer suggests that a new center yoke locking nut be used when the center bearing is removed.*

REAR AXLE

Identification

A sticker indicating the gear ratio is attached to the axle housing.

Axle shaft, Bearing and Seal

REMOVAL AND INSTALLATION

1. Jack up the vehicle and support it on stands.

2. Remove the rear wheels and brake drums.

3. Disconnect the brake line from the wheel cylinder and plug it to prevent fluid loss.

4. Remove the four nuts behind the brake backing plate holding the bearing case to the axle housing assembly.

5. Remove the braking plate, bearing case and the axle shaft as an assembly.

NOTE: *It may be necessary to use a slide hammer to remove the assembly.*

6. Remove the "O" ring and the bearing

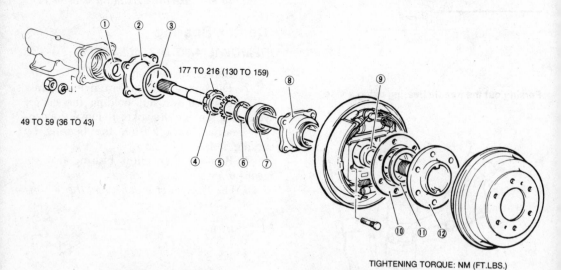

TIGHTENING TORQUE: NM (FT.LBS.)

1. Rear axle shaft oil seal (Inner)
2. Shim
3. O Ring
4. Lock nut
5. Lock washer
6. Washer
7. Rear axle shaft bearing
8. Bearing case
9. Rear axle shaft oil seal (Outer)
10. Dust cover
11. Packing
12. Rear axle shaft

Exploded view of rear axle shaft

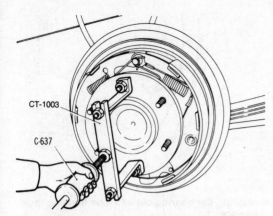

Pulling out the axle shaft using a slide hammer

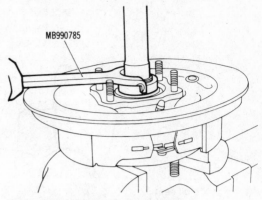

Removing the axle bearing locknut

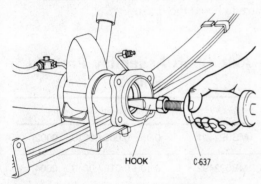

Removing the oil seal with a slide hammer and a hook attachment

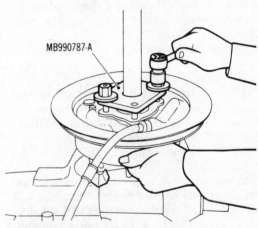

Removing the bearing case

preload shims. Save the preload shims, as you will need them for reassembly.

7. Remove the oil seal with a hooked slide hammer.

8. To remove the axle shaft bearing, remove the notched locknut. This calls for a special tool, but you should be able to use a brass drift to knock it loose.

9. Remove the lock washer and plain washer.

10. Screw the lock nut back on to the axle shaft about three turns.

11. It will be necessary to fabricate a metal plate that fits over the axle shaft and butts the lock nut. Drill four holes in the plate that align with the four bearing case studs and fit the plate. Refit two nuts and washers to the bearing case studs diagonally across from each other and tighten them evenly to free the bearing case and the bearing.

12. Use a hammer and drift to remove the bearing outer race from the bearing case.

13. Remove the outer oil seal from the bearing case.

To assemble:

NOTE: *Always use new "O" rings and check the condition of all oil seals and dust covers.*

14. Apply grease to the outer surface on the bearing outer race and to the lip of the outer oil seal, and drive them into the bearing case from each side.

15. Slide the bearing case and bearing over the rear axle shaft. Apply grease on the bearing rollers and fit the inner race by pressing it into place.

CAUTION: *Be careful not to damage or deform the dust cover.*

16. Pack the bearing with grease.

17. Install the washer, the crowned lock washer and the lock nut in the order just given and tighten the lock nut to 130–159 ft. lb. if possible.

18. Bend the tab on the lock washer into the groove on the lock nut. If the tab and the groove do not line up, slightly tighten the lock nut until they do.

19. Drive the new inner oil seal into place after greasing it and refit the assembly. Be

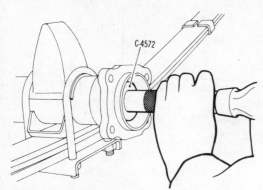

Driving in the oil seal

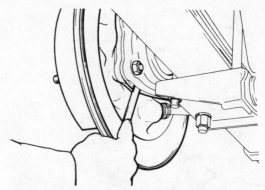

Measuring the bearing case to axle housing face clearance

sure to fit the "O" ring and shim and apply silicone rubber sealant to the bearing case face.

NOTE: *Be sure to bleed the brakes before road testing!*

To adjust preload:

1. Begin with the left side rear axle assembly and insert a 0.04 in. shim between the bearing case and the axle shaft housing. Tighten the four nuts to 36–43 ft. lb.

NOTE: *Be sure to fit the "O" ring and apply sealant.*

2. Install the right side axle assembly into the right side housing without its shim and "O" ring. Tighten the four nuts to 0.4 ft. lb.

3. Using a flat blade feeler gauge, measure the gap between the bearing case and the axle housing face. It should range between 0.002–0.008 in. Record the measurement.

4. Remove the axle shaft and select a shim that is the same thickness as the gap between the faces just measured, plus a shim with a thickness from 0.002–0.0079 in. and install them on the housing. Fit the "O" ring and apply sealant. Fit the axle assembly and tighten the four nuts to 36–43 ft. lb.

5. Assemble remaining components. Be sure to bleed the brakes!

Axle Shaft Assembly Preload Shims

Part No.	Thickness of shim mm (in).
MB092491	0.05 ± 0.005 (.0020 ± .0002)
MB092492	0.10 ± 0.010 (.0040 ± .0004)
MB092493	0.20 ± 0.015 (.0079 ± .0006)
MB092494	0.30 ± 0.020 (.0118 ± .0008)
MB092495	0.50 ± 0.025 (.0197 ± .0010)
MB092496	1.00 ± 0.040 (.0394 ± .0016)
MB092497	1.50 ± 0.050 (.0591 ± .0020)
MB092498	2.00 ± 0.055 (.0787 ± .0022)

Suspension and Steering

FRONT SUSPENSION

All models are equipped with a Wishbone type front suspension.

Coil Spring

REMOVAL AND INSTALLATION

1. Raise the front of the vehicle and support it on jack stands.
2. Remove the wheel.
3. Remove the shock absorber (see below for procedures).
4. Remove stabilizer and strut bar (see below for procedures).
5. Compress the coil spring with a spring compressor.
6. Remove the relay rod from the steering arm.
7. Remove the upper and lower ball joints using a ball joint remover.
8. Remove the coil spring.

Installation is the reverse of removal.

NOTE: *The coil springs are color coded. The left side spring has a green band on it and the right side spring has a pink band on it. Do not mix the left and right springs.*

9. Tighten the ball joint castle nuts to: upper, 43–65 ft. lb; lower, 87–130 ft. lb.

Stabilizer and Strut Bar

REMOVAL AND INSTALLATION

1. Raise the vehicle and support it on jack stands.
2. Remove the wheels.
3. Disconnect the stabilizer and the strut bars from the lower control arms.

CAUTION: *When removing the strut bar, loosen the adjusting nut at the other end of the bar before loosening the bolts at the control arm.*

NOTE: *Before removing stabilizer bar, note the order and direction of the rubber cushion washers and their metal caps for reassembly.*

4. Remove the nut and spacers at the threaded end of the strut bar and remove the bar.
5. Remove the two stabilizer brackets and remove the stabilizer.

Installation is the reverse of removal. Observe the following.

There is a letter "L" on the left side strut bar, do not confuse it with the right side bar. The rubber cushions on the front of the strut bar are different; the cushion with a protruded lip is mounted at the front and the regular cushion is mounted at the back.

When installing the strut bar, set the standard distance (A) in illustration to 3.8 in.

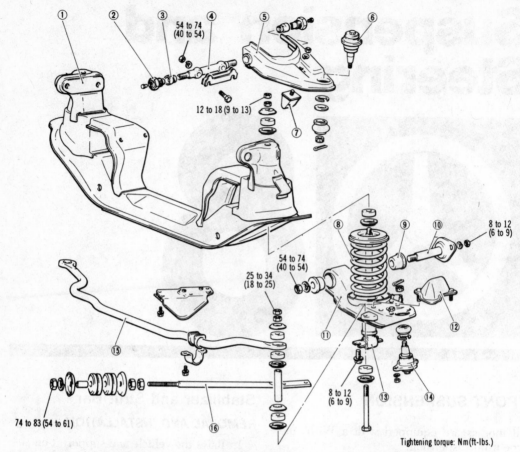

Tightening torque: Nm(ft-lbs.)

1. Crossmember
2. Pivot bushing
3. Dust seal
4. Upper arm shaft
5. Upper arm
6. Upper ball joint
7. Rebound stop
8. Front coil spring
9. Lower arm bushing
10. Lower arm shaft
11. Lower arm
12. Bump stop
13. Shock absorber
14. Lower ball joint
15. Stabilizer
16. Strut bar

Front suspension—exploded view

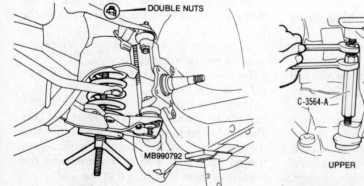

Compressing the front spring

UPPER

LOWER

Loosening the connection at the ball joint and knuckle

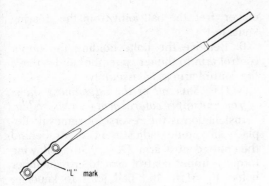

"L" mark

Strut bar installing position

from the tip of the threaded end of the bar to the rear face of the rear double nut. Lower the vehicle to the ground and tighten all nuts and bolts.

CAUTION: *Make sure you check the front wheel alignment after installing the strut bar in order to obtain the correct caster, and then re-adjust the distance (A) (see illustration) as required.*

When installing both ends of the stabilizer, tighten the first nut (adjustment nut) to obtain length (B) (see illustration) 00.87–0.94 in., then tighten the lock nut to 18–25 ft. lb.

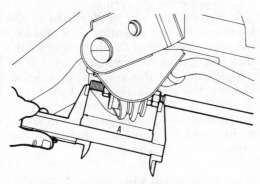

Installed dimension of the strut bar

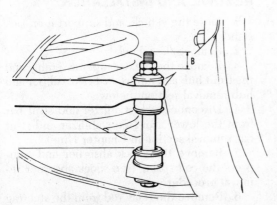

Installing the stabilizer

Shock Absorbers
BOUNCE TEST

Each shock absorber can be tested by bouncing the corner of the vehicle until maximum up and down movement is obtained. Release the car. It should stop bouncing in one or two bounces. Compare both front corners or both rear corners but do not compare the front to the rear. If one corner bounces longer than the other it should be inspected for damage and possibly be replaced.

REMOVAL AND INSTALLATION

1. Raise the vehicle and support it on jack stands.
2. Remove the wheel.
3. Remove the double lock nuts at the top of the shock absorber along with the rubber washer and its metal caps.
4. Remove the two bolts at the bottom of the shock absorber and withdraw the shock absorber through the bottom arm.

Installation is the reverse of removal.

5. Be sure to refit all of the rubber cushion washers and their metal caps in the correct order. Tighten the upper shock absorber nut to 9–13 ft. lb. and install the lock nut. Tighten the two lower shock absorber bolts to 6–9 ft. lb.

Upper Ball Joint
REMOVAL AND INSTALLATION

1. Remove the upper control arm from the vehicle (see procedure).
2. Remove the ball joint dust seal by prying up the dust seal ring evenly with a screwdriver.

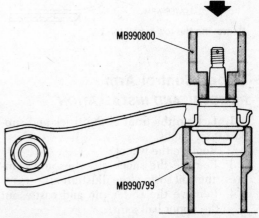

MB990800

MB990799

Removing the upper ball joint using special tools

3. Remove the snap ring using snap ring pliers.

4. Using a ball joint remover and installer tool, press off the ball joint.

NOTE: *A minimum of 2200 lb. pressure will be required to remove the upper ball joint from the control arm.*

5. To install the ball joint, press it into the burred hole, with the ball joint and upper arm mating marks aligned.

6. Make sure the ball joint snap ring is a tight fit and install the dust cover.

Lower Ball Joint
REMOVAL AND INSTALLATION

1. Jack up the vehicle and remove the wheel.

2. Remove the coil spring (see procedure).

3. If you have not already done so, free the lower ball joint from the steering knuckle using a ball joint remover. Remove the dust cover from the ball joint.

4. Unbolt and remove the ball joint.

5. Installation is the reverse of removal. Install the ball joint with its tab side pointing to the rear of the vehicle. Tighten the ball joint to lower control arm bolts to 22–30 ft. lb.

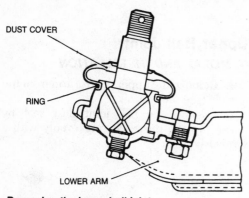

DUST COVER

RING

LOWER ARM

Removing the lower ball joint

Upper Control Arm
REMOVAL AND INSTALLATION

1. Jack up the front of the truck and support it on stands.

2. Remove the wheel.

3. Remove the shock absorber and compress the coil spring (see illustration).

4. Remove the cotter pin and castle nut from the upper ball joint.

5. Using a gear puller or ball joint re-

mover, free the ball joint from the steering knuckle.

6. Remove the bolts holding the upper control arm to the crossmember and remove the control arm as an assembly.

NOTE: *Save all of the adjustment shims from the upper control arm for reassembly.*

Installation is the reverse of removal. Replace all camber adjustment shims behind the upper control arm. Observe the following torques: upper control arm to crossmember bolts, 40–54 ft. lb.; ball joint to knuckle, 43–65 ft. lb.

Lower Control Arm
REMOVAL AND INSTALLATION

1. Raise the front of the truck and support it on jackstands.

2. Remove the wheel.

3. Remove the shock absorber and compress the coil spring (see procedure).

4. Remove the stabilizer and strut bar (see below for procedures).

5. Remove the cotter pin and castle nut from the lower ball joint and separate the ball joint from the steering knuckle using a ball joint remover.

6. Remove the coil spring.

7. Remove the nut in the front of the lower control arm mounting shaft. Remove the nuts at the rear of the shaft. Remove the shaft and remove the lower arm.

Installation is the reverse of removal. Tighten the front mounting shaft nut to 40–54 ft. lb. Tighten the rear nut to 6–9 ft. lb. Tighten the ball joint castle nut to 87–130 ft. lb. Tighten control arm shaft only after truck is on the ground.

Steering Knuckle
REMOVAL AND INSTALLATION

1. Raise the vehicle and support it on jack stands.

2. Remove the wheel.

3. Remove the brake caliper assembly and the front hub assembly (see brake caliper and hub removal section, below).

4. Disconnect the stabilizer and strut bar from the lower arm (see stabilizer and strut bar removal section in Chapter Nine).

5. Remove the shock absorber and compress the coil spring (see shock absorber removal procedure).

6. Remove the relay rod from the steering arm using a ball joint remover.

7. Remove the cotter pins and castle nuts from the steering knuckle ball joints, and using either a gear puller or a ball joint remover, free the ball joints from the knuckle. Remove the knuckle.

When installing, tighten the upper ball joint castle nut to 43–65 ft. lb. and the lower ball joint nut to 87–130 ft. lb. Tighten the tie rod end ball joint nut to 25–33 ft. lb. Fit new cotter keys. Installation is the reverse of removal.

Front End Alignment

CASTER AND CAMBER

To adjust caster, adjust the tightening of the upper arm shaft. A half turn of the upper arm shaft will cause 0.049 in. play in the upper arm shaft resulting in a ¼ degree caster adjustment. The standard caster value and other wheel alignment specifications can be found at the beginning of this chapter.

To adjust the camber, it is necessary to adjust the number and thickness of the shims under the upper arm shaft. A total of 0.16 in. shim thickness between the upper arm shaft

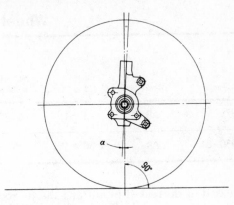

Caster dimension

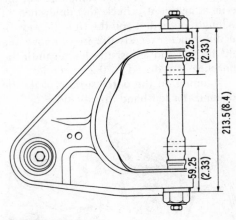

Adjusting caster

and the crossmember is normally required for standard camber. A 0.024 in. adjustment in thickness of shims will provide about 8 minutes adjustment of camber.

TOE-IN

Toe-in can be adjusted by screwing the left tie rod turnbuckle in or out. One revolution of the turnbuckle will vary in about 0.3 in. of toe-in adjustment. The toe-in may be in-

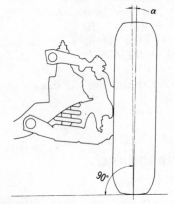

Camber dimension

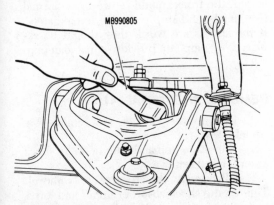

Adjusting camber

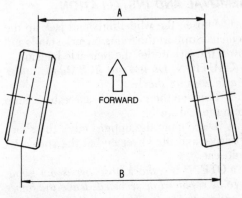

Toe-in dimension

Wheel Alignment

Year	Model	Caster (deg)	Camber (deg)	Toe-in (in.)	Steering Angle		King Pin Angle
					Inner Wheel (deg)	Outer Wheel (deg)	
1979	All	3° ± 1°	1° ± 30'	0.08–0.35	37°	30.5°	8°
1980–81	All	2°30' ± 1°	1° ± 30'	0.08–0.35	37°	30.5°	8°

creased or decreased by turning the tie rod turnbuckle toward the front or the rear of the vehicle respectively. After completion of the toe-in adjustment, check the difference in the length of the left and the right tie rods. If the difference exceeds 0.2 in., remove the right tie rod and adjust the length until the difference is reduced to 0.2 in. or less. An "L" stamped on the outer surface of the tie rod stands for left-hand thread end.

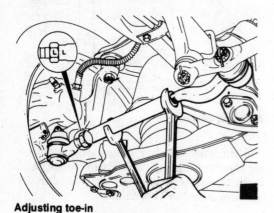

Adjusting toe-in

REAR SUSPENSION

Leaf Springs
REMOVAL AND INSTALLATION

1. Loosen the wheel nuts and jack up the vehicle. Support the frame on jack stands and lower the jack under the rear axle housing.
CAUTION: *Do not put jack stands under axle housing shafts.*
2. Remove the parking brake cable clamp from the leaf spring.
3. Disconnect the upper end of the shock absorber and the lower end at the spring U-bolt seat.
NOTE: *If the shock absorber is not going to be replaced or serviced, leave the lower end on the spring U-bolt seat.*

4. Loosen the U-bolt nuts and jack up the rear axle housing until it clears the spring seat. Remove the spring seat.
5. Remove the front spring pin and the rear shackle pin and remove the spring.
Installation is the reverse of removal. Observe the following:
6. Install the spring front eye bushings from both sides of the eye with the bushing flanges facing out. Insert the spring pin assembly from the wheel side and secure it to the hanger bracket with its bolt. Temporarily tighten the spring pin nut.
7. Repeat step 6 on the rear spring mount.
8. Align the center of the U-bolt seat with the center bolt hole in the spring. Tighten the U-bolts to 47–54 ft. lb.
NOTE: *Tighten the nuts on the U-bolts until all of the U-bolt threads protrude evenly.*
Tighten the spring pins and shackle pins to 22–33 ft. lb.

Shock Absorbers
TESTING

To test the shock absorbers, bounce the front of the truck by hand a few times. When released, the truck should return to its normal ride height and stop bouncing immediately. If the shocks are worn, they should be replaced in pairs to provide equal dampening.

REMOVAL AND INSTALLATION

1. Jack up the vehicle and remove the wheel.
2. Unbolt the top and bottom of the shock absorber and remove.
Installation is the reverse of removal. Tighten the shock absorber upper and lower mounting nuts to 13–18 ft. lb.

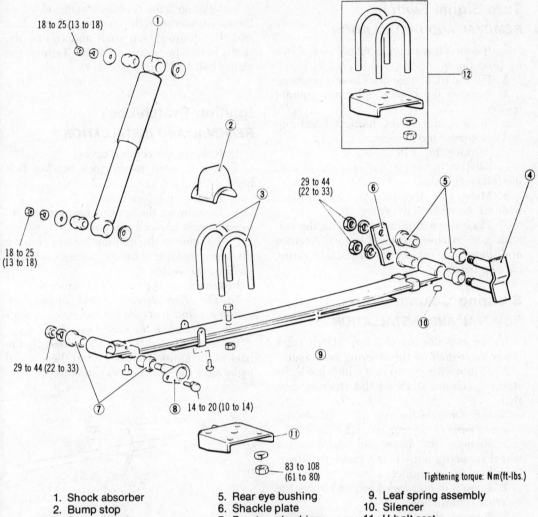

18 to 25 (13 to 18)

18 to 25
(13 to 18)

29 to 44 (22 to 33)

29 to 44
(22 to 33)

14 to 20 (10 to 14)

83 to 108
(61 to 80)

Tightening torque: Nm(ft-lbs.)

1. Shock absorber
2. Bump stop
3. Spring U-bolt
4. Spring shackle assembly
5. Rear eye bushing
6. Shackle plate
7. Front eye bushing
8. Spring pin assembly
9. Leaf spring assembly
10. Silencer
11. U-bolt seat
12. Repair kit, U-bolt

Exploded view of the rear suspension

STEERING

Steering Wheel

REMOVAL AND INSTALLATION

1. Pry off the steering wheel center foam pad.

2. Remove the steering wheel retaining nut.

3. Using a steering wheel puller, remove the wheel.

4. Be sure the front wheels are in a straight ahead position. Reverse the removal procedure for installation.

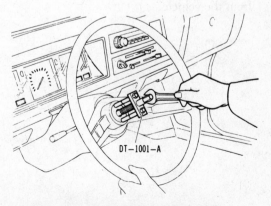

DT−1001−A

Removing the steering wheel using a puller

Turn Signal Switch
REMOVAL AND INSTALLATION

1. Remove the steering wheel (see above for procedure).
2. Put the tilt handle in its lowest position.
3. Remove the upper and lower column covers.
4. Remove the wiring harness band clip and disconnect the harness.
5. Remove the switch.

Installation is the reverse of removal with the following notes.

6. Make sure the column switch aligns with the steering shaft center.
7. Place the wiring harness along the column tube as close as possible to the center line. Be sure to replace the adjustable wiring harness bands.

Steering Column
REMOVAL AND INSTALLATION

1. Remove the air cleaner. Match mark the column shaft on the steering gear shaft.
2. Remove the clamp bolt which holds the steering column shaft on the steering gear shaft.

NOTE: *On vehicles with air conditioning, step 2 must be done from under the truck.*

3. Remove the horn pad and steering wheel retaining nut, then remove the steering wheel using a puller.
4. Loosen the tilt lock knob and lower the steering column fully.
5. Remove the steering column cover and disconnect the column wiring under the dashboard.
6. Remove the five bolts holding the base of the column at the fire wall.
7. Remove the four bolts holding the tilt column and remove the steering column from the vehicle.

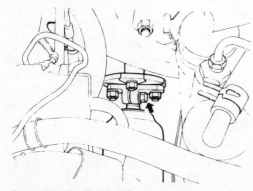

Removing the clamp bolt

Installation is the reverse of removal. Align the match marks on the steering column shaft and the steering gear shaft and couple the shafts before installing any bolts. Tighten the clamp bolt to 15–18 ft. lb.

Ignition Switch/Lock
REMOVAL AND INSTALLATION

1. Remove the column cover.
2. Cut a notch in the lock bracket bolt head with a hack saw.
3. Remove the lock bolts.
4. Disconnect the ignition harness and remove the switch/lock as a unit.
5. To remove the ignition switch, remove the screw holding it on the harness side and pull out the switch.

Installation is the reverse of removal.

NOTE: *The steering wheel upper lock bracket and bolts should be replaced with new parts when the unit is installed.*

Before fully tightening the screw in the back of the ignition switch, insert the key and make sure the switch works smoothly.

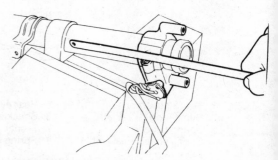

Cut a notch in the lock bracket bolt using a hack saw

Steering Linkage
REMOVAL AND INSTALLATION

1. Jack up the vehicle and support it on stands.
2. Remove the cotter pins and castle nuts holding the tie rod ends to the steering arms and the relay rod, and free the tie rods using either a suitable gear puller or a ball joint remover.
3. Unbolt and remove the relay rod in the same manner.
4. To remove the idler arm, remove the two bolts holding it to the frame and pull it out.

NOTE: *The outer tie rod end has a left hand thread and the inner tie rod has a right handed thread on the driver's side.*

Installation is the reverse of removal. Tighten all tie rod end nuts and relay rod nuts to 25–33 ft. lbs.

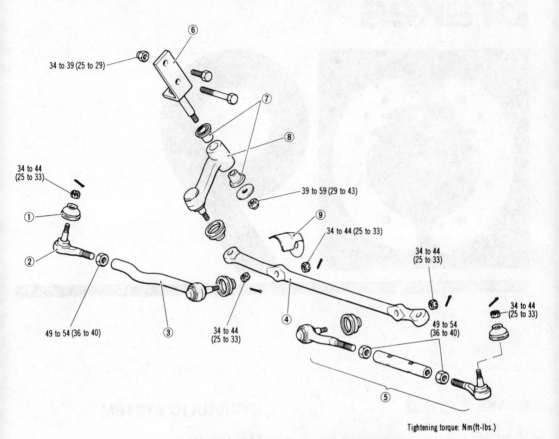

Tightening torque: Nm(ft-lbs.)

1. Tie rod end dust cover
2. Tie rod end, outer
3. Tie rod, R. H.
4. Relay rod
5. Tie rod assembly, L. H.
6. Idler arm bracket
7. Idler arm bushing
8. Idler arm
9. Heat protector

Steering linkage

Brakes

BRAKE SYSTEM

All models use the sliding caliper type disc brakes on the front and the duo-servo rear brakes with the automatic adjusters.

REAR BRAKE SHOE ADJUSTMENT

The rear brake shoe clearance is automatically adjusted by the movement of the brake shoe and no adjustment is required. However, if the brakes are disassembled or the adjuster fails, use the following procedure to adjust the shoes:

1. Turn the adjuster wheel in the opposite direction of the arrow until the shoes are pressed against the drum.

2. With the adjuster wheel free of the adjuster lever, turn the adjuster wheel in the direction of the arrow to adjust the clearance between the shoe lining and the drum (.010 to .016 in.).

3. Adjust the shoe clearance by moving the truck in reverse direction and depressing the brake pedal several times until the pedal stroke is constant.

HYDRAULIC SYSTEM

Master Cylinder

REMOVAL AND INSTALLATION

1. Remove all lines connected to the master cylinder. Slowly depress the brake pedal to remove the fluid.

2. Remove the master cylinder from the booster assembly.

3. Installation is the reverse of removal. Bleed the brakes.

OVERHAUL

1. Remove the stop ring, piston stop, primary piston assembly, secondary piston assembly and the secondary return spring in the given order.

2. Loosen the valve case and remove the check valve and the check valve spring.

3. Wash the master cylinder, pistons and cups in brake fluid. Use care not to damage the cylinder, piston or cups.

CAUTION: *Do not attempt to disassemble the primary piston assembly; its length is factory adjusted.*

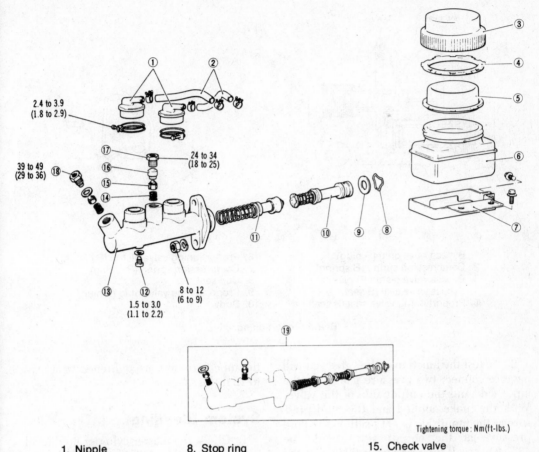

2.4 to 3.9
(1.8 to 2.9)

24 to 34
(18 to 25)

39 to 49
(29 to 36)

8 to 12
(6 to 9)

1.5 to 3.0
(1.1 to 2.2)

Tightening torque : Nm(ft-lbs.)

1. Nipple	8. Stop ring	15. Check valve
2. Reservoir hose	9. Piston stop	16. Tube seat
3. Reservoir cap	10. Primary piston assembly	17. Check valve cap
4. Slide ring	11. Secondary piston assembly	18. Valve case
5. Diaphragm	12. Secondary piston stop	19. Master cylinder kit
6. Fluid reservoir	13. Master cylinder	
7. Holder	14. Check valve spring	

Exploded view of the master cylinder

NOTE: *When any related parts such as the return spring, piston cup and piston require replacement, you must replace the entire piston assembly.*

To assemble:

4. Hone the master cylinder slightly. The cylinder bore inside diameter should be between 0.8748–0.8768 in. If not, replace cylinder. Coat the cylinder with brake fluid.

5. Measure the piston outside diameter. It should be between 0.8719–0.8732. If not, replace.

6. Assemble the master cylinder components in the master cylinder after coating the rubber seals with brake fluid. Bleed the brakes after installation.

NOTE: *Prime the cylinder by pouring a little fluid in the reservoirs and working the*

piston until fluid squirts out of the two brake line ports.

Blend Proportioning Valve

The blend proportioning valve is designed to improve efficiency within the normal braking range by distributing braking force most effectively to the front and rear wheels. It also increases braking force to the rear wheels by releasing decompressing effect if a large braking force is required, the vehicle is loaded, or in the event that a front brake line should burst.

REMOVAL AND INSPECTION

1. Check all line connections and plugs for fluid leakage and damage and tighten or replace any loose or defective parts.

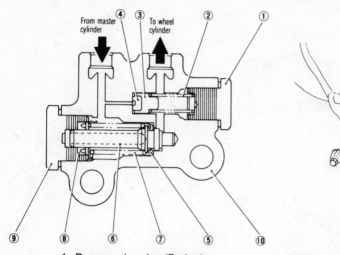
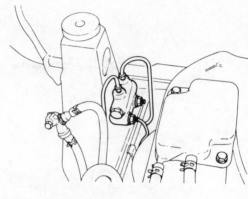

1. Bypass valve plug (B plug)
2. Compression spring (B spring)
3. Bypass valve piston (B piston)
4. Bypass valve seal (B seal)
5. Proportioning valve seal (P seal)
6. Proportioning valve piston (P piston)
7. Compression spring (P spring)
8. Cup seal
9. Proportioning valve plug (P plug)
10. Body

Blend proportioning valve

2. To test the function of the valve you will have to connect two pressure gauges to the input side and the output side of the valve. With the brake applied and the fluid pressure at the input side is 711 psi then the fluid pressure at the output side should be 437–494 psi. If the pressure is 996 psi at the input side then it should be 668–754 psi at the output side.

Replace the valve if the measured value is not within the range.

NOTE: *The valve should not be disassembled, because its performance significantly depends on the setting loads of springs.*

3. When installing the valve make sure the tube flare nuts are tightened to at least 9 to 12 ft. lbs.

System Bleeding

1. Check the master cylinder fluid level.
2. Remove the cap from the bleeder screw of the wheel farthest from the master cylinder.
3. Connect a length of rubber tubing to the screw and place the other end in a jar half full of clean brake fluid.
4. Pump the brake pedal until no bubbles are visible in the container.
5. Hold the pedal in the depressed posi-

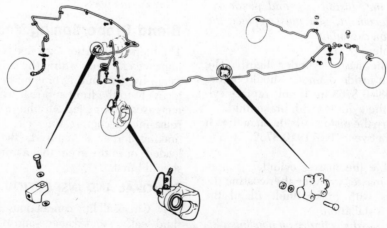

Brake tubing system

tion and tighten the screw. Replace the cap and proceed to each wheel in turn.

NOTE: *Periodically check the master cylinder during the bleeding operation to check that the fluid level does not go too low. If it does, air will enter the master cylinder and it will have to be bled as well.*

FRONT DISC BRAKES

INSPECTION

The remaining thickness of the pads can be easily checked through the inspection hole in the caliper assembly after removing the wheel. The standard thickness of the pads are .41 in. and the service limit is .04 in.

REMOVAL AND INSTALLATION

1. Remove the wheel and expose the caliper.

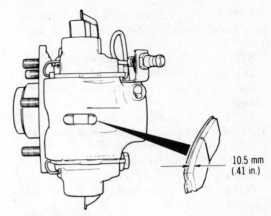

Pad inspection

2. Remove approximately ½ the fluid from the master cylinder reservoir.

3. Remove the spring (spigot) pin and pull the stopper plug from the upper end of the caliper.

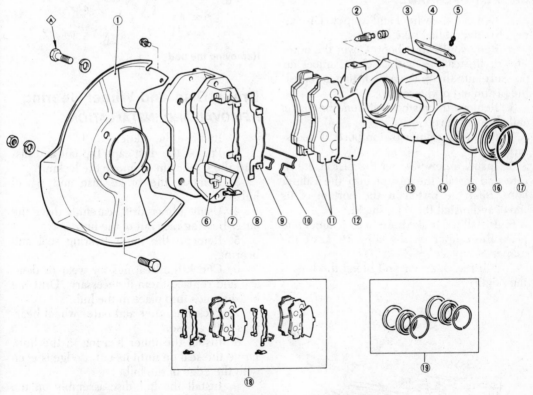

1. Dust cover
2. Bleeder screw
3. Pad support plate
4. Stopper plug
5. Spigot pin
6. Caliper support
7. Pad clip (inner)
8. Pad clip B
9. Pad clip (outer)
10. Anti-rattle spring
11. Brake pad
12. Anti-squeak shim
13. Caliper body
14. Piston
15. Piston seal
16. Dust boot
17. Boot ring
18. Pad repair kit
19. Seal and boot repair kit
⟨A⟩ Tightening torque: Nm (ft. lbs.) 69 to 88 (51 to 65)

Exploded view of the disc brake assembly

4. Move the caliper back and forth to loosen and remove it from the caliper support.

NOTE: *The hydraulic brake hose need not be removed from the caliper, but do not allow the caliper weight to hang from the hose.*

5. To install, push the piston into its original position in the caliper, using a piston expander tool or a hammer handle.

NOTE: *The bleeder may have to be opened to allow the piston to bottom.*

6. Install the pads, pad clip B, and pad clips inner and outer.

7. Slip the caliper over the pads and install the pad support plate, stopper plug, and the spring pin.

8. Check the brake drag torque after the brakes have been applied several times on a test drive. The torque should be 29 in. lbs., measured at a wheel mounting bolt.

CALIPER OVERHAUL

1. Remove the wheel and caliper. Disconnect the hydraulic brake line.

2. Remove the dust boot. Cover the outer side of the caliper with a cloth, inject air pressure into the brake hose fitting and push the piston out of the caliper.

3. Remove the piston seal from the piston and clean all parts.

4. Hone the caliper piston bore, if necessary.

5. Install a new seal on the piston, lubricate and install the piston into the caliper bore. Seat the piston at the bottom of its travel and install the dust shield.

6. Install the brake hose to the caliper and place the caliper on the support. Lock the caliper into place.

7. Fill the reservoir and bleed the brakes thoroughly.

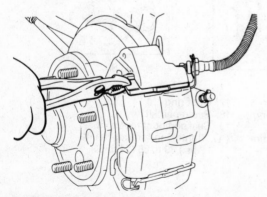

Removing the stopper plug

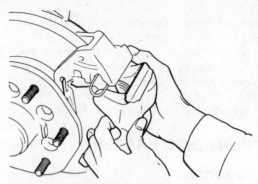

Removing the caliper assembly

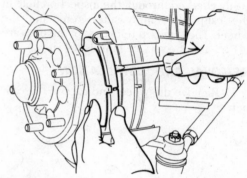

Removing the pad

Brake Disc and Wheel Bearing
REMOVAL AND INSTALLATION

1. Remove the caliper.

2. Pry off the dust cap. Tap out and discard the cotter pin. Remove the locknut.

3. Remove the brake disc and wheel hub.

4. Using a brass drift, carefully drive the outer bearing race out of the hub.

5. Remove the inner bearing seal and bearing.

6. Check the bearings for wear or damage and replace them if necessary. Drift the bearing race into place in the hub.

7. Pack the inner and outer wheel bearings with grease.

8. Install the inner bearing in the hub. Drive the seal on until its outer edge is even with the edge of the hub.

9. Install the hub/disc assembly on the spindle, being careful not to damage the oil seal.

10. Install the outer bearing, washer, and spindle nut. Adjust the bearing.

ADJUSTMENT

1. Tighten the spindle nut to 22 ft. lbs. and then loosen it.

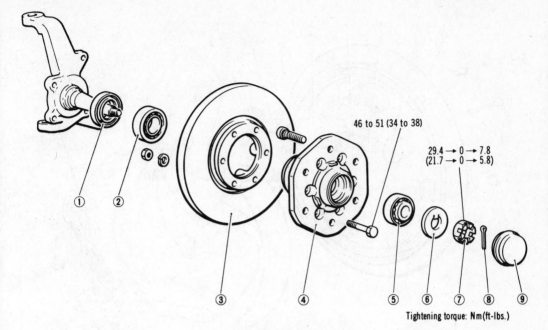

46 to 51 (34 to 38)

29.4 → 0 → 7.8
(21.7 → 0 → 5.8)

Tightening torque: Nm(ft-lbs.)

1. Oil seal
2. Wheel bearing (Inner)
3. Brake disc
4. Wheel hub
5. Wheel bearing (Outer)
6. Plain washer
7. Hub nut
8. Cotter pin
9. Hub cap

Front axle hub assembly

2. Tighten the nut to 6 ft. lbs.
3. Install the cap on the nut. Do not back off the nut more than 30° for cotter pin hole-to-slot alignment.

REAR DRUM BRAKES

Brake Drum
REMOVAL AND INSTALLATION

1. Release the parking brake. Block the front wheels.
2. Jack up the rear of the truck and support it on stands.
3. Remove the wheel.
4. Remove the brake drum.
Installation is the reverse of removal.

INSPECTION

Check the inner wall of the brake drum for groove wear and the presence of oil which could mean a leaking wheel cylinder.

Brake Shoes
REMOVAL AND INSTALLATION

1. Remove the wheel and the brake drum.
2. Using a standard brake return spring tool, remove the return spring.

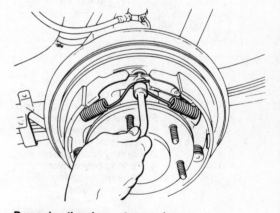

Removing the shoe return spring

3. Remove the adjusting spring and the adjusting lever.
4. Remove the brake shoes and the adjusting assembly then remove the cable from the parking brake lever.

Installation is the reverse of removal with the following notes.

5. After the primary shoes have been installed, install the parking brake cable. Set the adjuster assembly, then secure the secondary shoes.

NOTE: *Grease the threaded area on the adjuster assembly and make sure it turns smoothly.*

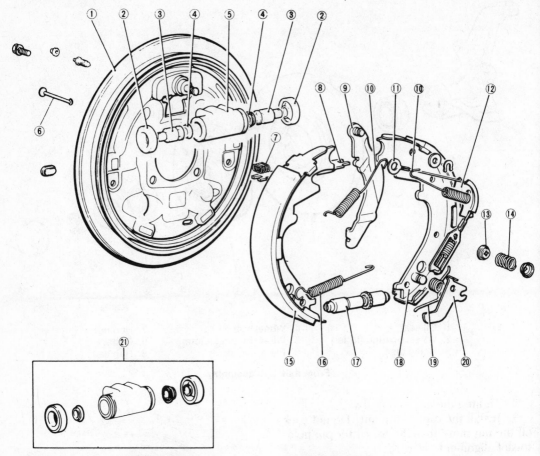

1. Backing plate
2. Wheel cylinder boot
3. Wheel cylinder piston
4. Wheel cylinder piston cup
5. Wheel cylinder body
6. Shoe hold-down pin
7. Anti-rattle spring
8. Parking brake strut
9. Parking brake lever
10. Shoe return spring
11. Adjusting cable
12. Cable guide
13. Shoe hold-down cup
14. Shoe hold-down spring
15. Primary shoe assembly
16. Adjusting spring
17. Adjuster assembly
18. Secondary shoe assembly
19. Adjuster spring
20. Autoadjuster lever
21. Wheel cylinder repair kit

Exploded view of the rear brake assembly

6. Install the primary shoe return springs, adjusting cable and the secondary shoe return springs in the given order.

NOTE: *The spring for the primary shoe is colored green, while the spring for the secondary shoe is gray. Do not mix them, as they are different lengths.*

7. To check the adjuster assembly operation: pull the adjuster cable toward you to see if the adjuster lever goes into mesh with the next tooth on the adjuster wheel. Make sure that when the cable is released, the adjuster lever returns to its original position after the adjuster wheel has moved a tooth ahead.

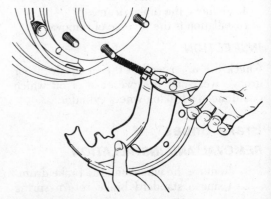

Removing the parking brake cable

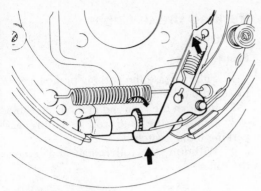

Brake shoe adjuster

Wheel Cylinder
REMOVAL AND INSTALLATION

1. Remove brake shoes (see above for procedures).
2. Disconnect the brake pipe from the rear of the wheel cylinder and plug it to prevent it from leaking fluid.
3. Remove the wheel cylinder from the brake backing plate.

Installation is the reverse of removal.

OVERHAUL

1. Remove dust caps from both ends of the wheel cylinder.
2. Pull out the plungers, rubber seals and piston cups.

Clean and lightly hone the wheel cylinder.

Assembly is the reverse of disassembly. Lubricate all parts with brake fluid before assembly.

Power Brake Unit
REMOVAL AND INSTALLATION

1. Remove the master cylinder.
2. Disconnect the vacuum hose from the power brake.

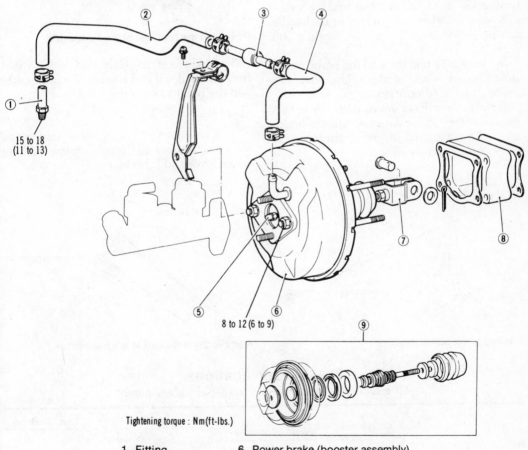

Tightening torque : Nm(ft-lbs.)

1. Fitting
2. Vacuum hose
3. Check valve
4. Vacuum hose
5. Push rod
6. Power brake (booster assembly)
7. Yoke
8. Booster spacer
9. Brake booster repair kit

Exploded view of the power brake unit

3. Remove the pin connecting the power brake operating rod to the pedal.

4. Loosen the nuts attaching the power brake to the fire wall and remove the power brake.

Installation is the reverse of removal. Apply sealer to all mounting surfaces before assembling.

Parking Brake
ADJUSTMENT

1. Relese the parking brake.

2. Jack up the vehicles and support it on jack stands.

3. Make sure the balancer that the front of the cable rides in is parallel with the center line of the truck. The clearance between the balancer and the crossmember should be about 8 in.

4. Adjust the parking brake by turning the turnbuckle on the cable. The brake is properly adjusted when the parking brake handle can be pulled 16 to 17 notches (approx. 4.3 in.)

5. After adjusting the parking brake, make sure there is slack in the cable when the brake is in the off position.

If the brake will not adjust correctly or fails on a hill, the rear brake shoes should be inspected for wear, oil or grease covered surfaces or malfunction.

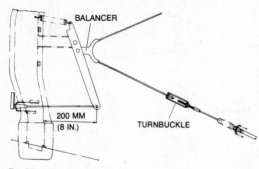

Parking brake adjustment

Parking Brake Cable
REMOVAL
Front

1. Fully release the parking brake lever to loosen the cable.

2. Remove the rear end of the front cable.

3. Remove the pull rod assembly and parking brake switch.

4. Withdraw the roller shaft and remove the roller.

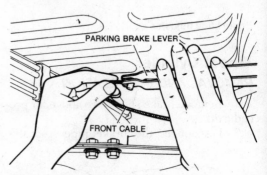

Removing the rear end of the front cable

5. Disconnect the front end of the cable from the pull rod and remove the front cable and the pull rod from the tube.

Rear

1. Disconnect the rear cable under the floor and remove the return spring, parking brake lever and cable clamp.

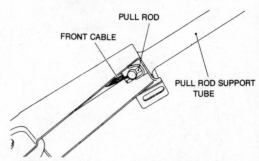

Remove the front end of the front cable

Brake Specifications
(All measurements are given in inches unless noted)

Model	Year	Lug Nut Torque (ft. lb.)	Master Cylinder Bore	Brake Disc Thickness			Brake Drum		Lining Thickness	
				Std	Min	Runout	Diameter	Maximum Wear	Front Min	Rear Min
All	1979–81	51–58	7/8	0.79	0.72	0.006	9.5	9.579	0.04 ①	0.04 ①

① Due to the variations in state inspection regulations, the minimum allowable lining thickness may be different from that recommended by the manufacturer.

2. Disassemble the rear brakes and remove the cable.

INSTALLATION
Front and Rear

1. Using the turnbuckle, adjust the cable length, so the balancer is parallel with the center line of the vehicle and the brake shoe does not drag.

2. When installing the cable make sure it is not twisted and apply an appropriate amount of chassis grease to all sliding parts.

3. Adjust the parking brake.

Body

10

You can repair most minor auto body damage yourself. Minor damage usually falls into one of several categories: (1) small scratches and dings in the paint that can be repaired without the use of body filler, (2) deep scratches and dents that require body filler, but do not require pulling, or hammering metal back into shape and (3) rust-out repairs. The repair sequences illustrated in this chapter are typical of these types of repairs. If you want to get involved in more complicated repairs including pulling or hammering sheet metal back into shape, you will probably need more detailed instructions. Chilton's *Minor Auto Body Repair, 2nd Edition* is a comprehensive guide to repairing auto body damage yourself.

TOOLS AND SUPPLIES

The list of tools and equipment you may need to fix minor body damage ranges from very basic hand tools to a wide assortment of specialized body tools. Most minor scratches, dings and rust holes can be fixed using an electric drill, wire wheel or grinder attachment, half-round plastic file, sanding block, various grades of sandpaper (#36, which is coarse through #600, which is fine) in both wet and dry types, auto body plastic,

primer, touch-up paint, spreaders, newspaper and masking tape.

Most manufacturers of auto body repair products began supplying materials to professionals. Their knowledge of the best, most-used products has been translated into body repair kits for the do-it-yourselfer. Kits are available from a number of manufacturers and contain the necessary materials in the required amounts for the repair identified on the package.

Kits are available for a wide variety of uses, including:

- Rusted out metal
- All purpose kit for dents and holes
- Dents and deep scratches
- Fiberglass repair kit
- Epoxy kit for restyling.

Kits offer the advantage of buying what you need for the job. There is little waste and little chance of materials going bad from not being used. The same manufacturers also merchandise all of the individual products used—spreaders, dent pullers, fiberglass cloth, polyester resin, cream hardener, body filler, body files, sandpaper, sanding discs and holders, primer, spray paint, etc.

CAUTION: *Most of the products you will be using contain harmful chemicals, so be extremely careful. Always read the complete label before opening the containers. When* *you put them away for future use, be sure they are out of children's reach!*

Most auto body repair kits contain all the materials you need to do the job right in the kit. So, if you have a small rust spot or dent you want to fix, check the contents of the kit before you run out and buy any additional tools.

ALIGNING BODY PANELS

Doors

There are several methods of adjusting doors. Your vehicle will probably use one of those illustrated.

Whenever a door is removed and is to be reinstalled, you should matchmark the position of the hinges on the door pillars. The holes of the hinges and/or the hinge attaching points are usually oversize to permit alignment of doors. The striker plate is also moveable, through oversize holes, permitting up-and-down, in-and-out and fore-and-aft movement. Fore-and-aft movement is made by adding or subtracting shims from behind the striker and pillar post. The striker should be adjusted so that the door closes fully and remains closed, yet enters the lock freely.

DOOR HINGES

Don't try to cover up poor door adjustment with a striker plate adjustment. The gap on each side of the door should be equal and uniform and there should be no metal-to-metal contact as the door is opened or closed.

1. Determine which hinge bolts must be loosened to move the door in the desired direction.

2. Loosen the hinge bolt(s) just enough to allow the door to be moved with a padded pry bar.

3. Move the door a small amount and check the fit, after tightening the bolts. Be sure that there is no bind or interference with adjacent panels.

4. Repeat this until the door is properly positioned, and tighten all the bolts securely.

Hood, Trunk or Tailgate

As with doors, the outline of hinges should be scribed before removal. The hood and trunk can be aligned by loosening the hinge bolts in their slotted mounting holes and moving the hood or trunk lid as necessary.

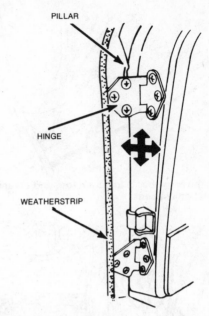

Door hinge adjustment

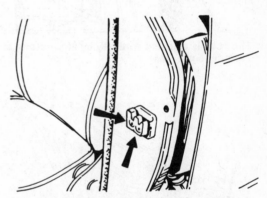

Move the door striker as indicated by arrows

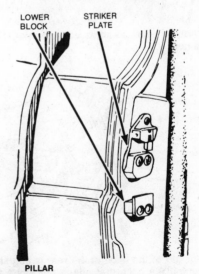

Striker plate and lower block

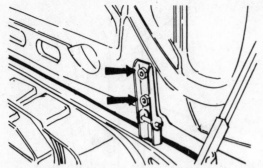

Loosen the hinge boots to permit fore-and-aft and horizontal adjustment

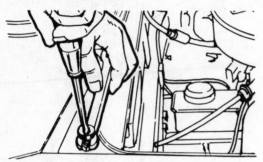

The hood is adjusted vertically by stop-screws at the front and/or rear

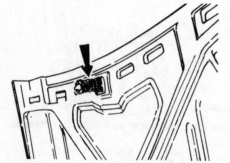

The hood pin can be adjusted for proper lock engagement

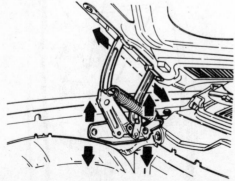

The height of the hood at the rear is adjusted by loosening the bolts that attach the hinge to the body and moving the hood up or down

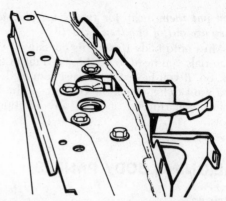

The base of the hood lock can also be re-positioned slightly to give more positive lock engagement

The hood and trunk have adjustable catch locations to regulate lock engagement. Bumpers at the front and/or rear of the hood provide a vertical adjustment and the hood lockpin can be adjusted for proper engagement.

The tailgate on the station wagon can be adjusted by loosening the hinge bolts in their slotted mounting holes and moving the tailgate on its hinges. The latchplate and latch striker at the bottom of the tailgate opening can be adjusted to stop rattle. An adjustable bumper is located on each side.

RUST, UNDERCOATING, AND RUSTPROOFING

Rust

Rust is an electrochemical process. It works on ferrous metals (iron and steel) from the inside out due to exposure of unprotected surfaces to air and moisture. The possibility of rust exists practically nationwide—anywhere humidity, industrial pollution or chemical salts are present, rust can form. In coastal areas, the problem is high humidity and salt air; in snowy areas, the problem is chemical salt (de-icer) used to keep the roads clear, and in industrial areas, sulphur dioxide is present in the air from industrial pollution and is changed to sulphuric acid when it rains. The rusting process is accelerated by high temperatures, especially in snowy areas, when vehicles are driven over slushy roads and then left overnight in a heated garage.

Automotive styling also can be a contributor to rust formation. Spot welding of panels creates small pockets that trap moisture and form an environment for rust formation. Fortunately, auto manufacturers have been working hard to increase the corrosion protection of their products. Galvanized sheet metal enjoys much wider use, along with the increased use of plastic and various rust retardant coatings. Manufacturers are also designing out areas in the body where rust-forming moisture can collect.

To prevent rust, you must stop it before it gets started. On new vehicles, there are two ways to accomplish this.

First, the car or truck should be treated with a commercial rustproofing compound. There are many different brands of franchised rustproofers, but most processes involve spraying a waxy "self-healing" compound under the chassis, inside rocker panels, inside doors and fender liners and similar places where rust is likely to form. Prices for a quality rustproofing job range from $100–$250, depending on the area, the brand name and the size of the vehicle.

Ideally, the vehicle should be rustproofed as soon as possible following the purchase. The surfaces of the car or truck have begun to oxidize and deteriorate during shipping. In addition, the car may have sat on a dealer's lot or on a lot at the factory, and once the rust has progressed past the stage of light, powdery surface oxidation rustproofing is not likely to be worthwhile. Professional rustproofers feel that once rust has formed, rustproofing will simply seal in moisture already present. Most franchised rustproofing operations offer a 3–5 year warranty against rust-through, but will not support that warranty if the rustproofing is not applied within three months of the date of manufacture.

Undercoating should not be mistaken for rustproofing. Undercoating is a black, tar-like substance that is applied to the underside of a vehicle. Its basic function is to deaden noises that are transmitted from under the car. It simply cannot get into the crevices and seams where moisture tends to collect. In fact, it may clog up drainage holes and ventilation passages. Some undercoatings also tend to crack or peel with age and only create more moisture and corrosion attracting pockets.

The second thing you should do immediately after purchasing the car is apply a paint sealant. A sealant is a petroleum based product marketed under a wide variety of brand names. It has the same protective properties as a good wax, but bonds to the paint with a chemically inert layer that seals it from the air. If air can't get at the surface, oxidation cannot start.

The paint sealant kit consists of a base coat and a conditioning coat that should be applied every 6–8 months, depending on the manufacturer. The base coat must be applied before waxing, or the wax must first be removed.

Third, keep a garden hose handy for your car in winter. Use it a few times on nice days during the winter for underneath areas, and it will pay big dividends when spring arrives. Spraying under the fenders and other areas which even car washes don't reach will help remove road salt, dirt and other build-ups which help breed rust. Adjust the nozzle to a high-force spray. An old brush will help break up residue, permitting it to be washed away more easily.

It's a somewhat messy job, but worth it in the long run because rust often starts in those hidden areas.

At the same time, wash grime off the door sills and, more importantly, the under portions of the doors, plus the tailgate if you have a station wagon or truck. Applying a coat of wax to those areas at least once before and once during winter will help fend off rust.

When applying the wax to the under parts of the doors, you will note small drain holes. These holes often are plugged with undercoating or dirt. Make sure they are cleaned out to prevent water build-up inside the doors. A small punch or penknife will do the job.

Water from the high-pressure sprays in car washes sometimes can get into the housings for parking and taillights, so take a close look. If they contain water merely loosen the retaining screws and the water should run out.

Repairing Scratches and Small Dents

Step 1. This dent (arrow) is typical of a deep scratch or minor dent. If deep enough, the dent or scratch can be pulled out or hammered out from behind. In this case no straightening is necessary

Step 2. Using an 80-grit grinding disc on an electric drill grind the paint from the surrounding area down to bare metal. This will provide a rough surface for the body filler to grab

Step 3. The area should look like this when you're finished grinding

Step 4. Mix the body filler and cream hardener according to the directions

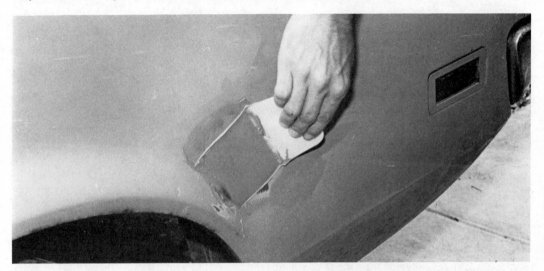

Step 5. Spread the body filler evenly over the entire area. Be sure to cover the area completely

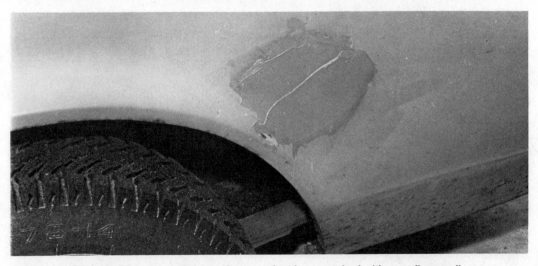

Step 6. Let the body filler dry until the surface can just be scratched with your fingernail

Step 7. Knock the high spots from the body filler with a body file

Step 8. Check frequently with the palm of your hand for high and low spots. If you wind up with low spots, you may have to apply another layer of filler

Step 9. Block sand the entire area with 320 grit paper

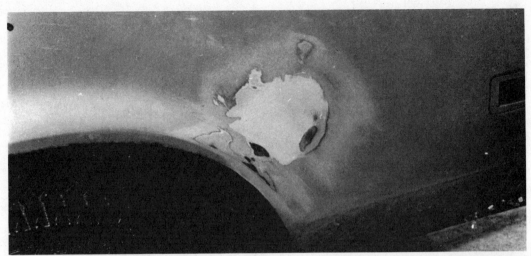

Step 10. When you're finished, the repair should look like this. Note the sand marks extending 2—3 inches out from the repaired area

Step 11. Prime the entire area with automotive primer

Step 12. The finished repair ready for the final paint coat. Note that the primer has covered the sanding marks (see Step 10). A repair of this size should be able to be spotpainted with good results

REPAIRING RUST HOLES

One thing you have to remember about rust: even if you grind away all the rusted metal in a panel, and repair the area with any of the kits available, *eventually* the rust will return. There are two reasons for this. One, rust is a chemical reaction that causes pressure under the repair from the inside out. That's how the blisters form. Two, the back side of the panel (and the repair) is wide open to moisture, and unpainted body filler acts like a sponge. That's why the best solution to rust problems is to remove the rusted panel and install a new one or have the rusted area cut out and a new piece of sheet metal welded in its place. The trouble with welding is the expense; sometimes it will cost more than the car or truck is worth.

One of the better solutions to do-it-yourself rust repair is the process using a fiberglass cloth repair kit (shown here). This will give a strong repair that resists cracking and moisture and is relatively easy to use. It can be used on large or small holes and also can be applied over contoured surfaces.

Step 1. Rust areas such as this are common and are easily fixed

Step 2. Grind away all traces of rust with a 24-grit grinding disc. Be sure to grind back 3—4 inches from the edge of the hole down to bare metal and be sure all traces of rust are removed

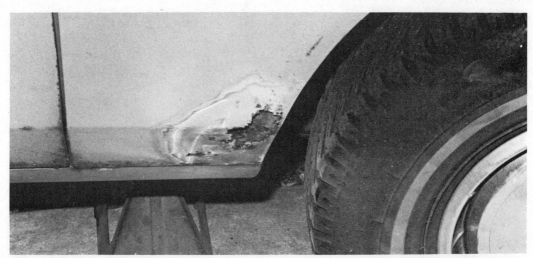

Step 3. Be sure all rust is removed from the edges of the metal. The edges must be ground back to un-rusted metal

Step 4. If you are going to use release film, cut a piece about 2″ larger than the area you have sanded. Place the film over the repair and mark the sanded area on the film. Avoid any unnecessary wrinkling of the film

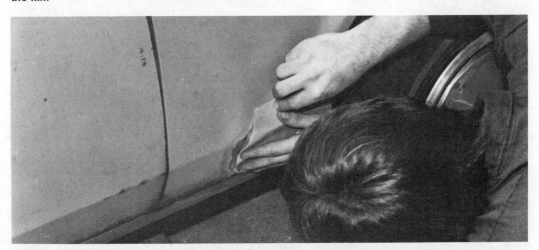

Step 5. Cut 2 pieces of fiberglass matte. One piece should be about 1″ smaller than the sanded area and the second piece should be 1″ smaller than the first. Use sharp scissors to avoid loose ends

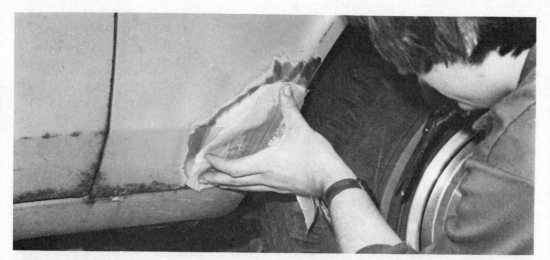

Step 6. Check the dimensions of the release film and cloth by holding them up to the repair area

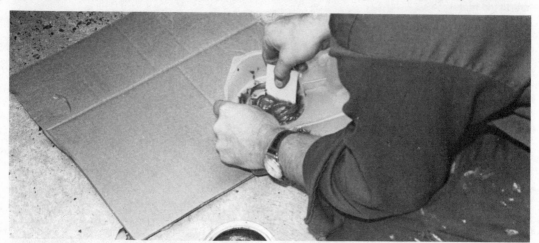

Step 7. Mix enough repair jelly and cream hardener in the mixing tray to saturate the fiberglass material or fill the repair area. Follow the directions on the container

Step 8. Lay the release sheet on a flat surface and spread an even layer of filler, large enough to cover the repair. Lay the smaller piece of fiberglass cloth in the center of the sheet and spread another layer of repair jelly over the fiberglass cloth. Repeat the operation for the larger piece of cloth. If the fiberglass cloth is not used, spread the repair jelly on the release film, concentrated in the middle of the repair

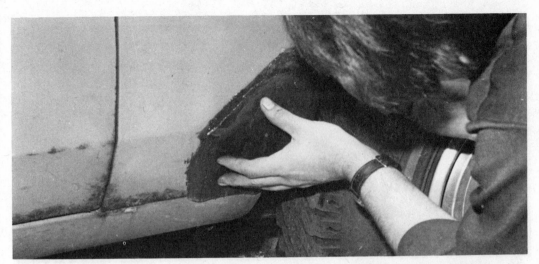

Step 9. Place the repair material over the repair area, with the release film facing outward

Step 10. Use a spreader and work from the center outward to smooth the material, following the body contours. Be sure to remove all air bubbles

Step 11. Wait until the repair has dried tack-free and peel off the release sheet. The ideal working temperature is 65—90° F. Cooler or warmer temperatures or high humidity may require additional curing time

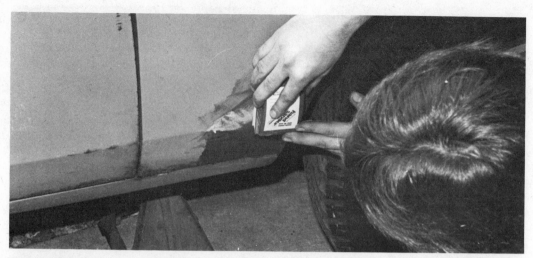

Step 12. Sand and feather-edge the entire area. The initial sanding can be done with a sanding disc on an electric drill if care is used. Finish the sanding with a block sander

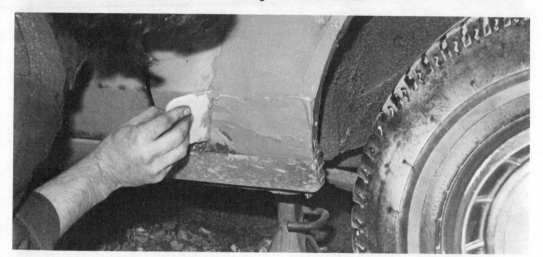

Step 13. When the area is sanded smooth, mix some topcoat and hardener and apply it directly with a spreader. This will give a smooth finish and prevent the glass matte from showing through the paint

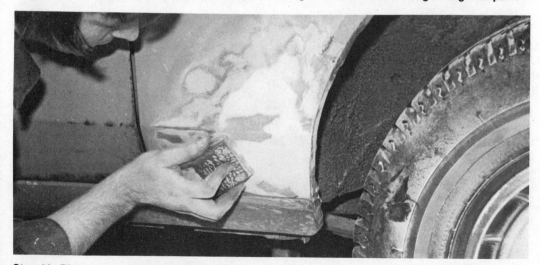

Step 14. Block sand the topcoat with finishing sandpaper

Step 15. To finish this repair, grind out the surface rust along the top edge of the rocker panel

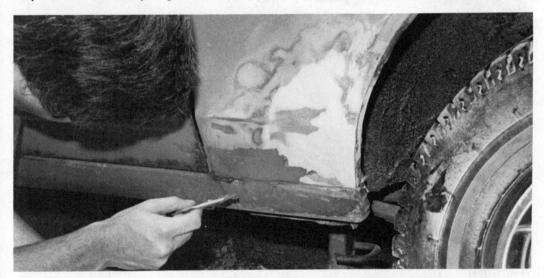

Step 16. Mix some more repair jelly and cream hardener and apply it directly over the surface

Step 17. When it dries tack-free, block sand the surface smooth

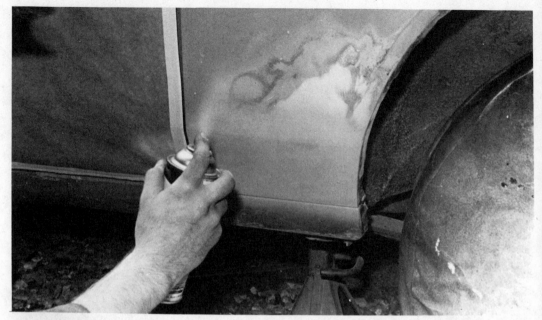

Step 18. If necessary, mask off adjacent panels and spray the entire repair with primer. You are now ready for a color coat

AUTO BODY CARE

There are hundreds—maybe thousands—of products on the market, all designed to protect or aid your car's finish in some manner. There are as many different products as there are ways to use them, but they all have one thing in common—the surface must be clean.

Washing

The primary ingredient for washing your car is water, preferably "soft" water. In many areas of the country, the local water supply is "hard" containing many minerals. The little rings or film that is left on your car's surface after it has dried is the result of "hard" water.

Since you usually can't change the local water supply, the next best thing is to dry the surface before it has a chance to dry itself.

Into the water you usually add soap. Don't use detergents or common, coarse soaps. Your car's paint never truly dries out, but is always evaporating residual oils into the air. Harsh detergents will remove these oils, causing the paint to dry faster than normal. Instead use warm water and a non-detergent soap made especially for waxed surfaces or a liquid soap made for waxed surfaces or a liquid soap made for washing dishes by hand.

Other products that can be used on painted surfaces include baking soda or plain soda water for stubborn dirt.

Wash the car completely, starting at the top, and rinse it completely clean. Abrasive grit should be loaded off under water pressure; scrubbing grit off will scratch the finish. The best washing tool is a sponge, cleaning mitt or soft towel. Whichever you choose, replace it often as each tends to absorb grease and dirt.

Other ways to get a better wash include:

• Don't wash your car in the sun or when the finish is hot.

• Use water pressure to remove caked-on dirt.

• Remove tree-sap and bird effluence immediately. Such substances will eat through wax, polish and paint.

One of the best implements to dry your car is a turkish towel or an old, soft bath towel. Anything with a deep nap will hold any dirt in suspension and not grind it into the paint.

Harder cloths will only grind the grit into the paint making more scratches. Always start drying at the top, followed by the hood and trunk and sides. You'll find there's always more dirt near the rocker panels and wheelwells which will wind up on the rest of the car if you dry these areas first.

Cleaners, Waxes and Polishes

Before going any farther you should know the function of various products.

Cleaners—remove the top layer of dead pigment or paint.

Rubbing or polishing compounds—used to remove stubborn dirt, get rid of minor scratches, smooth away imperfections and partially restore badly weathered paint.

Polishes—contain no abrasives or waxes; they shine the paint by adding oils to the paint.

Waxes—are a protective coating for the polish.

CLEANERS AND COMPOUNDS

Before you apply any wax, you'll have to remove oxidation, road film and other types of pollutants that washing alone will not remove.

The paint on your car never dries completely. There are always residual oils evaporating from the paint into the air. When enough oils are present in the paint, it has a healthy shine (gloss). When too many oils evaporate the paint takes on a whitish cast known as oxidation. The idea of polishing and waxing is to keep enough oil present in the painted surface to prevent oxidation; but when it occurs, the only recourse is to remove the top layer of "dead" paint, exposing the healthy paint underneath.

Products to remove oxidation and road film are sold under a variety of generic names—polishes, cleaner, rubbing compound, cleaner/polish, polish/cleaner, self-polishing wax, pre-wax cleaner, finish restorer and many more. Regardless of name there are two types of cleaners—abrasive cleaners (sometimes called polishing or rubbing compounds) that remove oxidation by grinding away the top layer of "dead" paint, or chemical cleaners that dissolve the "dead" pigment, allowing it to be wiped away.

Abrasive cleaners, by their nature, leave thousands of minute scratches in the finish, which must be polished out later. These should only be used in extreme cases, but are usually the only thing to use on badly oxidized paint finishes. Chemical cleaners are much milder but are not strong enough for severe cases of oxidation or weathered paint.

The most popular cleaners are liquid or paste abrasive polishing and rubbing compounds. Polishing compounds have a finer abrasive grit for medium duty work. Rubbing compounds are a coarser abrasive and for heavy duty work. Unless you are familiar with how to use compounds, be very careful. Excessive rubbing with any type of compound or cleaner can grind right through the paint to primer or bare metal. Follow the directions on the container—depending on type, the cleaner may or may not be OK for your paint. For example, some cleaners are not formulated for acrylic lacquer finishes.

When a small area needs compounding or heavy polishing, it's best to do the job by hand. Some people prefer a powered buffer for large areas. Avoid cutting through the paint along styling edges on the body. Small, hand operations where the compound is applied and rubbed using cloth folded into a thick ball allow you to work in straight lines along such edges.

To avoid cutting through on the edges when using a power buffer, try masking tape. Just cover the edge with tape while using power. Then finish the job by hand with the tape removed. Even then work carefully. The paint tends to be a lot thinner along the sharp ridges stamped into the panels.

Whether compounding by machine or by hand, only work on a small area and apply the compound sparingly. If the materials are spread too thin, or allowed to sit too long, they dry out. Once dry they lose the ability to deliver a smooth, clean finish. Also, dried out polish tends to cause the buffer to stick in one spot. This in turn can burn or cut through the finish.

WAXES AND POLISHES

Your car's finish can be protected in a number of ways. A cleaner/wax or polish/cleaner followed by wax or variations of each all provide good results. The two-step approach (polish followed by wax) is probably slightly better but consumes more time and effort. Properly fed with oils, your paint should never need cleaning, but despite the best polishing job, it won't last unless it's protected with wax. Without wax, polish must be renewed at least once a month to prevent oxidation. Years ago (some still swear by it today), the best wax was made from the Brazilian palm, the Carnuba, favored for its vegetable base and high melting point. However, modern synthetic waxes are harder, which means they protect against moisture better, and chemically inert silicone is used for a long lasting protection. The only problem with silicone wax is that it penetrates all layers of paint. To repaint or touch up a panel or car protected by silicone wax, you have to completely strip the finish to avoid "fisheyes."

Under normal conditions, silicone waxes will last 4–6 months, but you have to be careful of wax build-up from too much waxing. Too thick a coat of wax is just as bad as no wax at all; it stops the paint from breathing.

Combination cleaners/waxes have become popular lately because they remove the old layer of wax plus light oxidation, while putting on a fresh coat of wax at the same time. Some cleaners/waxes contain abrasive cleaners which require caution, although many cleaner/waxes use a chemical cleaner.

Applying Wax or Polish

You may view polishing and waxing your car as a pleasant way to spend an afternoon, or as a boring chore, but it has to be done to keep the paint on your car. Caring for the paint doesn't require special tools, but you should follow a few rules.

1. Use a good quality wax.

2. Before applying any wax or polish, be sure the surface is completely clean. Just because the car looks clean, doesn't mean it's ready for polish or wax.

3. If the finish on your car is weathered, dull, or oxidized, it will probably have to be compounded to remove the old or oxidized paint. If the paint is simply dulled from lack of care, one of the non-abrasive cleaners known as polishing compounds will do the trick. If the paint is severely scratched or really dull, you'll probably have to use a rubbing compound to prepare the finish for waxing. If you're not sure which one to use, use the polishing compound, since you can easily ruin the finish by using too strong a compound.

4. Don't apply wax, polish or compound in direct sunlight, even if the directions on the can say you can. Most waxes will not cure properly in bright sunlight and you'll probably end up with a blotchy looking finish.

5. Don't rub the wax off too soon. The result will be a wet, dull looking finish. Let the wax dry thoroughly before buffing it off.

6. A constant debate among car enthusiasts is how wax should be applied. Some maintain pastes or liquids should be applied in a circular motion, but body shop experts have long thought that this approach results in barely detectable circular abrasions, especially on cars that are waxed frequently. They advise rubbing in straight lines, especially if any kind of cleaner is involved.

7. If an applicator is not supplied with the wax, use a piece of soft cheesecloth or very soft lint-free material. The same applies to buffing the surface.

SPECIAL SURFACES

One-step combination cleaner and wax formulas shouldn't be used on many of the special surfaces which abound on cars. The one-step materials contain abrasives to achieve a clean surface under the wax top coat. The abrasives are so mild that you could clean a car every week for a couple of years without fear of rubbing through the paint. But this same level of abrasiveness might, through repeated use, damage decals used for special trim effects. This includes wide stripes, wood-grain trim and other appliques.

Painted plastics must be cleaned with care. If a cleaner is too aggressive it will cut through the paint and expose the primer. If bright trim such as polished aluminum or chrome is painted, cleaning must be performed with even greater care. If rubbing compound is being used, it will cut faster than polish.

Abrasive cleaners will dull an acrylic finish. The best way to clean these newer finishes is with a non-abrasive liquid polish. Only dirt and oxidation, not paint, will be removed.

Taking a few minutes to read the instructions on the can of polish or wax will help prevent making serious mistakes. Not all preparations will work on all surfaces. And some are intended for power application while others will only work when applied by hand.

Don't get the idea that just pouring on some polish and then hitting it with a buffer will suffice. Power equipment speeds the operation. But it also adds a measure of risk. It's very easy to damage the finish if you use the wrong methods or materials.

Caring for Chrome

Read the label on the container. Many products are formulated specifically for chrome, but others contain abrasives that will scratch the chrome finish. If it isn't recommended for chrome, don't use it.

Never use steel wool or kitchen soap pads to clean chrome. Be careful not to get chrome cleaner on paint or interior vinyl surfaces. If you do, get it off immediately.

Troubleshooting

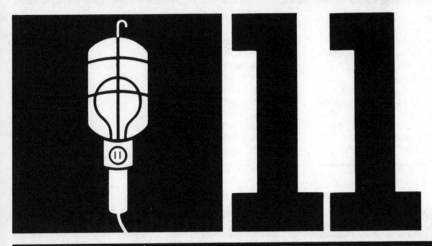

This section is designed to aid in the quick, accurate diagnosis of automotive problems. While automotive repairs can be made by many people, accurate troubleshooting is a rare skill for the amateur and professional alike.

In its simplest state, troubleshooting is an exercise in logic. It is essential to realize that an automobile is really composed of a series of systems. Some of these systems are interrelated; others are not. Automobiles operate within a framework of logical rules and physical laws, and the key to troubleshooting is a good understanding of all the automotive systems.

This section breaks the car or truck down into its component systems, allowing the problem to be isolated. The charts and diagnostic road maps list the most common problems and the most probable causes of trouble. Obviously it would be impossible to list every possible problem that could happen along with every possible cause, but it will locate MOST problems and eliminate a lot of unnecessary guesswork. The systematic format will locate problems within a given system, but, because many automotive systems are interrelated, the solution to your particular problem may be found in a number of systems on the car or truck.

USING THE TROUBLESHOOTING CHARTS

This book contains all of the specific information that the average do-it-yourself mechanic needs to repair and maintain his or her car or truck. The troubleshooting charts are designed to be used in conjunction with the specific procedures and information in the text. For instance, troubleshooting a point-type ignition system is fairly standard for all models, but you may be directed to the text to find procedures for troubleshooting an individual type of electronic ignition. You will also have to refer to the specification charts throughout the book for specifications applicable to your car or truck.

TOOLS AND EQUIPMENT

The tools illustrated in Chapter 1 (plus two more diagnostic pieces) will be adequate to troubleshoot most problems. The two other tools needed are a voltmeter and an ohmmeter. These can be purchased separately or in combination, known as a VOM meter.

In the event that other tools are required, they will be noted in the procedures.

Troubleshooting Engine Problems

See Chapters 2, 3, 4 for more information and service procedures.

Index to Systems

System	To Test	Group
Battery	Engine need not be running	1
Starting system	Engine need not be running	2
Primary electrical system	Engine need not be running	3
Secondary electrical system	Engine need not be running	4
Fuel system	Engine need not be running	5
Engine compression	Engine need not be running	6
Engine vacuum	Engine must be running	7
Secondary electrical system	Engine must be running	8
Valve train	Engine must be running	9
Exhaust system	Engine must be running	10
Cooling system	Engine must be running	11
Engine lubrication	Engine must be running	12

Index to Problems

Problem: Symptom	Begin at Specific Diagnosis, Number
Engine Won't Start:	
Starter doesn't turn	1.1, 2.1
Starter turns, engine doesn't	2.1
Starter turns engine very slowly	1.1, 2.4
Starter turns engine normally	3.1, 4.1
Starter turns engine very quickly	6.1
Engine fires intermittently	4.1
Engine fires consistently	5.1, 6.1
Engine Runs Poorly:	
Hard starting	3.1, 4.1, 5.1, 8.1
Rough idle	4.1, 5.1, 8.1
Stalling	3.1, 4.1, 5.1, 8.1
Engine dies at high speeds	4.1, 5.1
Hesitation (on acceleration from standing stop)	5.1, 8.1
Poor pickup	4.1, 5.1, 8.1
Lack of power	3.1, 4.1, 5.1, 8.1
Backfire through the carburetor	4.1, 8.1, 9.1
Backfire through the exhaust	4.1, 8.1, 9.1
Blue exhaust gases	6.1, 7.1
Black exhaust gases	5.1
Running on (after the ignition is shut off)	3.1, 8.1
Susceptible to moisture	4.1
Engine misfires under load	4.1, 7.1, 8.4, 9.1
Engine misfires at speed	4.1, 8.4
Engine misfires at idle	3.1, 4.1, 5.1, 7.1, 8.4

Sample Section

Test and Procedure	Results and Indications	Proceed to
4.1—Check for spark: Hold each spark plug wire approximately ¼″ from ground with gloves or a heavy, dry rag. Crank the engine and observe the spark.	If no spark is evident:	4.2
	If spark is good in some cases:	4.3
	If spark is good in all cases:	4.6

Specific Diagnosis

This section is arranged so that following each test, instructions are given to proceed to another, until a problem is diagnosed.

Section 1—Battery

Test and Procedure	Results and Indications	Proceed to
1.1—Inspect the battery visually for case condition (corrosion, cracks) and water level.	If case is cracked, replace battery:	**1.4**
	If the case is intact, remove corrosion with a solution of baking soda and water (**CAUTION:** *do not get the solution into the battery*), and fill with water:	**1.2**

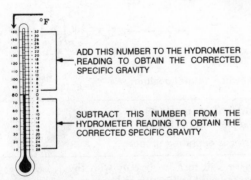

DIRT ON TOP OF BATTERY
CORROSION
PLUGGED VENT
LOOSE CABLE OR POSTS
CRACKS
LOW WATER LEVEL

Inspect the battery case

1.2—Check the battery cable connections: Insert a screwdriver between the battery post and the cable clamp. Turn the headlights on high beam, and observe them as the screwdriver is gently twisted to ensure good metal to metal contact.	If the lights brighten, remove and clean the clamp and post; coat the post with petroleum jelly, install and tighten the clamp:	**1.4**
	If no improvement is noted:	**1.3**

TESTING BATTERY CABLE CONNECTIONS USING A SCREWDRIVER

1.3—Test the state of charge of the battery using an individual cell tester or hydrometer.	If indicated, charge the battery. **NOTE:** *If no obvious reason exists for the low state of charge (i.e., battery age, prolonged storage), proceed to:*	**1.4**

°F

ADD THIS NUMBER TO THE HYDROMETER READING TO OBTAIN THE CORRECTED SPECIFIC GRAVITY

SUBTRACT THIS NUMBER FROM THE HYDROMETER READING TO OBTAIN THE CORRECTED SPECIFIC GRAVITY

Specific Gravity (@ 80° F.)

Minimum	Battery Charge
1.260	100% Charged
1.230	75% Charged
1.200	50% Charged
1.170	25% Charged
1.140	Very Little Power Left
1.110	Completely Discharged

The effects of temperature on battery specific gravity (left) and amount of battery charge in relation to specific gravity (right)

1.4—Visually inspect battery cables for cracking, bad connection to ground, or bad connection to starter.	If necessary, tighten connections or replace the cables:	**2.1**

Section 2—Starting System

See Chapter 3 for service procedures

Test and Procedure	Results and Indications	Proceed to
Note: Tests in Group 2 are performed with coil high tension lead disconnected to prevent accidental starting.		
2.1—Test the starter motor and solenoid: Connect a jumper from the battery post of the solenoid (or relay) to the starter post of the solenoid (or relay).	If starter turns the engine normally:	2.2
	If the starter buzzes, or turns the engine very slowly:	2.4
	If no response, replace the solenoid (or relay).	3.1
	If the starter turns, but the engine doesn't, ensure that the flywheel ring gear is intact. If the gear is undamaged, replace the starter drive.	3.1
2.2—Determine whether ignition override switches are functioning properly (clutch start switch, neutral safety switch), by connecting a jumper across the switch(es), and turning the ignition switch to "start".	If starter operates, adjust or replace switch:	3.1
	If the starter doesn't operate:	2.3
2.3—Check the ignition switch "start" position: Connect a 12V test lamp or voltmeter between the starter post of the solenoid (or relay) and ground. Turn the ignition switch to the "start" position, and jiggle the key.	If the lamp doesn't light or the meter needle doesn't move when the switch is turned, check the ignition switch for loose connections, cracked insulation, or broken wires. Repair or replace as necessary:	3.1
	If the lamp flickers or needle moves when the key is jiggled, replace the ignition switch.	3.3

Checking the ignition switch "start" position

STARTER RELAY
(IF EQUIPPED)

2.4—Remove and bench test the starter, according to specifications in the engine electrical section.	If the starter does not meet specifications, repair or replace as needed:	3.1
	If the starter is operating properly:	2.5
2.5—Determine whether the engine can turn freely: Remove the spark plugs, and check for water in the cylinders. Check for water on the dipstick, or oil in the radiator. Attempt to turn the engine using an 18″ flex drive and socket on the crankshaft pulley nut or bolt.	If the engine will turn freely only with the spark plugs out, and hydrostatic lock (water in the cylinders) is ruled out, check valve timing:	9.2
	If engine will not turn freely, and it is known that the clutch and transmission are free, the engine must be disassembled for further evaluation:	Chapter 3

Section 3—Primary Electrical System

Test and Procedure	Results and Indications	Proceed to
3.1—Check the ignition switch "on" position: Connect a jumper wire between the distributor side of the coil and ground, and a 12V test lamp between the switch side of the coil and ground. Remove the high tension lead from the coil. Turn the ignition switch on and jiggle the key.	If the lamp lights:	**3.2**
	If the lamp flickers when the key is jiggled, replace the ignition switch:	**3.3**
	If the lamp doesn't light, check for loose or open connections. If none are found, remove the ignition switch and check for continuity. If the switch is faulty, replace it:	**3.3**

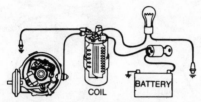

Checking the ignition switch "on" position

Test and Procedure	Results and Indications	Proceed to
3.2—Check the ballast resistor or resistance wire for an open circuit, using an ohmmeter. See Chapter 3 for specific tests.	Replace the resistor or resistance wire if the resistance is zero. **NOTE:** *Some ignition systems have no ballast resistor.*	**3.3**

 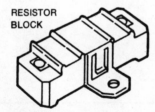

CALIBRATED
RESISTANCE
LEAD

RESISTOR
BLOCK

Two types of resistors

Test and Procedure	Results and Indications	Proceed to
3.3—On point-type ignition systems, visually inspect the breaker points for burning, pitting or excessive wear. Gray coloring of the point contact surfaces is normal. Rotate the crankshaft until the contact heel rests on a high point of the distributor cam and adjust the point gap to specifications. On electronic ignition models, remove the distributor cap and visually inspect the armature. Ensure that the armature pin is in place, and that the armature is on tight and rotates when the engine is cranked. Make sure there are no cracks, chips or rounded edges on the armature.	If the breaker points are intact, clean the contact surfaces with fine emery cloth, and adjust the point gap to specifications. If the points are worn, replace them. On electronic systems, replace any parts which appear defective. If condition persists:	**3.4**

Test and Procedure	Results and Indications	Proceed to
3.4—On point-type ignition systems, connect a dwell-meter between the distributor primary lead and ground. Crank the engine and observe the point dwell angle. On electronic ignition systems, conduct a stator (magnetic pickup assembly) test. See Chapter 3.	On point-type systems, adjust the dwell angle if necessary. **NOTE:** *Increasing the point gap decreases the dwell angle and vice-versa.*	**3.6**
	If the dwell meter shows little or no reading;	**3.5**
	On electronic ignition systems, if the stator is bad, replace the stator. If the stator is good, proceed to the other tests in Chapter 3.	

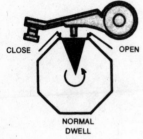 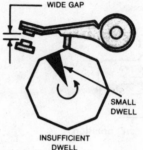 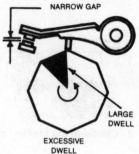

Dwell is a function of point gap

Test and Procedure	Results and Indications	Proceed to
3.5—On the point-type ignition systems, check the condenser for short: connect an ohmeter across the condenser body and the pigtail lead.	If any reading other than infinite is noted, replace the condenser	**3.6**

Checking the condenser for short

Test and Procedure	Results and Indications	Proceed to
3.6—Test the coil primary resistance: On point-type ignition systems, connect an ohmmeter across the coil primary terminals, and read the resistance on the low scale. Note whether an external ballast resistor or resistance wire is used. On electronic ignition systems, test the coil primary resistance as in Chapter 3.	Point-type ignition coils utilizing ballast resistors or resistance wires should have approximately 1.0 ohms resistance. Coils with internal resistors should have approximately 4.0 ohms resistance. If values far from the above are noted, replace the coil.	**4.1**

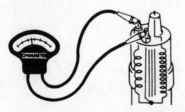

Check the coil primary resistance

Section 4—Secondary Electrical System
See Chapters 2–3 for service procedures

Test and Procedure	Results and Indications	Proceed to
4.1—Check for spark: Hold each spark plug wire approximately ¼″ from ground with gloves or a heavy, dry rag. Crank the engine, and observe the spark.	If no spark is evident:	**4.2**
	If spark is good in some cylinders:	**4.3**
	If spark is good in all cylinders:	**4.6**

Check for spark at the plugs

4.2—Check for spark at the coil high tension lead: Remove the coil high tension lead from the distributor and position it approximately ¼″ from ground. Crank the engine and observe spark. **CAUTION:** *This test should not be performed on engines equipped with electronic ignition.*	If the spark is good and consistent:	**4.3**
	If the spark is good but intermittent, test the primary electrical system starting at 3.3:	**3.3**
	If the spark is weak or non-existent, replace the coil high tension lead, clean and tighten all connections and retest. If no improvement is noted:	**4.4**
4.3—Visually inspect the distributor cap and rotor for burned or corroded contacts, cracks, carbon tracks, or moisture. Also check the fit of the rotor on the distributor shaft (where applicable).	If moisture is present, dry thoroughly, and retest per 4.1:	**4.1**
	If burned or excessively corroded contacts, cracks, or carbon tracks are noted, replace the defective part(s) and retest per 4.1:	**4.1**
	If the rotor and cap appear intact, or are only slightly corroded, clean the contacts thoroughly (including the cap towers and spark plug wire ends) and retest per 4.1:	
	If the spark is good in all cases:	**4.6**
	If the spark is poor in all cases:	**4.5**

Inspect the distributor cap and rotor

Test and Procedure	Results and Indications	Proceed to
4.4—Check the coil secondary resistance: On point-type systems connect an ohmmeter across the distributor side of the coil and the coil tower. Read the resistance on the high scale of the ohmmeter. On electronic ignition systems, see Chapter 3 for specific tests.	The resistance of a satisfactory coil should be between 4,000 and 10,000 ohms. If resistance is considerably higher (i.e., 40,000 ohms) replace the coil and retest per 4.1. **NOTE:** *This does not apply to high performance coils.*	

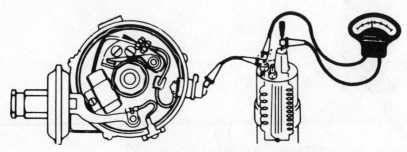

Testing the coil secondary resistance

4.5—Visually inspect the spark plug wires for cracking or brittleness. Ensure that no two wires are positioned so as to cause induction firing (adjacent and parallel). Remove each wire, one by one, and check resistance with an ohmmeter.	Replace any cracked or brittle wires. If any of the wires are defective, replace the entire set. Replace any wires with excessive resistance (over $8000\,\Omega$ per foot for suppression wire), and separate any wires that might cause induction firing.	**4.6**

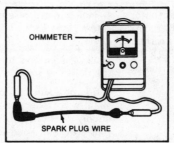

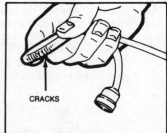

Misfiring can be the result of spark plug leads to adjacent, consecutively firing cylinders running parallel and too close together

On point-type ignition systems, check the spark plug wires as shown. On electronic ignitions, do not remove the wire from the distributor cap terminal; instead, test through the cap

Spark plug wires can be checked visually by bending them in a loop over your finger. This will reveal any cracks, burned or broken insulation. Any wire with cracked insulation should be replaced

4.6—Remove the spark plugs, noting the cylinders from which they were removed, and evaluate according to the color photos in the middle of this book.	See following.	**See following.**

Test and Procedure	Results and Indications	Proceed to

4.7—Examine the location of all the plugs.

The following diagrams illustrate some of the conditions that the location of plugs will reveal.

4.8

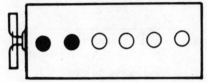

Two adjacent plugs are fouled in a 6-cylinder engine, 4-cylinder engine or either bank of a V-8. This is probably due to a blown head gasket between the two cylinders

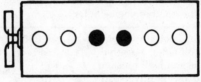

The two center plugs in a 6-cylinder engine are fouled. Raw fuel may be "boiled" out of the carburetor into the intake manifold after the engine is shut-off. Stop-start driving can also foul the center plugs, due to overly rich mixture. Proper float level, a new float needle and seat or use of an insulating spacer may help this problem

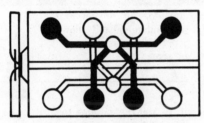

An unbalanced carburetor is indicated. Following the fuel flow on this particular design shows that the cylinders fed by the right-hand barrel are fouled from overly rich mixture, while the cylinders fed by the left-hand barrel are normal

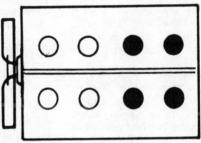

If the four rear plugs are overheated, a cooling system problem is suggested. A thorough cleaning of the cooling system may restore coolant circulation and cure the problem

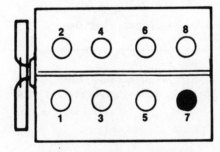

Finding one plug overheated may indicate an intake manifold leak near the affected cylinder. If the overheated plug is the second of two adjacent, consecutively firing plugs, it could be the result of ignition cross-firing. Separating the leads to these two plugs will eliminate cross-fire

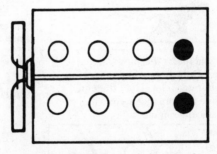

Occasionally, the two rear plugs in large, lightly used V-8's will become oil fouled. High oil consumption and smoky exhaust may also be noticed. It is probably due to plugged oil drain holes in the rear of the cylinder head, causing oil to be sucked in around the valve stems. This usually occurs in the rear cylinders first, because the engine slants that way

Test and Procedure	Results and Indications	Proceed to
4.8—Determine the static ignition timing. Using the crankshaft pulley timing marks as a guide, locate top dead center on the compression stroke of the number one cylinder.	The rotor should be pointing toward the No. 1 tower in the distributor cap, and, on electronic ignitions, the armature spoke for that cylinder should be lined up with the stator.	**4.8**
4.9—Check coil polarity: Connect a voltmeter negative lead to the coil high tension lead, and the positive lead to ground (**NOTE:** *Reverse the hook-up for positive ground systems*). Crank the engine momentarily. **Checking coil polarity**	If the voltmeter reads up-scale, the polarity is correct: If the voltmeter reads down-scale, reverse the coil polarity (switch the primary leads):	**5.1** **5.1**

Section 5—Fuel System
See Chapter 4 for service procedures

Test and Procedure	Results and Indications	Proceed to
5.1—Determine that the air filter is functioning efficiently: Hold paper elements up to a strong light, and attempt to see light through the filter.	Clean permanent air filters in solvent (or manufacturer's recommendation), and allow to dry. Replace paper elements through which light cannot be seen:	**5.2**
5.2—Determine whether a flooding condition exists: Flooding is identified by a strong gasoline odor, and excessive gasoline present in the throttle bore(s) of the carburetor.	If flooding is not evident: If flooding is evident, permit the gasoline to dry for a few moments and restart. If flooding doesn't recur: If flooding is persistent:	**5.3** **5.7** **5.5**
If the engine floods repeatedly, check the choke butterfly flap		
5.3—Check that fuel is reaching the carburetor: Detach the fuel line at the carburetor inlet. Hold the end of the line in a cup (not styrofoam), and crank the engine.	If fuel flows smoothly: If fuel doesn't flow (**NOTE:** *Make sure that there is fuel in the tank*), or flows erratically:	**5.7** **5.4**

Check the fuel pump by disconnecting the output line (fuel pump-to-carburetor) at the carburetor and operating the starter briefly

Test and Procedure	Results and Indications	Proceed to
5.4—Test the fuel pump: Disconnect all fuel lines from the fuel pump. Hold a finger over the input fitting, crank the engine (with electric pump, turn the ignition or pump on); and feel for suction.	If suction is evident, blow out the fuel line to the tank with low pressure compressed air until bubbling is heard from the fuel filler neck. Also blow out the carburetor fuel line (both ends disconnected):	**5.7**
	If no suction is evident, replace or repair the fuel pump: NOTE: *Repeated oil fouling of the spark plugs, or a no-start condition, could be the result of a ruptured vacuum booster pump diaphragm, through which oil or gasoline is being drawn into the intake manifold (where applicable).*	**5.7**
5.5—Occasionally, small specks of dirt will clog the small jets and orifices in the carburetor. With the engine cold, hold a flat piece of wood or similar material over the carburetor, where possible, and crank the engine.	If the engine starts, but runs roughly the engine is probably not run enough. If the engine won't start:	**5.9**
5.6—Check the needle and seat: Tap the carburetor in the area of the needle and seat.	If flooding stops, a gasoline additive (e.g., Gumout) will often cure the problem:	**5.7**
	If flooding continues, check the fuel pump for excessive pressure at the carburetor (according to specifications). If the pressure is normal, the needle and seat must be removed and checked, and/or the float level adjusted:	**5.7**
5.7—Test the accelerator pump by looking into the throttle bores while operating the throttle.	If the accelerator pump appears to be operating normally:	**5.8**
	If the accelerator pump is not operating, the pump must be reconditioned. Where possible, service the pump with the carburetor(s) installed on the engine. If necessary, remove the carburetor. Prior to removal:	**5.8**

Check for gas at the carburetor by looking down the carburetor throat while someone moves the accelerator

5.8—Determine whether the carburetor main fuel system is functioning: Spray a commercial starting fluid into the carburetor while attempting to start the engine.	If the engine starts, runs for a few seconds, and dies:	**5.9**
	If the engine doesn't start:	**6.1**

Test and Procedure	Results and Indications	Proceed to
5.9—Uncommon fuel system malfunctions: See below:	If the problem is solved:	6.1
	If the problem remains, remove and recondition the carburetor.	

Condition	Indication	Test	Prevailing Weather Conditions	Remedy
Vapor lock	Engine will not restart shortly after running.	Cool the components of the fuel system until the engine starts. Vapor lock can be cured faster by draping a wet cloth over a mechanical fuel pump.	Hot to very hot	Ensure that the exhaust manifold heat control valve is operating. Check with the vehicle manufacturer for the recommended solution to vapor lock on the model in question.
Carburetor icing	Engine will not idle, stalls at low speeds.	Visually inspect the throttle plate area of the throttle bores for frost.	High humidity, 32–40° F.	Ensure that the exhaust manifold heat control valve is operating, and that the intake manifold heat riser is not blocked.
Water in the fuel	Engine sputters and stalls; may not start.	Pump a small amount of fuel into a glass jar. Allow to stand, and inspect for droplets or a layer of water.	High humidity, extreme temperature changes.	For droplets, use one or two cans of commercial gas line anti-freeze. For a layer of water, the tank must be drained, and the fuel lines blown out with compressed air.

Section 6—Engine Compression
See Chapter 3 for service procedures

6.1—Test engine compression: Remove all spark plugs. Block the throttle wide open. Insert a compression gauge into a spark plug port, crank the engine to obtain the maximum reading, and record.	If compression is within limits on all cylinders:	7.1
	If gauge reading is extremely low on all cylinders:	6.2
	If gauge reading is low on one or two cylinders: (If gauge readings are identical and low on two or more adjacent cylinders, the head gasket must be replaced.)	6.2

Checking compression

6.2—Test engine compression (wet): Squirt approximately 30 cc. of engine oil into each cylinder, and retest per 6.1.	If the readings improve, worn or cracked rings or broken pistons are indicated:	See Chapter 3
	If the readings do not improve, burned or excessively carboned valves or a jumped timing chain are indicated:	7.1
	NOTE: *A jumped timing chain is often indicated by difficult cranking.*	

Section 7—Engine Vacuum
See Chapter 3 for service procedures

Test and Procedure	Results and Indications	Proceed to
7.1—Attach a vacuum gauge to the intake manifold beyond the throttle plate. Start the engine, and observe the action of the needle over the range of engine speeds.	See below.	**See below**

INDICATION: normal engine in good condition

Proceed to: 8.1

Normal engine
Gauge reading: steady, from 17–22 in./Hg.

INDICATION: sticking valves or ignition miss

Proceed to: 9.1, 8.3

Sticking valves
Gauge reading: intermittent fluctuation at idle

INDICATION: late ignition or valve timing, low compression, stuck throttle valve, leaking carburetor or manifold gasket

Proceed to: 6.1

Incorrect valve timing
Gauge reading: low (10–15 in./Hg) but steady

INDICATION: improper carburetor adjustment or minor intake leak.

Proceed to: 7.2

Carburetor requires adjustment
Gauge reading: drifting needle

INDICATION: ignition miss, blown cylinder head gasket, leaking valve or weak valve spring

Proceed to: 8.3, 6.1

Blown head gasket
Gauge reading: needle fluctuates as engine speed increases

INDICATION: burnt valve or faulty valve clearance. Needle will fall when defective valve operates

Proceed to: 9.1

Burnt or leaking valves
Gauge reading: steady needle, but drops regularly

INDICATION: choked muffler, excessive back pressure in system

Proceed to: 10.1

Clogged exhaust system
Gauge reading: gradual drop in reading at idle

INDICATION: worn valve guides

Proceed to: 9.1

Worn valve guides
Gauge reading: needle vibrates excessively at idle, but steadies as engine speed increases

White pointer = steady gauge hand

Black pointer = fluctuating gauge hand

Test and Procedure	Results and Indications	Proceed to
7.2—Attach a vacuum gauge per 7.1, and test for an intake manifold leak. Squirt a small amount of oil around the intake manifold gaskets, carburetor gaskets, plugs and fittings. Observe the action of the vacuum gauge.	If the reading improves, replace the indicated gasket, or seal the indicated fitting or plug:	**8.1**
	If the reading remains low:	**7.3**
7.3—Test all vacuum hoses and accessories for leaks as described in 7.2. Also check the carburetor body (dashpots, automatic choke mechanism, throttle shafts) for leaks in the same manner.	If the reading improves, service or replace the offending part(s):	**8.1**
	If the reading remains low:	**6.1**

Section 8—Secondary Electrical System
See Chapter 2 for service procedures

Test and Procedure	Results and Indications	Proceed to
8.1—Remove the distributor cap and check to make sure that the rotor turns when the engine is cranked. Visually inspect the distributor components.	Clean, tighten or replace any components which appear defective.	**8.2**
8.2—Connect a timing light (per manufacturer's recommendation) and check the dynamic ignition timing. Disconnect and plug the vacuum hose(s) to the distributor if specified, start the engine, and observe the timing marks at the specified engine speed.	If the timing is not correct, adjust to specifications by rotating the distributor in the engine: (Advance timing by rotating distributor opposite normal direction of rotor rotation, retard timing by rotating distributor in same direction as rotor rotation.)	**8.3**
8.3—Check the operation of the distributor advance mechanism(s): To test the mechanical advance, disconnect the vacuum lines from the distributor advance unit and observe the timing marks with a timing light as the engine speed is increased from idle. If the mark moves smoothly, without hesitation, it may be assumed that the mechanical advance is functioning properly. To test vacuum advance and/or retard systems, alternately crimp and release the vacuum line, and observe the timing mark for movement. If movement is noted, the system is operating.	If the systems are functioning:	**8.4**
	If the systems are not functioning, remove the distributor, and test on a distributor tester:	**8.4**
8.4—Locate an ignition miss: With the engine running, remove each spark plug wire, one at a time, until one is found that doesn't cause the engine to roughen and slow down.	When the missing cylinder is identified:	**4.1**

Section 9—Valve Train
See Chapter 3 for service procedures

Test and Procedure	Results and Indications	Proceed to
9.1—Evaluate the valve train: Remove the valve cover, and ensure that the valves are adjusted to specifications. A mechanic's stethoscope may be used to aid in the diagnosis of the valve train. By pushing the probe on or near push rods or rockers, valve noise often can be isolated. A timing light also may be used to diagnose valve problems. Connect the light according to manufacturer's recommendations, and start the engine. Vary the firing moment of the light by increasing the engine speed (and therefore the ignition advance), and moving the trigger from cylinder to cylinder. Observe the movement of each valve.	Sticking valves or erratic valve train motion can be observed with the timing light. The cylinder head must be disassembled for repairs.	**See Chapter 3**
9.2—Check the valve timing: Locate top dead center of the No. 1 piston, and install a degree wheel or tape on the crankshaft pulley or damper with zero corresponding to an index mark on the engine. Rotate the crankshaft in its direction of rotation, and observe the opening of the No. 1 cylinder intake valve. The opening should correspond with the correct mark on the degree wheel according to specifications.	If the timing is not correct, the timing cover must be removed for further investigation.	**See Chapter 3**

Section 10—Exhaust System

Test and Procedure	Results and Indications	Proceed to
10.1—Determine whether the exhaust manifold heat control valve is operating: Operate the valve by hand to determine whether it is free to move. If the valve is free, run the engine to operating temperature and observe the action of the valve, to ensure that it is opening.	If the valve sticks, spray it with a suitable solvent, open and close the valve to free it, and retest. If the valve functions properly: If the valve does not free, or does not operate, replace the valve:	**10.2** **10.2**
10.2—Ensure that there are no exhaust restrictions: Visually inspect the exhaust system for kinks, dents, or crushing. Also note that gases are flowing freely from the tailpipe at all engine speeds, indicating no restriction in the muffler or resonator.	Replace any damaged portion of the system:	**11.1**

Section 11—Cooling System
See Chapter 3 for service procedures

Test and Procedure	Results and Indications	Proceed to
11.1—Visually inspect the fan belt for glazing, cracks, and fraying, and replace if necessary. Tighten the belt so that the longest span has approximately ½″ play at its midpoint under thumb pressure (see Chapter 1).	Replace or tighten the fan belt as necessary:	**11.2**

Checking belt tension

11.2—Check the fluid level of the cooling system.	If full or slightly low, fill as necessary:	**11.5**
	If extremely low:	**11.3**
11.3—Visually inspect the external portions of the cooling system (radiator, radiator hoses, thermostat elbow, water pump seals, heater hoses, etc.) for leaks. If none are found, pressurize the cooling system to 14–15 psi.	If cooling system holds the pressure:	**11.5**
	If cooling system loses pressure rapidly, reinspect external parts of the system for leaks under pressure. If none are found, check dipstick for coolant in crankcase. If no coolant is present, but pressure loss continues:	**11.4**
	If coolant is evident in crankcase, remove cylinder head(s), and check gasket(s). If gaskets are intact, block and cylinder head(s) should be checked for cracks or holes.	
	If the gasket(s) is blown, replace, and purge the crankcase of coolant:	**12.6**
	NOTE: *Occasionally, due to atmospheric and driving conditions, condensation of water can occur in the crankcase. This causes the oil to appear milky white. To remedy, run the engine until hot, and change the oil and oil filter.*	
11.4—Check for combustion leaks into the cooling system: Pressurize the cooling system as above. Start the engine, and observe the pressure gauge. If the needle fluctuates, remove each spark plug wire, one at a time, noting which cylinder(s) reduce or eliminate the fluctuation.	Cylinders which reduce or eliminate the fluctuation, when the spark plug wire is removed, are leaking into the cooling system. Replace the head gasket on the affected cylinder bank(s).	

Pressurizing the cooling system

Test and Procedure	Results and Indications	Proceed to
11.5—Check the radiator pressure cap: Attach a radiator pressure tester to the radiator cap (wet the seal prior to installation). Quickly pump up the pressure, noting the point at which the cap releases.	If the cap releases within ± 1 psi of the specified rating, it is operating properly:	**11.6**
	If the cap releases at more than ± 1 psi of the specified rating, it should be replaced:	**11.6**

Checking radiator pressure cap

Test and Procedure	Results and Indications	Proceed to
11.6—Test the thermostat: Start the engine cold, remove the radiator cap, and insert a thermometer into the radiator. Allow the engine to idle. After a short while, there will be a sudden, rapid increase in coolant temperature. The temperature at which this sharp rise stops is the thermostat opening temperature.	If the thermostat opens at or about the specified temperature:	**11.7**
	If the temperature doesn't increase: (If the temperature increases slowly and gradually, replace the thermostat.)	**11.7**
11.7—Check the water pump: Remove the thermostat elbow and the thermostat, disconnect the coil high tension lead (to prevent starting), and crank the engine momentarily.	If coolant flows, replace the thermostat and retest per 11.6:	**11.6**
	If coolant doesn't flow, reverse flush the cooling system to alleviate any blockage that might exist. If system is not blocked, and coolant will not flow, replace the water pump.	

Section 12—Lubrication
See Chapter 3 for service procedures

Test and Procedure	Results and Indications	Proceed to
12.1—Check the oil pressure gauge or warning light: If the gauge shows low pressure, or the light is on for no obvious reason, remove the oil pressure sender. Install an accurate oil pressure gauge and run the engine momentarily.	If oil pressure builds normally, run engine for a few moments to determine that it is functioning normally, and replace the sender.	—
	If the pressure remains low:	**12.2**
	If the pressure surges:	**12.3**
	If the oil pressure is zero:	**12.3**
12.2—Visually inspect the oil: If the oil is watery or very thin, milky, or foamy, replace the oil and oil filter.	If the oil is normal:	**12.3**
	If after replacing oil the pressure remains low:	**12.3**
	If after replacing oil the pressure becomes normal:	—

Test and Procedure	Results and Indications	Proceed to
12.3—Inspect the oil pressure relief valve and spring, to ensure that it is not sticking or stuck. Remove and thoroughly clean the valve, spring, and the valve body.	If the oil pressure improves: If no improvement is noted:	— **12.4**
12.4—Check to ensure that the oil pump is not cavitating (sucking air instead of oil): See that the crankcase is neither over nor underfull, and that the pickup in the sump is in the proper position and free from sludge.	Fill or drain the crankcase to the proper capacity, and clean the pickup screen in solvent if necessary. If no improvement is noted:	**12.5**
12.5—Inspect the oil pump drive and the oil pump:	If the pump drive or the oil pump appear to be defective, service as necessary and retest per 12.1: If the pump drive and pump appear to be operating normally, the engine should be disassembled to determine where blockage exists:	**12.1** **See Chapter 3**
12.6—Purge the engine of ethylene glycol coolant: Completely drain the crankcase and the oil filter. Obtain a commercial butyl cellosolve base solvent, designated for this purpose, and follow the instructions precisely. Following this, install a new oil filter and refill the crankcase with the proper weight oil. The next oil and filter change should follow shortly thereafter (1000 miles).		

TROUBLESHOOTING EMISSION CONTROL SYSTEMS

See Chapter 4 for procedures applicable to individual emission control systems used on specific combinations of engine/transmission/model.

TROUBLESHOOTING THE CARBURETOR

See Chapter 4 for service procedures

Carburetor problems cannot be effectively isolated unless all other engine systems (particularly ignition and emission) are functioning properly and the engine is properly tuned.

Condition	Possible Cause
Engine cranks, but does not start	1. Improper starting procedure 2. No fuel in tank 3. Clogged fuel line or filter 4. Defective fuel pump 5. Choke valve not closing properly 6. Engine flooded 7. Choke valve not unloading 8. Throttle linkage not making full travel 9. Stuck needle or float 10. Leaking float needle or seat 11. Improper float adjustment
Engine stalls	1. Improperly adjusted idle speed or mixture **Engine hot** 2. Improperly adjusted dashpot 3. Defective or improperly adjusted solenoid 4. Incorrect fuel level in fuel bowl 5. Fuel pump pressure too high 6. Leaking float needle seat 7. Secondary throttle valve stuck open 8. Air or fuel leaks 9. Idle air bleeds plugged or missing 10. Idle passages plugged **Engine Cold** 11. Incorrectly adjusted choke 12. Improperly adjusted fast idle speed 13. Air leaks 14. Plugged idle or idle air passages 15. Stuck choke valve or binding linkage 16. Stuck secondary throttle valves 17. Engine flooding—high fuel level 18. Leaking or misaligned float
Engine hesitates on acceleration	1. Clogged fuel filter 2. Leaking fuel pump diaphragm 3. Low fuel pump pressure 4. Secondary throttle valves stuck, bent or misadjusted 5. Sticking or binding air valve 6. Defective accelerator pump 7. Vacuum leaks 8. Clogged air filter 9. Incorrect choke adjustment (engine cold)
Engine feels sluggish or flat on acceleration	1. Improperly adjusted idle speed or mixture 2. Clogged fuel filter 3. Defective accelerator pump 4. Dirty, plugged or incorrect main metering jets 5. Bent or sticking main metering rods 6. Sticking throttle valves 7. Stuck heat riser 8. Binding or stuck air valve 9. Dirty, plugged or incorrect secondary jets 10. Bent or sticking secondary metering rods. 11. Throttle body or manifold heat passages plugged 12. Improperly adjusted choke or choke vacuum break.
Carburetor floods	1. Defective fuel pump. Pressure too high. 2. Stuck choke valve 3. Dirty, worn or damaged float or needle valve/seat 4. Incorrect float/fuel level 5. Leaking float bowl

Condition	Possible Cause
Engine idles roughly and stalls	1. Incorrect idle speed 2. Clogged fuel filter 3. Dirt in fuel system or carburetor 4. Loose carburetor screws or attaching bolts 5. Broken carburetor gaskets 6. Air leaks 7. Dirty carburetor 8. Worn idle mixture needles 9. Throttle valves stuck open 10. Incorrectly adjusted float or fuel level 11. Clogged air filter
Engine runs unevenly or surges	1. Defective fuel pump 2. Dirty or clogged fuel filter 3. Plugged, loose or incorrect main metering jets or rods 4. Air leaks 5. Bent or sticking main metering rods 6. Stuck power piston 7. Incorrect float adjustment 8. Incorrect idle speed or mixture 9. Dirty or plugged idle system passages 10. Hard, brittle or broken gaskets 11. Loose attaching or mounting screws 12. Stuck or misaligned secondary throttle valves
Poor fuel economy	1. Poor driving habits 2. Stuck choke valve 3. Binding choke linkage 4. Stuck heat riser 5. Incorrect idle mixture 6. Defective accelerator pump 7. Air leaks 8. Plugged, loose or incorrect main metering jets 9. Improperly adjusted float or fuel level 10. Bent, misaligned or fuel-clogged float 11. Leaking float needle seat 12. Fuel leak 13. Accelerator pump discharge ball not seating properly 14. Incorrect main jets
Engine lacks high speed performance or power	1. Incorrect throttle linkage adjustment 2. Stuck or binding power piston 3. Defective accelerator pump 4. Air leaks 5. Incorrect float setting or fuel level 6. Dirty, plugged, worn or incorrect main metering jets or rods 7. Binding or sticking air valve 8. Brittle or cracked gaskets 9. Bent, incorrect or improperly adjusted secondary metering rods 10. Clogged fuel filter 11. Clogged air filter 12. Defective fuel pump

TROUBLESHOOTING FUEL INJECTION PROBLEMS

Each fuel injection system has its own unique components and test procedures, for which it is impossible to generalize. Refer to Chapter 4 of this Repair & Tune-Up Guide for specific test and repair procedures, if the vehicle is equipped with fuel injection.

TROUBLESHOOTING ELECTRICAL PROBLEMS

See Chapter 5 for service procedures

For any electrical system to operate, it must make a complete circuit. This simply means that the power flow from the battery must make a complete circle. When an electrical component is operating, power flows from the battery to the component, passes through the component causing it to perform its function (lighting a light bulb), and then returns to the battery through the ground of the circuit. This ground is usually (but not always) the metal part of the car or truck on which the electrical component is mounted.

Perhaps the easiest way to visualize this is to think of connecting a light bulb with two wires attached to it to the battery. If one of the two wires attached to the light bulb were attached to the negative post of the battery and the other were attached to the positive post of the battery, you would have a complete circuit. Current from the battery would flow to the light bulb, causing it to light, and return to the negative post of the battery.

The normal automotive circuit differs from this simple example in two ways. First, instead of having a return wire from the bulb to the battery, the light bulb returns the current to the battery through the chassis of the vehicle. Since the negative battery cable is attached to the chassis and the chassis is made of electrically conductive metal, the chassis of the vehicle can serve as a ground wire to complete the circuit. Secondly, most automotive circuits contain switches to turn components on and off as required.

Every complete circuit from a power source must include a component which is using the power from the power source. If you were to disconnect the light bulb from the wires and touch the two wires together (don't do this) the power supply wire to the component would be grounded before the normal ground connection for the circuit.

Because grounding a wire from a power source makes a complete circuit—less the required component to use the power—this phenomenon is called a short circuit. Common causes are: broken insulation (exposing the metal wire to a metal part of the car or truck), or a shorted switch.

Some electrical components which require a large amount of current to operate also have a relay in their circuit. Since these circuits carry a large amount of current, the thickness of the wire in the circuit (gauge size) is also greater. If this large wire were connected from the component to the control switch on the instrument panel, and then back to the component, a voltage drop would occur in the circuit. To prevent this potential drop in voltage, an electromagnetic switch (relay) is used. The large wires in the circuit are connected from the battery to one side of the relay, and from the opposite side of the relay to the component. The relay is normally open, preventing current from passing through the circuit. An additional, smaller, wire is connected from the relay to the control switch for the circuit. When the control switch is turned on, it grounds the smaller wire from the relay and completes the circuit. This closes the relay and allows current to flow from the battery to the component. The horn, headlight, and starter circuits are three which use relays.

It is possible for larger surges of current to pass through the electrical system of your car or truck. If this surge of current were to reach an electrical component, it could burn it out. To prevent this, fuses, circuit breakers or fusible links are connected into the current supply wires of most of the major electrical systems. When an electrical current of excessive power passes through the component's fuse, the fuse blows out and breaks the circuit, saving the component from destruction.

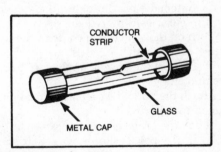

Typical automotive fuse

A circuit breaker is basically a self-repairing fuse. The circuit breaker opens the circuit the same way a fuse does. However, when either the short is removed from the circuit or the surge subsides, the circuit breaker resets itself and does not have to be replaced as a fuse does.

A fuse link is a wire that acts as a fuse. It is normally connected between the starter relay and the main wiring harness. This connection is usually under the hood. The fuse link (if installed) protects all the

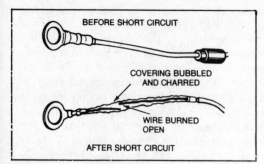

BEFORE SHORT CIRCUIT

COVERING BUBBLED
AND CHARRED

WIRE BURNED
OPEN

AFTER SHORT CIRCUIT

Most fusible links show a charred, melted insulation when they burn out

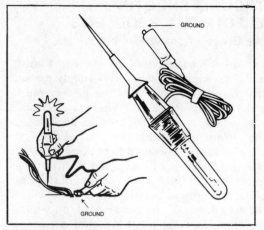

GROUND

GROUND

The test light will show the presence of current when touched to a hot wire and grounded at the other end

chassis electrical components, and is the probable cause of trouble when none of the electrical components function, unless the battery is disconnected or dead.

Electrical problems generally fall into one of three areas:

1. The component that is not functioning is not receiving current.

2. The component itself is not functioning.

3. The component is not properly grounded.

The electrical system can be checked with a test light and a jumper wire. A test light is a device that looks like a pointed screwdriver with a wire attached to it and has a light bulb in its handle. A jumper wire is a piece of insulated wire with an alligator clip attached to each end.

If a component is not working, you must follow a systematic plan to determine which of the three causes is the villain.

1. Turn on the switch that controls the inoperable component.

2. Disconnect the power supply wire from the component.

3. Attach the ground wire on the test light to a good metal ground.

4. Touch the probe end of the test light to the end of the power supply wire that was disconnected from the component. If the component is receiving current, the test light will go on.

NOTE: *Some components work only when the ignition switch is turned on.*

If the test light does not go on, then the problem is in the circuit between the battery and the component. This includes all the switches, fuses, and relays in the system. Follow the wire that runs back to the battery. The problem is an open circuit between the

battery and the component. If the fuse is blown and, when replaced, immediately blows again, there is a short circuit in the system which must be located and repaired. If there is a switch in the system, bypass it with a jumper wire. This is done by connecting one end of the jumper wire to the power supply wire into the switch and the other end of the jumper wire to the wire coming out of the switch. If the test light lights with the jumper wire installed, the switch or whatever was bypassed is defective.

NOTE: *Never substitute the jumper wire for the component, since it is required to use the power from the power source.*

5. If the bulb in the test light goes on, then the current is getting to the component that is not working. This eliminates the first of the three possible causes. Connect the power supply wire and connect a jumper wire from the component to a good metal ground. Do this with the switch which controls the component turned on, and also the ignition switch turned on if it is required for the component to work. If the component works with the jumper wire installed, then it has a bad ground. This is usually caused by the metal area on which the component mounts to the chassis being coated with some type of foreign matter.

6. If neither test located the source of the trouble, then the component itself is defective. Remember that for any electrical system to work, all connections must be clean and tight.

Troubleshooting Basic Turn Signal and Flasher Problems
See Chapter 5 for service procedures

Most problems in the turn signals or flasher system can be reduced to defective flashers or bulbs, which are easily replaced. Occasionally, the turn signal switch will prove defective.

F = Front   R = Rear   ● = Lights off   ○ = Lights on

Condition	Possible Cause
Turn signals light, but do not flash	Defective flasher
	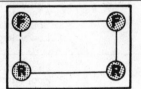
No turn signals light on either side	Blown fuse. Replace if defective. Defective flasher. Check by substitution. Open circuit, short circuit or poor ground.
	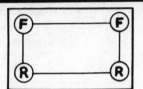
Both turn signals on one side don't work	Bad bulbs. Bad ground in both (or either) housings.
	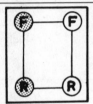
One turn signal light on one side doesn't work	Defective bulb. Corrosion in socket. Clean contacts. Poor ground at socket.
	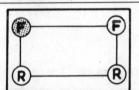
Turn signal flashes too fast or too slowly	Check any bulb on the side flashing too fast. A heavy-duty bulb is probably installed in place of a regular bulb. Check the bulb flashing too slowly. A standard bulb was probably installed in place of a heavy-duty bulb. Loose connections or corrosion at the bulb socket.
	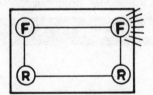
Indicator lights don't work in either direction	Check if the turn signals are working. Check the dash indicator lights. Check the flasher by substitution.

One indicator light doesn't light	On systems with one dash indicator: See if the lights work on the same side. Often the filaments have been reversed in systems combining stoplights with taillights and turn signals. Check the flasher by substitution. On systems with two indicators: Check the bulbs on the same side. Check the indicator light bulb. Check the flasher by substitution.

Troubleshooting Lighting Problems
See Chapter 5 for service procedures

Condition	Possible Cause
One or more lights don't work, but others do	1. Defective bulb(s) 2. Blown fuse(s) 3. Dirty fuse clips or light sockets 4. Poor ground circuit
Lights burn out quickly	1. Incorrect voltage regulator setting or defective regulator 2. Poor battery/alternator connections
Lights go dim	1. Low/discharged battery 2. Alternator not charging 3. Corroded sockets or connections 4. Low voltage output
Lights flicker	1. Loose connection 2. Poor ground. (Run ground wire from light housing to frame) 3. Circuit breaker operating (short circuit)
Lights "flare"—Some flare is normal on acceleration—If excessive, see "Lights Burn Out Quickly"	High voltage setting
Lights glare—approaching drivers are blinded	1. Lights adjusted too high 2. Rear springs or shocks sagging 3. Rear tires soft

Troubleshooting Dash Gauge Problems
Most problems can be traced to a defective sending unit or faulty wiring. Occasionally, the gauge itself is at fault. See Chapter 5 for service procedures.

Condition	Possible Cause
COOLANT TEMPERATURE GAUGE	
Gauge reads erratically or not at all	1. Loose or dirty connections 2. Defective sending unit. 3. Defective gauge. To test a bi-metal gauge, remove the wire from the sending unit. Ground the wire for an instant. If the gauge registers, replace the sending unit. To test a magnetic gauge, disconnect the wire at the sending unit. With ignition ON gauge should register COLD. Ground the wire; gauge should register HOT.
AMMETER GAUGE—TURN HEADLIGHTS ON (DO NOT START ENGINE). NOTE REACTION	
Ammeter shows charge Ammeter shows discharge Ammeter does not move	1. Connections reversed on gauge 2. Ammeter is OK 3. Loose connections or faulty wiring 4. Defective gauge

Condition	Possible Cause

OIL PRESSURE GAUGE

| Gauge does not register or is inaccurate | 1. On mechanical gauge, Bourdon tube may be bent or kinked.
2. Low oil pressure. Remove sending unit. Idle the engine briefly. If no oil flows from sending unit hole, problem is in engine.
3. Defective gauge. Remove the wire from the sending unit and ground it for an instant with the ignition ON. A good gauge will go to the top of the scale.
4. Defective wiring. Check the wiring to the gauge. If it's OK and the gauge doesn't register when grounded, replace the gauge.
5. Defective sending unit. |

ALL GAUGES

| All gauges do not operate

All gauges read low or erratically
All gauges pegged | 1. Blown fuse
2. Defective instrument regulator
3. Defective or dirty instrument voltage regulator
4. Loss of ground between instrument voltage regulator and frame
5. Defective instrument regulator |

WARNING LIGHTS

| Light(s) do not come on when ignition is ON, but engine is not started

Light comes on with engine running | 1. Defective bulb
2. Defective wire
3. Defective sending unit. Disconnect the wire from the sending unit and ground it. Replace the sending unit if the light comes on with the ignition ON.
4. Problem in individual system
5. Defective sending unit |

Troubleshooting Clutch Problems

It is false economy to replace individual clutch components. The pressure plate, clutch plate and throwout bearing should be replaced as a set, and the flywheel face inspected, whenever the clutch is overhauled. See Chapter 6 for service procedures.

Condition	Possible Cause
Clutch chatter	1. Grease on driven plate (disc) facing 2. Binding clutch linkage or cable 3. Loose, damaged facings on driven plate (disc) 4. Engine mounts loose 5. Incorrect height adjustment of pressure plate release levers 6. Clutch housing or housing to transmission adapter misalignment 7. Loose driven plate hub
Clutch grabbing	1. Oil, grease on driven plate (disc) facing 2. Broken pressure plate 3. Warped or binding driven plate. Driven plate binding on clutch shaft
Clutch slips	1. Lack of lubrication in clutch linkage or cable (linkage or cable binds, causes incomplete engagement) 2. Incorrect pedal, or linkage adjustment 3. Broken pressure plate springs 4. Weak pressure plate springs 5. Grease on driven plate facings (disc)

Troubleshooting Clutch Problems (cont.)

Condition	Possible Cause
Incomplete clutch release	1. Incorrect pedal or linkage adjustment or linkage or cable binding 2. Incorrect height adjustment on pressure plate release levers 3. Loose, broken facings on driven plate (disc) 4. Bent, dished, warped driven plate caused by overheating
Grinding, whirring grating noise when pedal is depressed	1. Worn or defective throwout bearing 2. Starter drive teeth contacting flywheel ring gear teeth. Look for milled or polished teeth on ring gear.
Squeal, howl, trumpeting noise when pedal is being released (occurs during first inch to inch and one-half of pedal travel)	Pilot bushing worn or lack of lubricant. If bushing appears OK, polish bushing with emery cloth, soak lube wick in oil, lube bushing with oil, apply film of chassis grease to clutch shaft pilot hub, reassemble. NOTE: Bushing wear may be due to misalignment of clutch housing or housing to transmission adapter
Vibration or clutch pedal pulsation with clutch disengaged (pedal fully depressed)	1. Worn or defective engine transmission mounts 2. Flywheel run out. (Flywheel run out at face not to exceed 0.005″) 3. Damaged or defective clutch components

Troubleshooting Manual Transmission Problems
See Chapter 6 for service procedures

Condition	Possible Cause
Transmission jumps out of gear	1. Misalignment of transmission case or clutch housing. 2. Worn pilot bearing in crankshaft. 3. Bent transmission shaft. 4. Worn high speed sliding gear. 5. Worn teeth or end-play in clutch shaft. 6. Insufficient spring tension on shifter rail plunger. 7. Bent or loose shifter fork. 8. Gears not engaging completely. 9. Loose or worn bearings on clutch shaft or mainshaft. 10. Worn gear teeth. 11. Worn or damaged detent balls.
Transmission sticks in gear	1. Clutch not releasing fully. 2. Burred or battered teeth on clutch shaft, or sliding sleeve. 3. Burred or battered transmission mainshaft. 4. Frozen synchronizing clutch. 5. Stuck shifter rail plunger. 6. Gearshift lever twisting and binding shifter rail. 7. Battered teeth on high speed sliding gear or on sleeve. 8. Improper lubrication, or lack of lubrication. 9. Corroded transmission parts. 10. Defective mainshaft pilot bearing. 11. Locked gear bearings will give same effect as stuck in gear.
Transmission gears will not synchronize	1. Binding pilot bearing on mainshaft, will synchronize in high gear only. 2. Clutch not releasing fully. 3. Detent spring weak or broken. 4. Weak or broken springs under balls in sliding gear sleeve. 5. Binding bearing on clutch shaft, or binding countershaft. 6. Binding pilot bearing in crankshaft. 7. Badly worn gear teeth. 8. Improper lubrication. 9. Constant mesh gear not turning freely on transmission mainshaft. Will synchronize in that gear only.

Condition	Possible Cause 0
Gears spinning when shifting into gear from neutral	1. Clutch not releasing fully. 2. In some cases an extremely light lubricant in transmission will cause gears to continue to spin for a short time after clutch is released. 3. Binding pilot bearing in crankshaft.
Transmission noisy in all gears	1. Insufficient lubricant, or improper lubricant. 2. Worn countergear bearings. 3. Worn or damaged main drive gear or countergear. 4. Damaged main drive gear or mainshaft bearings. 5. Worn or damaged countergear anti-lash plate.
Transmission noisy in neutral only	1. Damaged main drive gear bearing. 2. Damaged or loose mainshaft pilot bearing. 3. Worn or damaged countergear anti-lash plate. 4. Worn countergear bearings.
Transmission noisy in one gear only	1. Damaged or worn constant mesh gears. 2. Worn or damaged countergear bearings. 3. Damaged or worn synchronizer.
Transmission noisy in reverse only	1. Worn or damaged reverse idler gear or idler bushing. 2. Worn or damaged mainshaft reverse gear. 3. Worn or damaged reverse countergear. 4. Damaged shift mechanism.

TROUBLESHOOTING AUTOMATIC TRANSMISSION PROBLEMS

Keeping alert to changes in the operating characteristics of the transmission (changing shift points, noises, etc.) can prevent small problems from becoming large ones. If the problem cannot be traced to loose bolts, fluid level, misadjusted linkage, clogged filters or similar problems, you should probably seek professional service.

Transmission Fluid Indications

The appearance and odor of the transmission fluid can give valuable clues to the overall condition of the transmission. Always note the appearance of the fluid when you check the fluid level or change the fluid. Rub a small amount of fluid between your fingers to feel for grit and smell the fluid on the dipstick.

If the fluid appears:	It indicates:
Clear and red colored	Normal operation
Discolored (extremely dark red or brownish) or smells burned	Band or clutch pack failure, usually caused by an overheated transmission. Hauling very heavy loads with insufficient power or failure to change the fluid often result in overheating. Do not confuse this appearance with newer fluids that have a darker red color and a strong odor (though not a burned odor).
Foamy or aerated (light in color and full of bubbles)	1. The level is too high (gear train is churning oil) 2. An internal air leak (air is mixing with the fluid). Have the transmission checked professionally.
Solid residue in the fluid	Defective bands, clutch pack or bearings. Bits of band material or metal abrasives are clinging to the dipstick. Have the transmission checked professionally.
Varnish coating on the dipstick	The transmission fluid is overheating

TROUBLESHOOTING DRIVE AXLE PROBLEMS

First, determine when the noise is most noticeable.

Drive Noise: Produced under vehicle acceleration.

Coast Noise: Produced while coasting with a closed throttle.

Float Noise: Occurs while maintaining constant speed (just enough to keep speed constant) on a level road.

External Noise Elimination

It is advisable to make a thorough road test to determine whether the noise originates in the rear axle or whether it originates from the tires, engine, transmission, wheel bearings or road surface. Noise originating from other places cannot be corrected by servicing the rear axle.

ROAD NOISE

Brick or rough surfaced concrete roads produce noises that seem to come from the rear axle. Road noise is usually identical in Drive or Coast and driving on a different type of road will tell whether the road is the problem.

TIRE NOISE

Tire noise can be mistaken as rear axle noise, even though the tires on the front are at fault. Snow tread and mud tread tires or tires worn unevenly will frequently cause vibrations which seem to originate elsewhere; *temporarily, and for test purposes only*, inflate the tires to 40–50 lbs. This will significantly alter the noise produced by the tires, but will not alter noise from the rear axle. Noises from the rear axle will normally cease at speeds below 30 mph on coast, while tire noise will continue at lower tone as speed is decreased. The rear axle noise will usually change from drive conditions to coast conditions, while tire noise will not. Do not forget to lower the tire pressure to normal after the test is complete.

ENGINE/TRANSMISSION NOISE

Determine at what speed the noise is most pronounced, then stop in a quiet place. With the transmission in Neutral, run the engine through speeds corresponding to road speeds where the noise was noticed. Noises produced with the vehicle standing still are coming from the engine or transmission.

FRONT WHEEL BEARINGS

Front wheel bearing noises, sometimes confused with rear axle noises, will not change when comparing drive and coast conditions. While holding the speed steady, lightly apply the footbrake. This will often cause wheel bearing noise to lessen, as some of the weight is taken off the bearing. Front wheel bearings are easily checked by jacking up the wheels and spinning the wheels. Shaking the wheels will also determine if the wheel bearings are excessively loose.

REAR AXLE NOISES

Eliminating other possible sources can narrow the cause to the rear axle, which normally produces noise from worn gears or bearings. Gear noises tend to peak in a narrow speed range, while bearing noises will usually vary in pitch with engine speeds.

Noise Diagnosis

The Noise Is:	Most Probably Produced By:
1. Identical under Drive or Coast	Road surface, tires or front wheel bearings
2. Different depending on road surface	Road surface or tires
3. Lower as speed is lowered	Tires
4. Similar when standing or moving	Engine or transmission
5. A vibration	Unbalanced tires, rear wheel bearing, unbalanced driveshaft or worn U-joint
6. A knock or click about every two tire revolutions	Rear wheel bearing
7. Most pronounced on turns	Damaged differential gears
8. A steady low-pitched whirring or scraping, starting at low speeds	Damaged or worn pinion bearing
9. A chattering vibration on turns	Wrong differential lubricant or worn clutch plates (limited slip rear axle)
10. Noticed only in Drive, Coast or Float conditions	Worn ring gear and/or pinion gear

Troubleshooting Steering & Suspension Problems

Condition	Possible Cause
Hard steering (wheel is hard to turn)	1. Improper tire pressure 2. Loose or glazed pump drive belt 3. Low or incorrect fluid 4. Loose, bent or poorly lubricated front end parts 5. Improper front end alignment (excessive caster) 6. Bind in steering column or linkage 7. Kinked hydraulic hose 8. Air in hydraulic system 9. Low pump output or leaks in system 10. Obstruction in lines 11. Pump valves sticking or out of adjustment 12. Incorrect wheel alignment
Loose steering (too much play in steering wheel)	1. Loose wheel bearings 2. Faulty shocks 3. Worn linkage or suspension components 4. Loose steering gear mounting or linkage points 5. Steering mechanism worn or improperly adjusted 6. Valve spool improperly adjusted 7. Worn ball joints, tie-rod ends, etc.
Veers or wanders (pulls to one side with hands off steering wheel)	1. Improper tire pressure 2. Improper front end alignment 3. Dragging or improperly adjusted brakes 4. Bent frame 5. Improper rear end alignment 6. Faulty shocks or springs 7. Loose or bent front end components 8. Play in Pitman arm 9. Steering gear mountings loose 10. Loose wheel bearings 11. Binding Pitman arm 12. Spool valve sticking or improperly adjusted 13. Worn ball joints
Wheel oscillation or vibration transmitted through steering wheel	1. Low or uneven tire pressure 2. Loose wheel bearings 3. Improper front end alignment 4. Bent spindle 5. Worn, bent or broken front end components 6. Tires out of round or out of balance 7. Excessive lateral runout in disc brake rotor 8. Loose or bent shock absorber or strut
Noises (see also "Troubleshooting Drive Axle Problems")	1. Loose belts 2. Low fluid, air in system 3. Foreign matter in system 4. Improper lubrication 5. Interference or chafing in linkage 6. Steering gear mountings loose 7. Incorrect adjustment or wear in gear box 8. Faulty valves or wear in pump 9. Kinked hydraulic lines 10. Worn wheel bearings
Poor return of steering	1. Over-inflated tires 2. Improperly aligned front end (excessive caster) 3. Binding in steering column 4. No lubrication in front end 5. Steering gear adjusted too tight
Uneven tire wear (see "How To Read Tire Wear")	1. Incorrect tire pressure 2. Improperly aligned front end 3. Tires out-of-balance 4. Bent or worn suspension parts

HOW TO READ TIRE WEAR

The way your tires wear is a good indicator of other parts of the suspension. Abnormal wear patterns are often caused by the need for simple tire maintenance, or for front end alignment.

Excessive wear at the center of the tread indicates that the air pressure in the tire is consistently too high. The tire is riding on the center of the tread and wearing it prematurely. Occasionally, this wear pattern can result from outrageously wide tires on narrow rims. The cure for this is to replace either the tires or the wheels.

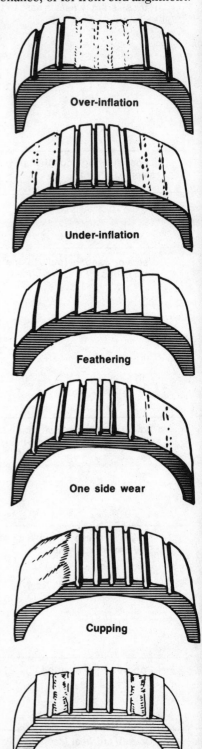

Over-inflation

This type of wear usually results from consistent under-inflation. When a tire is under-inflated, there is too much contact with the road by the outer treads, which wear prematurely. When this type of wear occurs, and the tire pressure is known to be consistently correct, a bent or worn steering component or the need for wheel alignment could be indicated.

Under-inflation

Feathering is a condition when the edge of each tread rib develops a slightly rounded edge on one side and a sharp edge on the other. By running your hand over the tire, you can usually feel the sharper edges before you'll be able to see them. The most common causes of feathering are incorrect toe-in setting or deteriorated bushings in the front suspension.

Feathering

When an inner or outer rib wears faster than the rest of the tire, the need for wheel alignment is indicated. There is excessive camber in the front suspension, causing the wheel to lean too much putting excessive load on one side of the tire. Misalignment could also be due to sagging springs, worn ball joints, or worn control arm bushings. Be sure the vehicle is loaded the way it's normally driven when you have the wheels aligned.

One side wear

Cups or scalloped dips appearing around the edge of the tread almost always indicate worn (sometimes bent) suspension parts. Adjustment of wheel alignment alone will seldom cure the problem. Any worn component that connects the wheel to the suspension can cause this type of wear. Occasionally, wheels that are out of balance will wear like this, but wheel imbalance usually shows up as bald spots between the outside edges and center of the tread.

Cupping

Second-rib wear is usually found only in radial tires, and appears where the steel belts end in relation to the tread. It can be kept to a minimum by paying careful attention to tire pressure and frequently rotating the tires. This is often considered normal wear but excessive amounts indicate that the tires are too wide for the wheels.

Second-rib wear

Troubleshooting Disc Brake Problems

Condition	Possible Cause
Noise—groan—brake noise emanating when slowly releasing brakes (creep-groan)	Not detrimental to function of disc brakes—no corrective action required. (This noise may be eliminated by slightly increasing or decreasing brake pedal efforts.)
Rattle—brake noise or rattle emanating at low speeds on rough roads, (front wheels only).	1. Shoe anti-rattle spring missing or not properly positioned. 2. Excessive clearance between shoe and caliper. 3. Soft or broken caliper seals. 4. Deformed or misaligned disc. 5. Loose caliper.
Scraping	1. Mounting bolts too long. 2. Loose wheel bearings. 3. Bent, loose, or misaligned splash shield.
Front brakes heat up during driving and fail to release	1. Operator riding brake pedal. 2. Stop light switch improperly adjusted. 3. Sticking pedal linkage. 4. Frozen or seized piston. 5. Residual pressure valve in master cylinder. 6. Power brake malfunction. 7. Proportioning valve malfunction.
Leaky brake caliper	1. Damaged or worn caliper piston seal. 2. Scores or corrosion on surface of cylinder bore.
Grabbing or uneven brake action—Brakes pull to one side	1. Causes listed under "Brakes Pull". 2. Power brake malfunction. 3. Low fluid level in master cylinder. 4. Air in hydraulic system. 5. Brake fluid, oil or grease on linings. 6. Unmatched linings. 7. Distorted brake pads. 8. Frozen or seized pistons. 9. Incorrect tire pressure. 10. Front end out of alignment. 11. Broken rear spring. 12. Brake caliper pistons sticking. 13. Restricted hose or line. 14. Caliper not in proper alignment to braking disc. 15. Stuck or malfunctioning metering valve. 16. Soft or broken caliper seals. 17. Loose caliper.
Brake pedal can be depressed without braking effect	1. Air in hydraulic system or improper bleeding procedure. 2. Leak past primary cup in master cylinder. 3. Leak in system. 4. Rear brakes out of adjustment. 5. Bleeder screw open.
Excessive pedal travel	1. Air, leak, or insufficient fluid in system or caliper. 2. Warped or excessively tapered shoe and lining assembly. 3. Excessive disc runout. 4. Rear brake adjustment required. 5. Loose wheel bearing adjustment. 6. Damaged caliper piston seal. 7. Improper brake fluid (boil). 8. Power brake malfunction. 9. Weak or soft hoses.

Troubleshooting Disc Brake Problems (cont.)

Condition	Possible Cause
Brake roughness or chatter (pedal pumping)	1. Excessive thickness variation of braking disc. 2. Excessive lateral runout of braking disc. 3. Rear brake drums out-of-round. 4. Excessive front bearing clearance.
Excessive pedal effort	1. Brake fluid, oil or grease on linings. 2. Incorrect lining. 3. Frozen or seized pistons. 4. Power brake malfunction. 5. Kinked or collapsed hose or line. 6. Stuck metering valve. 7. Scored caliper or master cylinder bore. 8. Seized caliper pistons.
Brake pedal fades (pedal travel increases with foot on brake)	1. Rough master cylinder or caliper bore. 2. Loose or broken hydraulic lines/connections. 3. Air in hydraulic system. 4. Fluid level low. 5. Weak or soft hoses. 6. Inferior quality brake shoes or fluid. 7. Worn master cylinder piston cups or seals.

Troubleshooting Drum Brakes

Condition	Possible Cause
Pedal goes to floor	1. Fluid low in reservoir. 2. Air in hydraulic system. 3. Improperly adjusted brake. 4. Leaking wheel cylinders. 5. Loose or broken brake lines. 6. Leaking or worn master cylinder. 7. Excessively worn brake lining.
Spongy brake pedal	1. Air in hydraulic system. 2. Improper brake fluid (low boiling point). 3. Excessively worn or cracked brake drums. 4. Broken pedal pivot bushing.
Brakes pulling	1. Contaminated lining. 2. Front end out of alignment. 3. Incorrect brake adjustment. 4. Unmatched brake lining. 5. Brake drums out of round. 6. Brake shoes distorted. 7. Restricted brake hose or line. 8. Broken rear spring. 9. Worn brake linings. 10. Uneven lining wear. 11. Glazed brake lining. 12. Excessive brake lining dust. 13. Heat spotted brake drums. 14. Weak brake return springs. 15. Faulty automatic adjusters. 16. Low or incorrect tire pressure.

Condition	Possible Cause
Squealing brakes	1. Glazed brake lining. 2. Saturated brake lining. 3. Weak or broken brake shoe retaining spring. 4. Broken or weak brake shoe return spring. 5. Incorrect brake lining. 6. Distorted brake shoes. 7. Bent support plate. 8. Dust in brakes or scored brake drums. 9. Linings worn below limit. 10. Uneven brake lining wear. 11. Heat spotted brake drums.
Chirping brakes	1. Out of round drum or eccentric axle flange pilot.
Dragging brakes	1. Incorrect wheel or parking brake adjustment. 2. Parking brakes engaged or improperly adjusted. 3. Weak or broken brake shoe return spring. 4. Brake pedal binding. 5. Master cylinder cup sticking. 6. Obstructed master cylinder relief port. 7. Saturated brake lining. 8. Bent or out of round brake drum. 9. Contaminated or improper brake fluid. 10. Sticking wheel cylinder pistons. 11. Driver riding brake pedal. 12. Defective proportioning valve. 13. Insufficient brake shoe lubricant.
Hard pedal	1. Brake booster inoperative. 2. Incorrect brake lining. 3. Restricted brake line or hose. 4. Frozen brake pedal linkage. 5. Stuck wheel cylinder. 6. Binding pedal linkage. 7. Faulty proportioning valve.
Wheel locks	1. Contaminated brake lining. 2. Loose or torn brake lining. 3. Wheel cylinder cups sticking. 4. Incorrect wheel bearing adjustment. 5. Faulty proportioning valve.
Brakes fade (high speed)	1. Incorrect lining. 2. Overheated brake drums. 3. Incorrect brake fluid (low boiling temperature). 4. Saturated brake lining. 5. Leak in hydraulic system. 6. Faulty automatic adjusters.
Pedal pulsates	1. Bent or out of round brake drum.
Brake chatter and shoe knock	1. Out of round brake drum. 2. Loose support plate. 3. Bent support plate. 4. Distorted brake shoes. 5. Machine grooves in contact face of brake drum (Shoe Knock). 6. Contaminated brake lining. 7. Missing or loose components. 8. Incorrect lining material. 9. Out-of-round brake drums. 10. Heat spotted or scored brake drums. 11. Out-of-balance wheels.

Troubleshooting Drum Brakes (cont.)

Condition	Possible Cause
Brakes do not self adjust	1. Adjuster screw frozen in thread. 2. Adjuster screw corroded at thrust washer. 3. Adjuster lever does not engage star wheel. 4. Adjuster installed on wrong wheel.
Brake light glows	1. Leak in the hydraulic system. 2. Air in the system. 3. Improperly adjusted master cylinder pushrod. 4. Uneven lining wear. 5. Failure to center combination valve or proportioning valve.

Appendix

General Conversion Table

Multiply by	To convert	To	
2.54	Inches	Centimeters	.3937
30.48	Feet	Centimeters	.0328
.914	Yards	Meters	1.094
1.609	Miles	Kilometers	.621
.645	Square inches	Square cm.	.155
.836	Square yards	Square meters	1.196
16.39	Cubic inches	Cubic cm.	.061
28.3	Cubic feet	Liters	.0353
.4536	Pounds	Kilograms	2.2045
4.226	Gallons	Liters	.264
.068	Lbs./sq. in. (psi)	Atmospheres	14.7
.138	Foot pounds	Kg. m.	7.23
1.014	H.P. (DIN)	H.P. (SAE)	.9861
—	To obtain	From	Multiply by

Note: 1 cm. equals 10 mm.; 1 mm. equals .0394".

Conversion—Common Fractions to Decimals and Millimeters

Common Fractions	Decimal Fractions	Millimeters (approx.)	Common Fractions	Decimal Fractions	Millimeters (approx.)	Common Fractions	Decimal Fractions	Millimeters (approx.)
1/128	.008	0.20	11/32	.344	8.73	43/64	.672	17.07
1/64	.016	0.40	23/64	.359	9.13	11/16	.688	17.46
1/32	.031	0.79	3/8	.375	9.53	45/64	.703	17.86
3/64	.047	1.19	25/64	.391	9.92	23/32	.719	18.26
1/16	.063	1.59	13/32	.406	10.32	47/64	.734	18.65
5/64	.078	1.98	27/64	.422	10.72	3/4	.750	19.05
3/32	.094	2.38	7/16	.438	11.11	49/64	.766	19.45
7/64	.109	2.78	29/64	.453	11.51	25/32	.781	19.84
1/8	.125	3.18	15/32	.469	11.91	51/64	.797	20.24
9/64	.141	3.57	31/64	.484	12.30	13/16	.813	20.64
5/32	.156	3.97	1/2	.500	12.70	53/64	.828	21.03
11/64	.172	4.37	33/64	.516	13.10	27/32	.844	21.43
3/16	.188	4.76	17/32	.531	13.49	55/64	.859	21.83
13/64	.203	5.16	35/64	.547	13.89	7/8	.875	22.23
7/32	.219	5.56	9/16	.563	14.29	57/64	.891	22.62
15/64	.234	5.95	37/64	.578	14.68	29/32	.906	23.02
1/4	.250	6.35	19/32	.594	15.08	59/64	.922	23.42
17/64	.266	6.75	39/64	.609	15.48	15/16	.938	23.81
9/32	.281	7.14	5/8	.625	15.88	61/64	.953	24.21
19/64	.297	7.54	41/64	.641	16.27	31/32	.969	24.61
5/16	.313	7.94	21/32	.656	16.67	63/64	.984	25.00
21/64	.328	8.33						

Conversion—Millimeters to Decimal Inches

mm	inches	mm	inches	mm	inches	mm	inches	mm	inches
1	.039 370	31	1.220 470	61	2.401 570	91	3.582 670	210	8.267 700
2	.078 740	32	1.259 840	62	2.440 940	92	3.622 040	220	8.661 400
3	.118 110	33	1.299 210	63	2.480 310	93	3.661 410	230	9.055 100
4	.157 480	34	1.338 580	64	2.519 680	94	3.700 780	240	9.448 800
5	.196 850	35	1.377 949	65	2.559 050	95	3.740 150	250	9.842 500
6	.236 220	36	1.417 319	66	2.598 420	96	3.779 520	260	10.236 200
7	.275 590	37	1.456 689	67	2.637 790	97	3.818 890	270	10.629 900
8	.314 960	38	1.496 050	68	2.677 160	98	3.858 260	280	11.032 600
9	.354 330	39	1.535 430	69	2.716 530	99	3.897 630	290	11.417 300
10	.393 700	40	1.574 800	70	2.755 900	100	3.937 000	300	11.811 000
11	.433 070	41	1.614 170	71	2.795 270	105	4.133 848	310	12.204 700
12	.472 440	42	1.653 540	72	2.834 640	110	4.330 700	320	12.598 400
13	.511 810	43	1.692 910	73	2.874 010	115	4.527 550	330	12.992 100
14	.551 180	44	1.732 280	74	2.913 380	120	4.724 400	340	13.385 800
15	.590 550	45	1.771 650	75	2.952 750	125	4.921 250	350	13.779 500
16	.629 920	46	1.811 020	76	2.992 120	130	5.118 100	360	14.173 200
17	.669 290	47	1.850 390	77	3.031 490	135	5.314 950	370	14.566 900
18	.708 660	48	1.889 760	78	3.070 860	140	5.511 800	380	14.960 600
19	.748 030	49	1.929 130	79	3.110 230	145	5.708 650	390	15.354 300
20	.787 400	50	1.968 500	80	3.149 600	150	5.905 500	400	15.748 000
21	.826 770	51	2.007 870	81	3.188 970	155	6.102 350	500	19.685 000
22	.866 140	52	2.047 240	82	3.228 340	160	6.299 200	600	23.622 000
23	.905 510	53	2.086 610	83	3.267 710	165	6.496 050	700	27.559 000
24	.944 880	54	2.125 980	84	3.307 080	170	6.692 900	800	31.496 000
25	.984 250	55	2.165 350	85	3.346 450	175	6.889 750	900	35.433 000
26	1.023 620	56	2.204 720	86	3.385 820	180	7.086 600	1000	39.370 000
27	1.062 990	57	2.244 090	87	3.425 190	185	7.283 450	2000	78.740 000
28	1.102 360	58	2.283 460	88	3.464 560	190	7.480 300	3000	118.110 000
29	1.141 730	59	2.322 830	89	3.503 903	195	7.677 150	4000	157.480 000
30	1.181 100	60	2.362 200	90	3.543 300	200	7.874 000	5000	196.850 000

To change decimal millimeters to decimal inches, position the decimal point where desired on either side of the millimeter measurement shown and reset the inches decimal by the same number of digits in the same direction. For example, to convert 0.001 mm to decimal inches, reset the decimal behind the 1 mm (shown on the chart) to 0.001; change the decimal inch equivalent (0.039″ shown) to 0.000039″.

Tap Drill Sizes

Screw & Tap Size	National Fine or S.A.E. Threads Per Inch	Use Drill Number
No. 5	44	37
No. 6	40	33
No. 8	36	29
No. 10	32	21
No. 12	28	15
1/4	28	3
5/16	24	1
3/8	24	Q
7/16	20	W
1/2	20	29/64
9/16	18	33/64
5/8	18	37/64
3/4	16	11/16
7/8	14	13/16
1 1/8	12	1 3/64
1 1/4	12	1 11/64
1 1/2	12	1 27/64

Tap Drill Sizes

Screw & Tap Size	National Coarse or U.S.S. Threads Per Inch	Use Drill Number
No. 5	40	39
No. 6	32	36
No. 8	32	29
No. 10	24	25
No. 12	24	17
1/4	20	8
5/16	18	F
3/8	16	5/16
7/16	14	U
1/2	13	27/64
9/16	12	31/64
5/8	11	17/32
3/4	10	21/32
7/8	9	49/64
1	8	7/8
1 1/8	7	63/64
1 1/4	7	1 7/64
1 1/2	6	1 11/32

Decimal Equivalent Size of the Number Drills

Drill No.	Decimal Equivalent	Drill No.	Decimal Equivalent	Drill No.	Decimal Equivalent
80	.0135	53	.0595	26	.1470
79	.0145	52	.0635	25	.1495
78	.0160	51	.0670	24	.1520
77	.0180	50	.0700	23	.1540
76	.0200	49	.0730	22	.1570
75	.0210	48	.0760	21	.1590
74	.0225	47	.0785	20	.1610
73	.0240	46	.0810	19	.1660
72	.0250	45	.0820	18	.1695
71	.0260	44	.0860	17	.1730
70	.0280	43	.0890	16	.1770
69	.0292	42	.0935	15	.1800
68	.0310	41	.0960	14	.1820
67	.0320	40	.0980	13	.1850
66	.0330	39	.0995	12	.1890
65	.0350	38	.1015	11	.1910
64	.0360	37	.1040	10	.1935
63	.0370	36	.1065	9	.1960
62	.0380	35	.1100	8	.1990
61	.0390	34	.1110	7	.2010
60	.0400	33	.1130	6	.2040
59	.0410	32	.1160	5	.2055
58	.0420	31	.1200	4	.2090
57	.0430	30	.1285	3	.2130
56	.0465	29	.1360	2	.2210
55	.0520	28	.1405	1	.2280
54	.0550	27	.1440		

Decimal Equivalent Size of the Letter Drills

Letter Drill	Decimal Equivalent	Letter Drill	Decimal Equivalent	Letter Drill	Decimal Equivalent
A	.234	J	.277	S	.348
B	.238	K	.281	T	.358
C	.242	L	.290	U	.368
D	.246	M	.295	V	.377
E	.250	N	.302	W	.386
F	.257	O	.316	X	.397
G	.261	P	.323	Y	.404
H	.266	Q	.332	Z	.413
I	.272	R	.339		

Anti-Freeze Chart

Temperatures Shown in Degrees Fahrenheit +32 is Freezing

Cooling System Capacity Quarts	Quarts of ETHYLENE GLYCOL Needed for Protection to Temperatures Shown Below													
	1	2	3	4	5	6	7	8	9	10	11	12	13	14
10	+24°	+16°	+ 4°	−12°	−34°	−62°								
11	+25	+18	+ 8	− 6	−23	−47								
12	+26	+19	+10	0	−15	−34	−57°							
13	+27	+21	+13	+ 3	− 9	−25	−45							
14			+15	+ 6	− 5	−18	−34							
15			+16	+ 8	0	−12	−26							
16			+17	+10	+ 2	− 8	−19	−34	−52°					
17				+18	+12	+ 5	− 4	−14	−27	−42				
18				+19	+14	+ 7	0	−10	−21	−34	−50°			
19				+20	+15	+ 9	+ 2	− 7	−16	−28	−42			
20					+16	+10	+ 4	− 3	−12	−22	−34	−48°		
21					+17	+12	+ 6	0	− 9	−17	−28	−41		
22					+18	+13	+ 8	+ 2	− 6	−14	−23	−34	−47°	
23					+19	+14	+ 9	+ 4	− 3	−10	−19	−29	−40	
24					+19	+15	+10	+ 5	0	− 8	−15	−23	−34	−46°
25					+20	+16	+12	+ 7	+ 1	− 5	−12	−20	−29	−40	−50°
26					+17	+13	+ 8	+ 3	− 3	− 9	−16	−25	−34	−44
27					+18	+14	+ 9	+ 5	− 1	− 7	−13	−21	−29	−39
28					+18	+15	+10	+ 6	+ 1	− 5	−11	−18	−25	−34
29					+19	+16	+12	+ 7	+ 2	− 3	− 8	−15	−22	−29
30					+20	+17	+13	+ 8	+ 4	− 1	− 6	−12	−18	−25

For capacities over 30 quarts divide true capacity by 3. Find quarts Anti-Freeze for the ⅓ and multiply by 3 for quarts to add.

For capacities under 10 quarts multiply true capacity by 3. Find quarts Anti-Freeze for the tripled volume and divide by 3 for quarts to add.

To Increase the Freezing Protection of Anti-Freeze Solutions Already Installed

Cooling System Capacity Quarts	Number of Quarts of ETHYLENE GLYCOL Anti-Freeze Required to Increase Protection														
	From +20° F. to					From +10° F. to					From 0° F. to			
	0°	−10°	−20°	−30°	−40°	0°	−10°	−20°	−30°	−40°	−10°	−20°	−30°	−40°
10	1¾	2¼	3	3½	3¾	¾	1½	2¼	2¾	3¼	¾	1½	2	2½
12	2	2¾	3½	4	4½	1	1¾	2½	3¼	3¾	1	1¾	2½	3¼
14	2¼	3¼	4	4¾	5½	1¼	2	3	3¾	4½	1	2	3	3½
16	2½	3½	4½	5¼	6	1¼	2½	3½	4¼	5¼	1¼	2¼	3¼	4
18	3	4	5	6	7	1½	2¾	4	5	5¾	1½	2½	3¾	4¾
20	3¼	4½	5¾	6¾	7½	1¾	3	4¼	5½	6½	1½	2¾	4¼	5¼
22	3½	5	6¼	7¼	8¼	1¾	3¼	4¾	6	7¼	1¾	3¼	4½	5½
24	4	5½	7	8	9	2	3½	5	6½	7½	1¾	3½	5	6
26	4¼	6	7½	8¾	10	2	4	5½	7	8¼	2	3¾	5½	6¾
28	4½	6¼	8	9½	10½	2¼	4¼	6	7½	9	2	4	5¾	7¼
30	5	6¾	8½	10	11½	2½	4½	6½	8	9½	2¼	4¼	6¼	7¾

Test radiator solution with proper hydrometer. Determine from the table the number of quarts of solution to be drawn off from a full cooling system and replace with undiluted anti-freeze, to give the desired increased protection. For example, to increase protection of a 22-quart cooling system containing Ethylene Glycol (permanent type) anti-freeze, from +20° F. to −20° F. will require the replacement of 6¼ quarts of solution with undiluted anti-freeze.

Index

Chilton's Repair & Tune-Up Guides

The Complete line covers domestic cars, imports, trucks, vans, RV's and 4-wheel drive vehicles.

RTUG Title	Part No.
AMC 1975-82 Covers all U.S. and Canadian models	7199
Aspen/Volare 1976-80 Covers all U.S. and Canadian models	6637
Audi 1970-73 Covers all U.S. and Canadian models.	5902
Audi 4000/5000 1978-81 Covers all U.S. and Canadian models including turbocharged and diesel engines	7028
Barracuda/Challenger 1965-72 Covers all U.S. and Canadian models	5807
Blazer/Jimmy 1969-82 Covers all U.S. and Canadian 2- and 4-wheel drive models, including diesel engines	6931
BMW 1970-82 Covers U.S. and Canadian models	6844
Buick/Olds/Pontiac 1975-85 Covers all U.S. and Canadian full size rear wheel drive models	7308
Cadillac 1967-84 Covers all U.S. and Canadian rear wheel drive models	7462
Camaro 1967-81 Covers all U.S. and Canadian models	6735
Camaro 1982-85 Covers all U.S. and Canadian models	7317
Capri 1970-77 Covers all U.S. and Canadian models	6695
Caravan/Voyager 1984-85 Covers all U.S. and Canadian models	7482
Century/Regal 1975-85 Covers all U.S. and Canadian rear wheel drive models, including turbocharged engines	7307
Champ/Arrow/Sapporo 1978-83 Covers all U.S. and Canadian models	7041
Chevette/1000 1976-86 Covers all U.S. and Canadian models	6836
Chevrolet 1968-85 Covers all U.S. and Canadian models	7135
Chevrolet 1968-79 Spanish	7082
Chevrolet/GMC Pick-Ups 1970-82 Spanish	7468
Chevrolet/GMC Pick-Ups and Suburban 1970-86 Covers all U.S. and Canadian 1/2, 3/4 and 1 ton models, including 4-wheel drive and diesel engines	6936
Chevrolet LUV 1972-81 Covers all U.S. and Canadian models	6815
Chevrolet Mid-Size 1964-86 Covers all U.S. and Canadian models of 1964-77 Chevelle, Malibu and Malibu SS; 1974-77 Laguna; 1978-85 Malibu; 1970-86 Monte Carlo; 1964-84 El Camino, including diesel engines	6840
Chevrolet Nova 1986 Covers all U.S. and Canadian models	7658
Chevy/GMC Vans 1967-84 Covers all U.S. and Canadian models of 1/2, 3/4, and 1 ton vans, cutaways, and motor home chassis, including diesel engines	6930
Chevy S-10 Blazer/GMC S-15 Jimmy 1982-85 Covers all U.S. and Canadian models	7383
Chevy S-10/GMC S-15 Pick-Ups 1982-85 Covers all U.S. and Canadian models	7310
Chevy II/Nova 1962-79 Covers all U.S. and Canadian models	6841
Chrysler K- and E-Car 1981-85 Covers all U.S. and Canadian front wheel drive models	7163
Colt/Challenger/Vista/Conquest 1971-85 Covers all U.S. and Canadian models	7037
Corolla/Carina/Tercel/Starlet 1970-85 Covers all U.S. and Canadian models	7036
Corona/Cressida/Crown/Mk.II/Camry/Van 1970-84 Covers all U.S. and Canadian models	7044

RTUG Title	Part No.
Corvair 1960-69 Covers all U.S. and Canadian models	6691
Corvette 1953-62 Covers all U.S. and Canadian models	6576
Corvette 1963-84 Covers all U.S. and Canadian models	6843
Cutlass 1970-85 Covers all U.S. and Canadian models	6933
Dart/Demon 1968-76 Covers all U.S. and Canadian models	6324
Datsun 1961-72 Covers all U.S. and Canadian models of Nissan Patrol; 1500, 1600 and 2000 sports cars; Pick-Ups; 410, 411, 510, 1200 and 240Z	5790
Datsun 1973-80 Spanish	7083
Datsun/Nissan F-10, 310, Stanza, Pulsar 1977-86 Covers all U.S. and Canadian models	7196
Datsun/Nissan Pick-Ups 1970-84 Covers all U.S and Canadian models	6816
Datsun/Nissan Z & ZX 1970-86 Covers all U.S. and Canadian models	6932
Datsun/Nissan 1200, 210, Sentra 1973-86 Covers all U.S. and Canadian models	7197
Datsun/Nissan 200SX, 510, 610, 710, 810, Maxima 1973-84 Covers all U.S. and Canadian models	7170
Dodge 1968-77 Covers all U.S. and Canadian models	6554
Dodge Charger 1967-70 Covers all U.S. and Canadian models	6486
Dodge/Plymouth Trucks 1967-84 Covers all 1/2, 3/4, and 1 ton 2- and 4-wheel drive U.S. and Canadian models, including diesel engines	7459
Dodge/Plymouth Vans 1967-84 Covers all 1/2, 3/4, and 1 ton U.S. and Canadian models of vans, cutaways and motor home chassis	6934
D-50/Arrow Pick-Up 1979-81 Covers all U.S. and Canadian models	7032
Fairlane/Torino 1962-75 Covers all U.S. and Canadian models	6320
Fairmont/Zephyr 1978-83 Covers all U.S. and Canadian models	6965
Fiat 1969-81 Covers all U.S. and Canadian models	7042
Fiesta 1978-80 Covers all U.S. and Canadian models	6846
Firebird 1967-81 Covers all U.S. and Canadian models	5996
Firebird 1982-85 Covers all U.S. and Canadian models	7345
Ford 1968-79 Spanish	7084
Ford Bronco 1966-83 Covers all U.S. and Canadian models	7140
Ford Bronco II 1984 Covers all U.S. and Canadian models	7408
Ford Courier 1972-82 Covers all U.S. and Canadian models	6983
Ford/Mercury Front Wheel Drive 1981-85 Covers all U.S. and Canadian models Escort, EXP, Tempo, Lynx, LN-7 and Topaz	7055
Ford/Mercury/Lincoln 1968-85 Covers all U.S. and Canadian models of FORD Country Sedan, Country Squire, Crown Victoria, Custom, Custom 500, Galaxie 500, LTD through 1982, Ranch Wagon, and XL; MERCURY Colony Park, Commuter, Marquis through 1982, Gran Marquis, Monterey and Park Lane; LINCOLN Continental and Towne Car	6842
Ford/Mercury/Lincoln Mid-Size 1971-85 Covers all U.S. and Canadian models of FORD Elite, 1983-85 LTD, 1977-79 LTD II, Ranchero, Torino, Gran Torino, 1977-85 Thunderbird; MERCURY 1972-85 Cougar,	6696

continued on next page

RTUG Title	Part No.	RTUG Title	Part No.
1983-85 Marquis, Montego, 1980-85 XR-7; LINCOLN 1982-85 Continental, 1984-85 Mark VII, 1978-80 Versailles		**Mercedes-Benz 1974-84** Covers all U.S. and Canadian models	6809
Ford Pick-Ups 1965-86 6913 Covers all $1/2$, $3/4$ and 1 ton, 2- and 4-wheel drive U.S. and Canadian pick-up, chassis cab and camper models, including diesel engines	6913	**Mitsubishi, Cordia, Tredia, Starion, Galant 1983-85** Covers all U.S. and Canadian models	7583
Ford Pick-Ups 1965-82 Spanish	7469	**MG 1961-81** Covers all U.S. and Canadian models	6780
Ford Ranger 1983-84 Covers all U.S. and Canadian models	7338	**Mustang/Capri/Merkur 1979-85**	6963
Ford Vans 1961-86 Covers all U.S. and Canadian $1/2$, $3/4$ and 1 ton van and cutaway chassis models, including diesel engines	6849	**Mustang/Cougar 1965-73** Covers all U.S. and Canadian models	6542
GM A-Body 1982-85 Covers all front wheel drive U.S. and Canadian models of BUICK Century, CHEVROLET Celebrity, OLDSMOBILE Cutlass Ciera and PONTIAC 6000	7309	**Mustang II 1974-78** Covers all U.S. and Canadian models	6812
GM C-Body 1985 Covers all front wheel drive U.S. and Canadian models of BUICK Electra Park Avenue and Electra T-Type, CADILLAC Fleetwood and deVille, OLDSMOBILE 98 Regency and Regency Brougham	7587	**Omni/Horizon/Rampage 1978-84** Covers all U.S. and Canadian models of DODGE omni, Miser, 024, Charger 2.2; PLYMOUTH Horizon, Miser, TC3, TC3 Tourismo; Rampage	6845
GM J-Car 1982-85 Covers all U.S. and Canadian models of BUICK Skyhawk, CHEVROLET Cavalier, CADILLAC Cimarron, OLDSMOBILE Firenza and PONTIAC 2000 and Sunbird	7059	**Opel 1971-75** Covers all U.S. and Canadian models	6575
		Peugeot 1970-74 Covers all U.S. and Canadian models	5982
GM N-Body 1985-86 Covers all U.S. and Canadian models of front wheel drive BUICK Somerset and Skylark, OLDSMOBILE Calais, and PONTIAC Grand Am	7657	**Pinto/Bobcat 1971-80** Covers all U.S. and Canadian models	7027
		Plymouth 1968-76 Covers all U.S. and Canadian models	6552
GM X-Body 1980-85 Covers all U.S. and Canadian models of BUICK Skylark, CHEVROLET Citation, OLDSMOBILE Omega and PONTIAC Phoenix	7049	**Pontiac Fiero 1984-85** Covers all U.S. and Canadian models	7571
		Pontiac Mid-Size 1974-83 Covers all U.S. and Canadian models of Ventura, Grand Am, LeMans, Grand LeMans, GTO, Phoenix, and Grand Prix	7346
GM Subcompact 1971-80 Covers all U.S. and Canadian models of BUICK Skyhawk (1975-80), CHEVROLET Vega and Monza, OLDSMOBILE Starfire, and PONTIAC Astre and 1975-80 Sunbird	6935	**Porsche 924/928 1976-81** Covers all U.S. and Canadian models	7048
		Renault 1975-85 Covers all U.S. and Canadian models	7165
Granada/Monarch 1975-82 Covers all U.S. and Canadian models	6937	**Roadrunner/Satellite/Belvedere/GTX 1968-73** Covers all U.S. and Canadian models	5821
Honda 1973-84 Covers all U.S. and Canadian models	6980	**RX-7 1979-81** Covers all U.S. and Canadian models	7031
International Scout 1967-73 Covers all U.S. and Canadian models	5912	**SAAB 99 1969-75** Covers all U.S. and Canadian models	5988
Jeep 1945-87 Covers all U.S. and Canadian CJ-2A, CJ-3A, CJ-3B, CJ-5, CJ-6, CJ-7, Scrambler and Wrangler models	6817	**SAAB 900 1979-85** Covers all U.S. and Canadian models	7572
		Snowmobiles 1976-80 Covers all Arctic Cat, John Deere, Kawasaki, Polaris, Ski-Doo and Yamaha	6978
Jeep Wagoneer, Commando, Cherokee, Truck 1957-86 Covers all U.S. and Canadian models of Wagoneer, Cherokee, Grand Wagoneer, Jeepster, Jeepster Commando, J-100, J-200, J-300, J-10, J20, FC-150 and FC-170	6739	**Subaru 1970-84** Covers all U.S. and Canadian models	6982
		Tempest/GTO/LeMans 1968-73 Covers all U.S. and Canadian models	5905
		Toyota 1966-70 Covers all U.S. and Canadian models of Corona, MkII, Corolla, Crown, Land Cruiser, Stout and Hi-Lux	5795
Laser/Daytona 1984-85 Covers all U.S. and Canadian models	7563	**Toyota 1970-79 Spanish**	7467
Maverick/Comet 1970-77 Covers all U.S. and Canadian models	6634	**Toyota Celica/Supra 1971-85** Covers all U.S. and Canadian models	7043
Mazda 1971-84 Covers all U.S. and Canadian models of RX-2, RX-3, RX-4, 808, 1300, 1600, Cosmo, GLC and 626	6981	**Toyota Trucks 1970-85** Covers all U.S. and Canadian models of pick-ups, Land Cruiser and 4Runner	7035
		Valiant/Duster 1968-76 Covers all U.S. and Canadian models	6326
Mazda Pick-Ups 1972-86 Covers all U.S. and Canadian models	7659	**Volvo 1956-69** Covers all U.S. and Canadian models	6529
Mercedes-Benz 1959-70 Covers all U.S. and Canadian models	6065	**Volvo 1970-83** Covers all U.S. and Canadian models	7040
Mereceds-Benz 1968-73 Covers all U.S. and Canadian models	5907	**VW Front Wheel Drive 1974-85** Covers all U.S. and Canadian models	6962
		VW 1949-71 Covers all U.S. and Canadian models	5796
		VW 1970-79 Spanish	7081
		VW 1970-81 Covers all U.S. and Canadian Beetles, Karmann Ghia, Fastback, Squareback, Vans, 411 and 412	6837

Chilton's Repair & Tune-Up Guides are available at your local retailer or by mailing a check or money order for **$13.95** plus **$3.25** to cover postage and handling to:

Chilton Book Company
Dept. DM
Radnor, PA 19089

NOTE: When ordering be sure to include your name & address, book part No. & title.